The Language of Queen Elizabeth I: A Sociolinguistic Perspective on Royal Style and Identity

Publications of the Philological Society, 46

WILEY
Blackwell

The Language of Queen Elizabeth I:
A Sociolinguistic Perspective on
Royal Style and Identity

Mel Evans

Publications of the Philological Society, 46

This edition first published 2013

© 2013 The Philological Society

Blackwell Publishing was acquired by John Wiley & Sons in February 2007. Blackwell's publishing program has been merged with Wiley's global Scientific, Technical, and Medical business to form Wiley-Blackwell.

Registered Office

John Wiley & Sons Ltd, The Atrium, Southern Gate, Chichester, West Sussex, PO19 8SQ, United Kingdom

Editorial Offices

350 Main Street, Malden, MA 02148-5020, USA

9600 Garsington Road, Oxford, OX4 2DQ, UK

The Atrium, Southern Gate, Chichester, West Sussex, PO19 8SQ, UK

For details of our global editorial offices, for customer services, and for information about how to apply for permission to reuse the copyright material in this book please see our website at www.wiley.com/wiley-blackwell.

The right of Mel Evans to be identified as the author of this work has been asserted in accordance with the UK Copyright, Designs and Patents Act 1988.

Wiley also publishes its books in a variety of electronic formats. Some content that appears in print may not be available in electronic books.

Designations used by companies to distinguish their products are often claimed as trademarks. All brand names and product names used in this book are trade names, service marks, trademarks or registered trademarks of their respective owners. The publisher is not associated with any product or vendor mentioned in this book. This publication is designed to provide accurate and authoritative information in regard to the subject matter covered. It is sold on the understanding that the publisher is not engaged in rendering professional services. If professional advice or other expert assistance is required, the services of a competent professional should be sought.

Library of Congress Cataloging-in-Publication Data

Library of Congress Cataloging-in-Publication Data is available for this work.

ISBN 978-1-118-67287-7

A catalogue record for this book is available from the British Library.

Set in Times by SPS (P) Ltd., Chennai, India

Printed in Singapore

1 2013

CONTENTS

CONTENTS

ACKNOWLEDGMENTS

The present work could not have been completed without the support and advice of many people, who between them have helped to improve my thinking about sociolinguistics, Queen Elizabeth I, and the relationship between the two. Professor Sylvia Adamson has provided invaluable advice and support, encouraging me to explore new directions within the data and across the disciplines. Her guidance and continued patience are truly appreciated. I would also like to thank Professor Steven W. May for the selfless sharing of his knowledge and expertise as a scholar of Queen Elizabeth I, and Professor Joan Beal and Professor Jeremy Smith, who have each offered vital constructive criticism and advice. My thanks also extend to faculty members in the School of English at the University of Sheffield, where this project originated and was funded by a University of Sheffield PhD scholarship. Particular mention should go to Dr Alan Bryson for his help with manuscripts and Elizabethan handwriting, Professor Cathy Shrank for guidance on various aspects of the thesis, and to Dr Sara Whiteley, Dr Alison Gibbons and Dr Gavin Shwartz-Leper for their amicable support.

I also owe my gratitude to Dr Alison Wiggins, University of Glasgow, and Professor James Daybell, University of Plymouth, for sharing their expertise at various stages of the project. The VARIENG team at the University of Helsinki have continually developed and challenged what it means to investigate historical sociolinguistics in Early Modern English; Professor Terttu Nevalainen, Professor Helena Raumolin-Brunberg, Dr Anni Sairio, Dr Tanja Saïly, Teo Juvenen and Samuli Kaislaniemi have each enlightened my thinking and my approach to the language of Queen Elizabeth I. My thanks also go to the staff at the British Library manuscript reading room for their help and assistance when I was preparing the electronic corpus, and to my colleagues in the Department of English at the University of Birmingham for their insight and support in the latter stages of research. I wish to thank Allegra Holbrook and Giney Sapera for their crucial assistance in preparing the manuscript for publication, and the Philological Society and the team at Wiley-Blackwell for guiding me through the final stages. All remaining errors are my own. Finally, I would like to express my gratitude to Rich, who has proved an irreplaceable silent partner throughout.

I dedicate this book to the memory of my mum, whose passion for history first introduced me to Tudor England.

Dr Mel Evans
University of Birmingham

LIST OF ABBREVIATIONS

BL	British Library, London
CED	Corpus of English Dialogues
CEEC	Corpus of Early English Correspondence
EModE	Early Modern English
HC	Helsinki Corpus
LALME	A Linguistic Atlas of Late Medieval English
LModE	Late Modern English
ME	Middle English
ODNB	Oxford Dictionary of National Biography
OE	Old English
OED	Oxford English Dictionary
PCEEC	Parsed Corpus of Early English Correspondence
PDE	Present Day English
PostA	Post-accession period (1559–1603)
PreA	Pre-accession period (1544–1558)
QEIC	Queen Elizabeth I Corpus
QEISC	Queen Elizabeth I Spelling Corpus
VARIENG	Research Unit for Variation, Contacts and Change in English (University of Helsinki)

PART I

INTRODUCTION

The life and reign of Queen Elizabeth I are an enduring focal point of scholarly and popular interest. As a Tudor queen, Elizabeth represented and opposed the norms of her age, with her biographical make-up (social status, gender, education and life-experiences) a contradictory combination in Tudor society. The conflicts that eschewed throughout her reign, and beyond, as well as the various attempts at resolution, echo across the Early Modern political, cultural and literary domains (Montrose 2002). Elizabeth's position and her actions as queen were the preserve of all to discuss and evaluate; as Elizabeth herself once commented: 'We Princes, I tell you, are set on stages' (May 2004a: 65). Posthumously, the queen's 'afterlife', as Helen Hackett (2009) terms it, has been similarly rich and multifaceted. Such is Elizabeth's appeal to modern audiences that her life is being repeatedly re-told and re-imagined, whether through fictionalised biographies, cinematic portrayals, or rather more comic interpretations as seen in BBC television's *Blackadder*.

However, the iconic status of Elizabeth and her reign creates problems for researchers who wish to investigate the queen's social identity and improve our understanding of her experiences and sense of self when located in such a unique and contradictory social position. The image of Elizabeth that survives in public consciousness today is a symbolic representation, constructed from 'a composite of texts' (Frye 1993: 7), a complex tapestry of historical evidence derived indiscriminately from fact, myth and memory. Any study that attempts to engage with Elizabeth rather than her legacy therefore needs to carefully determine the authenticity and origin of the material used for analysis. Viewed this way, the best surviving material for such an investigation is the writing of Elizabeth herself. Surviving in the archives of sixteenth-century English manuscripts are the queen's letters, speeches, translations, and shorter works including prayers and poetry, written throughout her life. The manuscripts, many of them autograph (i.e. surviving in the queen's own hand), are the best record of the queen's actions and engagement with her social contemporaries in their social context. Each text captures particular moments, specific social experiences, and preferred communicative acts. Significantly, these archival materials, as well as being the material remains of historical moments in Elizabeth's life, also (necessarily) capture and document the *language* of the queen herself.

These documents—the words and writings of Elizabeth I—are the focus of the present investigation.

More specifically, the approach expounded here is that the language of these texts represents the queen's IDIOLECT. The idiolect is a long-standing concept in SOCIOLINGUISTIC research. Bloch (1948: 7) offers an early (if not the earliest) linguistic definition of idiolect as 'the totality of the possible utterances of one speaker at one time in using a language to interact with one other speaker'. He goes on (1948: 7) to specify three points:

(a) that an idiolect is peculiar to one speaker;
(b) that a given speaker may have different idiolects at successive stages of his career; and
(c) that he may have two or more different idiolects at the same time.

Whilst introductory textbooks continue to acknowledge the concept (e.g. Wardhaugh 2010), the value of the idiolect for the study of linguistic variation and change has not been fully explored, and even less in the study of historical periods of a language. However, I propose here that approaching the writings of Elizabeth using a linguistic framework, specifically the principles and methods of VARIATIONIST SOCIOLINGUISTICS, will allow a new perspective on the queen by exploring the relationship between her language use and her social background. It should be noted that the present discussion modifies Bloch's definition, in order to treat the idiolect as a (singular) linguistic system specific to an individual. Rather than possessing a 'number' of idiolects a speaker, such as Elizabeth, modifies their idiolect for particular purposes.

My approach suggests that different aspects of Elizabeth's idiolect—both in their variation and consistency—will reflect and constitute the different components of her social identity: her rank, education, age, location, social contacts, experiences and relationships. The idiolectal data, it is hoped, will capture the intersection between social identity and linguistic meaning, and thus offer a new window from which to perceive and understand Elizabeth's sociolinguistic position in sixteenth-century society.

1. HISTORICAL SOCIOLINGUISTICS

HISTORICAL SOCIOLINGUISTICS, the study of historical language using socio-linguistic principles, is not conventionally associated with idiolectal analysis. As the youthful sibling to the more developed field of variationist sociolinguistics, the central aim has been to provide insight into 'the social embedding of real-time language change' by drawing on the diachronic span of historical data and investigating the correlation between linguistic variation and different social categories, such as age, gender, social status or region (Nevalainen & Raumolin-Brunberg (henceforth N&R-B) 2003: 11).

Historical sociolinguistics and sociolinguistics subscribe to the premise that linguistic variation can lead to language change, but that the mechanisms are both linguistic and social. Sociolinguistics posits that linguistic variants, which occur naturally in the process of human communication, can acquire a socially significant meaning. Once socially marked, the variant diffuses across linguistic contexts and the speech community, gaining acceptance within a community's repertoire and leading to language change.

The role of the individual speaker in accounts of language change is typically subsumed into mass social categories. Modern studies have attempted to justify this approach by noting that most speakers conform to the linguistic behaviour of the social group(s) with which they wish to affiliate, thus legitimising their treatment as speakers (plural) rather than as linguistically-independent, idiosyncratic individuals (Bayley 2002: 122).[1] The role of the individual in language change has also been downplayed because of the perception that an idiolect captures only a synchronic perspective of the language system (Romaine 1982: 246). Yet, there is a growing recognition that language change does occur, and can be captured and studied, within the lifetime of an individual. Whilst a number of contemporary panel studies are ongoing (e.g. Nahkola & Saanilahti 2004; Sankoff & Blondeau 2007), the necessary duration of real-time investigations means that the results will take years to be fully realised. Historical sociolinguistics, on the other hand, has no such limitations. Linguistic data from decades, even whole lifetimes, of individuals can be collated, assessed and explored, although historical data carries with it its own set of methodological challenges; see, for example, Raumolin-Brunberg (2005) and Nevalainen, Raumolin-Brunberg & Mannila (2011).

The hypothetical correlation between a speaker's social experiences and their language use is a central concept for the analysis of Elizabeth's idiolect. The patterns identified in her idiolect, and the degree of similarity between these patterns and particular social groups, could provide new information about Elizabeth I as a speaker and a social being. The analysis is orientated around three research questions that structure the following discussion:

- Does Elizabeth's idiolect change in response to her accession?
- Can a sociolinguistic analysis of Elizabeth's idiolect provide a useful means for assessing authorship?
- What can idiolectal analysis contribute to historical sociolinguistics?

The study is divided into three parts. In the remainder of the present section, I discuss the theoretical principles and existing studies that inform

---

[1] This account does recognise elements of individuation in language use such as intonation, but, as they have little social significance, considers them insignificant (Chambers 2003: 93; cf. Podesva 2007). See Milroy (2003) for a critique of the marginalised role of the speaker in linguistics more generally.

the three research questions, provide an overview of the data forming the main and comparative sources for the investigation, and summarise the methodology that will be used to interrogate this data. Part II presents the findings for ten linguistic features in Elizabeth I's idiolect, and Part III discusses and evaluates these findings in relation to each research question, identifying their implications for future work on historical idiolects, Early Modern English, and the sociolinguistic approach to language variation and change.

1.2 *Research Question 1: Does Elizabeth's idiolect change in response to her accession?*

Elizabeth's accession is consistently used by historians as a divide in Elizabeth's biography, separating her life into a 'before' and 'after' sequence of events. The division appears to have been largely accepted without criticism, with accounts repeatedly conceptualising Elizabeth's pre-accession (PreA) and post-accession (PostA) experiences as two, almost distinct, periods. For example, some works focus exclusively on Elizabeth's pre-accession life. The account of Thomas Heywood (1632) details 'the processe of her time from the Cradle to the Crowne', and the focus on Elizabeth's pre-accession life is also found in more recent publications, including Plowden (1971) and Starkey (2000). Elsewhere, some biographers disregard Elizabeth's pre-accession biography almost entirely. E.S. Beesly (1892) spends 235 pages exploring Elizabeth's reign, and grants the preceding 26 years of Elizabeth's 'early life (1533–1559)' a mere five pages. A number of biographies, of course, account for both periods in Elizabeth's life, particularly scholarly works such as Somerset (1991) and Perry (1990). Yet there is still a general sense of before and after that structures these reports, with the implication that Elizabeth's accession was a significant biographical event.

If the conceptualisation of Elizabeth's accession as a key moment in her biography is justified, then we might expect this event to have a noticeable impact on her language. Her accession certainly appears to have borne some influence upon her handwriting, at least, with the pre- and post-accession documents possessing notably different letterforms and levels of legibility (see Woudhuysen 2007 for a detailed discussion). However, whilst the emphasis placed on Elizabeth's accession is perhaps justified in a broad historical sense, it is unclear if there is a comparable impact at the idiolectal/biographical level. It may be that, in a life so rich and varied as Elizabeth's, there are other, more significant biographic experiences that have a greater affect on, and hence are more evident in, her idiolect. The diachronic analysis needs therefore to be sensitive to other potential links between patterns in her linguistic preferences and the socio-historical context.

In order to properly contextualise and interpret the idiolectal data, it is important to understand Elizabeth's experiences in both sub-periods. Fortunately, her life is well documented, and the following account offers a brief summary of the key biographical points most relevant to my analysis in Parts II and III. For a fuller account, I encourage the reader to consult Somerset (1991) and Perry (1990) in the first instance.

David Starkey (2000) describes Elizabeth's pre-accession life as an apprenticeship, a mildly hagiographical description that encapsulates the period's connection to, and distinction from, her later life as Queen of England. As part of her apprenticeship, Elizabeth experienced the privileges that came of being the daughter of a King. One clear benefit was her education. This began when she was aged only three or four, and its depth and breadth set her apart from many of her contemporaries in the mid-sixteenth century. The goal was not to prepare Elizabeth for the demands of sovereignty which, at this point, was an improbable occurrence given the birth of her brother Prince Edward, but rather to make the princess 'as learned as possible' (Somerset 1991: 15). Her early tutelage was largely a female-led affair. Her governess Kat Ashley reputedly taught her letters, the conventions and procedures of Tudor social etiquette, and Latin and Greek until 1542 (Borman 2009: 78).[2] Elizabeth's household also played an important role more generally in her formative years, her staff treating 'their young mistress with a mixture of parental indulgence and dominance' and providing her with 'emotional and political support' (McIntosh 2008: para.29).

From the mid-1540s onwards, Elizabeth's education was passed into the hands of male scholars affiliated with the universities: Dr. Richard Cox, Sir John Cheke, William Grindal and Roger Ascham. From this time, Elizabeth also came into consistent contact with the scholastic, religious and political affairs of the courts of her father and brother, and also the pious learned circle of her stepmother Catherine Parr. As well as being the only queen of Henry VIII to outlive the king, Parr was a groundbreaking scholar of her age, whose achievements have perhaps not always been recognised in the literature. Notably, she was the first woman 'to publish in print a work of her own under her own name' (Mueller 2011: 1), her *Prayers or Meditations* in 1545, and her devotional writings, activities and patronage were recognised and applauded by her contemporaries (see Mueller 2011). Parr is considered to have been an influential figure for Elizabeth until her early death in childbirth in 1548, encouraging some of Elizabeth's earliest displays of learning (such as her translation of Marguerite d'Navarre's *The Mirror of the Sinful Soul*) as well as providing her with a maternal figure (Demers 2005: 103; Borman 2009: 83).

---

[2] Anne Somerset, on the other hand, considers the evidence proving Ashley's competence in the Classical languages to be 'obscure' (1991: 14).

Some historians have emphasised Elizabeth's lack of autonomy during this period. As the female heir to the throne, Elizabeth occupied a privileged but uncertain position,

> vulnerable to a seemingly infinite assortment of competing interests holding considerable influence over her personal and political fate [...] continually subject to unpredictable and uncontrollable external forces (Cavanagh 1998: 9).

Elizabeth found herself in a number of serious predicaments during her adolescence and early adulthood. She was removed from the succession by her father in the late 1530s, and after a series of 'dizzying changes' was only restored in 1542 (Cavanagh 1998: 18). During her brother's reign, the Seymour affair posed a serious risk to Elizabeth's social standing. In January and February 1549 Elizabeth was interrogated over allegations that she had schemed to marry Thomas Seymour, Lord Admiral without King Edward VI's permission. Aged only 15, this proved a significant test of the young princess's resolve; it was also a test of her communication skills, as she wrote a series of letters to the Lord Protector stating her innocence. During her sister's reign, Elizabeth was again accused of treason and this time imprisoned in the Tower. Fearing for her life, she penned the "Tide" letter to her sister Mary I, pleading her loyalty. Tracy Borman (2009: 151) suggests that it was here Elizabeth learnt 'the strength of her own ability to talk—and write—her way out of danger'.

The learned, subservient girl of the pre-accession period contrasts with the post-accession Elizabeth, whom Starkey (2000: iii) has described as 'the bewigged and beruffed Gloriana'. As Queen, she moved geographically and socially to occupy the central position at Court, and surrounded herself with a core team of male councillors and advisers. The highly transitional nature of the outer Court ensured a steady stream of ambitious men attempting to gain Elizabeth's attention.[3] In this period, her power and political influence is more clearly defined than the uncertain status she held in her adolescence. In the latter half of the sixteenth century, Elizabeth's education was less unusual, and her high level of learning was shared by many of her courtiers. Elizabeth encouraged those around her to be the best and the brightest through her patronage and endorsement, and maintained her pre-accession scholarship through a number of translations and other literary writings.

But there was also political and ideological conflict. Queen Elizabeth was an unmarried female ruler in a traditionally male role, representing

---

[3] Roger Ascham provides an insightful description of the Court in a letter to Robert Dudley, the Earl of Leicester: 'The queen being last at Westminster, I was everyday in the privy chamber, and every day in your lordship's chamber, but the throng of your lordship's business and the thrust of importunate suitors kept me from speaking with your lordship', written 5th August 1564 (Giles 1864: 101).

a 'spectacular exception' to the norm, and 'a challenge to the homology between hierarchies of rule and gender [...] a cognitive dissonance with both political and affective consequences' (Montrose 2006: 1). As was noted above, Elizabeth's response to the conflict between her gender and position has been the focus of much scholarly attention in the last 30 years. Underlying this research is the perception that 'Elizabeth felt that monarchs created themselves through language' (Frye 1993: 4) and many studies subsequently examine Elizabeth's self-representation through her use of metaphor, analogy and other figurative devices. Research covers the spectrum of Elizabeth's writings, including her parliamentary speeches (Heisch 1975, 1980; Rose 2000), Latin University orations (Shenk 2003), other public orations (Green 1997), her prayers (May 2007), her poetry (Summit 1996), her letters (Doran 2000) and her translations (Archer 1995).

These analyses have produced no general consensus. Instead, a plurality of readings has emerged out of the semantic and rhetorical content of Elizabeth's writing. One of the earliest and best known proposals is the 'honorary male' concept, which suggests that the queen aligned herself with masculine social norms in order to deal with the gender pressures created by her role as monarch. Proponents of this interpretation suggest that Elizabeth embraced male characteristics such as 'dominance, aggression, and fearlessness' (Taylor-Smither 1984: 70), invoked the vocabulary of 'the male heroics of action' in her public speeches (Rose 2000: 1079–1080), 'did nothing to upset or interfere with male notions of how the world was or should be' and drew attention only to her gender's weaknesses (Heisch 1980: 53). Other accounts argue that the perspective of Elizabeth's adopted masculinity is too narrow, despite the legitimate argument that Elizabeth's role, at least, was traditionally male. Instead, they argue that Elizabeth's understanding of her social role and gender is more complex. Some studies describe Elizabeth's self-representation as androgynous, seen in her adoption of the neutral term 'prince' (Mueller 2001: 4). Others have identified feminine attributes, maternal and step-maternal imagery (Vanhoutte 2009), and of course Elizabeth's identification as 'the virginal Goddess', which allowed Elizabeth 'to derive special status as a female monarch' and claim affinity with other Biblical 'providential figures' (Doran 1998: 36). The sociolinguistic approach propounded here offers a different, complementary perspective on this on-going and complex debate.

The process of exploring, establishing and testing connections between the linguistic evidence and Elizabeth's biographical experiences is a fundamental component of the proposed idiolectal analysis, and a vital step if we are to properly assess the significance of Elizabeth's accession in relation to other potentially influential events in her biography.

1.3 *Research Question 2: Can a sociolinguistic analysis of Elizabeth's idiolect provide a useful means for assessing authorship?*

The second research question explores whether sociolinguistic idiolectal data can be used to establish the authorship of other texts purportedly written by Elizabeth. The field of authorship analysis is normally the concern of forensic linguistics (see Coulthard & Johnson 2007) and stylometry (e.g. Hoover 2010). The intention here is to assess what idiolectal data and the sociolinguistic framework can add to the analysis of historical documents. An evaluation of the merits and limitations of the different approaches for historical authorship analysis is beyond the remit of the present study, although such an investigation is highly desirable.

The applicability of a sociolinguistic approach for authorship analysis was first tested in Jonathan Hope's (1994) investigation of the language of William Shakespeare. Hope used quantitative methods to identify morphosyntactic features known to be undergoing change during Shakespeare's lifetime (e.g. relative clauses, periphrastic *do*) and establish the patterns of usage within plays of known and unknown authorship. Crucially, Hope's comparative method then accounted for the social factors that contribute to linguistic variation and change, such as age and social status, and also stylistic and contextual elements. Patterns could therefore be predicted, justified and explained by reference to the alleged author's biography, what Hope calls 'socio-historical linguistic evidence' (1994: xv); for example, the educational differences between Shakespeare and John Fletcher. The social significance of linguistic variation is a fundamental element of the sociolinguistic approach, and enables the analyst to evaluate the significance of the linguistic features in (or absent from) a text, and their relationship with the social identity of the proposed author. I consider Hope's method to be a persuasive demonstration of the possibilities of authorship analysis within a sociolinguistic framework, and indicative of the insight my own data may provide for analyses of Elizabeth's authorship.

Sociolinguistic studies of authorship since Hope have been surprisingly sparse, but important developments have been made in related areas. Since Hope's investigation, our documentation and understanding of macro-level linguistic trends in a sociolinguistic context has been greatly enhanced by the availability of socially stratified corpora, such as the Corpus of Early English Correspondence (henceforth CEEC). Now we are able to pinpoint specific elements of a trend by speakers' social groups and offer more rigorous and robust descriptions and interpretations of linguistic change. My analysis thus builds on the early techniques of Hope (1994) by incorporating the advances in source data, electronic methods and the better macro-level documentation of linguistic change and social stratification in the Early Modern period. The analysis of Elizabeth's idiolect documents a range of diachronic and synchronic characteristics that may prove valuable for authorship analysis. Hope's study was limited by the necessary focus on a single genre, dramatic dialogue, which has its own problems relating to the representativeness of the author's idiolect versus the voice of a fictional character. Elizabeth's idiolect is represented by a number of genres, permitting a well-rounded and detailed account of her language in different contexts.

A methodology that would enable authorial identification for a historical figure such as Elizabeth I would be a significant development. The rise of interest in 'the Queen's voice' (e.g. Clement 2008) testifies to the value of any technique that may allow texts of unidentified or dubious authorship to be confidently added or removed from the Elizabeth canon. The plethora of texts associated with Elizabeth's hand (and voice) requires a rigorous and flexible methodology. Even though we might assume that the assessment of autograph texts (i.e. those surviving in Elizabeth's hand) is a straightforward process, given her very distinctive handwriting (May 2004a: xviii), this is not a fail-proof measure. Henry Woudhuysen's investigation into Elizabeth's hand notes that a 1597 prayer could be the Queen's handwriting, but he cannot be certain (2007: 17–18). The idiolectal data is used to examine this text in Part III.

Other texts conventionally treated as canonical autographs would benefit from linguistic confirmation. Steven W. May (p.c.) questions the authenticity of the letters written to Edward Seymour, Lord Protector in 1549 during the Seymour affair. Whilst the letters are convincing examples of Elizabeth's pre-accession hand, May queries whether letters (in which Elizabeth shows 'as much skill and eloquence as the most highly trained lawyer' (Borman 2009: 120)), can be attributed to the sole composition of the 15-year-old. He believes that Elizabeth received extensive assistance from a third-party, either transcribing the letters from a draft text or from dictation. The Seymour letters comprise a significant portion of the extant pre-accession correspondence by Elizabeth, as well as offering a unique insight into her attitude towards these events. Determining the authenticity of these letters is an important step to confirm or deny the current accounts of Elizabeth's behaviour during this intense period of her youth. I include these letters in the pre-accession correspondence corpus, and reflect on the linguistic evidence for or against Elizabeth's authorship in Part III.

Elizabeth's participation in the production of scribal correspondence and other documents is also an appealing area of enquiry. Many of the official documents produced in Elizabeth's name during her reign survive in this state, and, although many carry her signature, it is unclear how involved Elizabeth was in their composition (i.e. through a full draft, through dictation, brief notes, or nothing at all). If the level of involvement could be determined, this would both extend the canon of Elizabeth's works and improve our knowledge of the relationship between Elizabeth and her administrative centre at Court.

1.4 *Research Question 3: What can idiolectal analysis contribute to historical sociolinguistics?*

The first two research questions investigate the potential benefits of a sociolinguistic idiolectal analysis for the study and understanding of Elizabeth I's life and reign. The third question takes a different tack, and asks what value the analysis of an idiolect has for the study of language variation and change. Can the data gathered from a diachronic investigation of Elizabeth's idiolect provide fresh perspectives or original insights for the field?

As noted above, historical sociolinguistics has conventionally focused on establishing macro-level social trends in historical language change. However, in the last few years there has been a growing recognition amongst scholars, both historical and contemporary, that the macro-level descriptive accounts are only the starting point, and the next step is to develop the means to enable linguistic change to be explained as well as described (N&R-B 2003: 19), such as pinpointing the factors at the actuation of a change, establishing the social differences between early adopters and mid-range users, or explaining why some linguistic changes 'take' (e.g. negative declarative *do*) and other do not (e.g. affirmative declarative *do*), amongst many other facets.

In response to this revised goal, sociolinguists have seized upon the individual speaker and the idiolect as a possible resource. Robert Podesva contends that

> [f]iner-grained analyses delving deep into an individual's linguistic performances, though they lack generalizability, may offer more insight into why speakers make the linguistic choices they do (Podesva 2007: 482).

Likewise, David Schreier believes the study of the individual speaker can offer an account of

> the socio-psychological underpinnings of variation—that is, the role and limits of linguistic accommodation, the relationship between group and individual, and also the inter-play of integration and assimilation, self-expression, and identity (Schreier 2006: 28).

In historical sociolinguistic research there is a growing appreciation that the next stage of research is to investigate 'how macro meets micro' (Palander-Collin, Nevala & Nurmi 2009: 1). Palander-Collin et al. propose that the existing framework can be enriched and enhanced by introducing the individual speaker, because they use language to communicate for specific purposes, to create his or her role in the situation and to maintain and form relationships with others. In other words, language variation and change are located at individual language users, who choose from a variety of options how to express themselves in a given situation and who eventually change language (Palander-Collin et al. 2009: 2–3).

The investigation of Elizabeth I's idiolect thus falls within the parameters proposed for a new historical sociolinguistic approach. In assessing Elizabeth's 'fit' with her social contemporaries, and tracking the change in her idiolect against her biographical experiences, the data represents the process of language variation and change at the site of the individual speaker, elucidating how Elizabeth draws on the 'variety of options' available to her to express herself 'in a given situation'.

Previous studies of historical idiolects within a sociolinguistic framework represent a small but valuable body of work, although with distinct emphases and approaches. Helena Raumolin-Brunberg's (1991) doctoral dissertation investigates sixteenth-century noun phrases based on the evidence from the idiolect of Sir Thomas More. Her interest lies in the stylistic or 'situationally conditioned linguistic variation' (1991: 18) of the noun phrase in EModE, and she assesses the different properties across a range of genres representing different levels of formality and literariness. Raumolin-Brunberg's study shows how More selects and modifies components of the noun-phrase in response to the different Early Modern genre conventions; for instance, the different syntactic positions of relative markers in his official and private correspondence reflect the different levels of formality of each genre (1991: 228–229). The scope of variation across More's writing demonstrates the importance of stylistic variation in an idiolect, and indicates how the individual speaker may participate in, and contribute to, language change affiliated with a particular register or style: a point that I also explore and address in the analysis of Elizabeth's writing.

Raumolin-Brunberg's decision to examine More's idiolect does not arise from a specific interest in More's language and its relation to his biography, but instead reflects the need to control 'speaker-dependent variables'. Raumolin-Brunberg argues that:

> the selection of one person as informant has held these variables (such as sex, education, domicile) constant, so that their possible effect on variation can be excluded from this research (Raumolin-Brunberg 1991: 24).

Later, she notes that the focus upon 'the language of one person only [...] can be very idiosyncratic', and she compensates for this 'drawback' by comparing More's usage with that of a larger corpus (1991: 42).

There are a number of points that arise from this analytical stance towards an idiolect. Firstly, as Raumolin-Brunberg's own analysis (2005, 2006) has subsequently shown, an idiolect is not a fixed entity. As well as the synchronic variation that emerges from stylistic variation, individual speakers are susceptible to diachronic change as well. Their linguistic preferences can show a dramatic change, such as the absolute loss or acquisition of a particular variant (i.e. the third-person singular verb ending, documented by Raumolin-Brunberg (2005)), or the evolution can be subtler, affecting the linguistic choices for a particular genre. Examples of both kinds are identified in Elizabeth's idiolect.

Traditionally, social (speaker) variation and stylistic (genre) variation are distinct approaches within historical sociolinguistics. Raumolin-Brunberg's study importantly demonstrates the scope for stylistic variation analysis at an idiolectal level, but she follows the existing divide and avoids any real consideration of how social and stylistic variation intersect. Nikolas Coupland has criticised the conventional division between social and stylistic factors, arguing that genre 'is a fundamental concept for the analysis of social meaning' (2007: 16). I concur with Coupland, and believe that the idiolect is a prime resource with which to break down the old barriers. The 'finer-grained' approach of an idiolectal analysis should surely include analysis of the interface of factors typically separated in larger, macro-level studies.

A more recent study of the individual speaker is Anni Sairio's (2009) analysis of another Elizabeth, Lady Montagu, who was a key individual in the eighteenth-century Bluestocking Network. Sairio investigates the social significance of three LModE linguistic variables: the development of the progressive, preposition stranding and the prominence of abbreviated spellings in past participles, all across a 40-year period. Sairio accounts for the biographical changes in Montagu's life, assessing her advancing age and the possible impact of widowhood upon her language use. However, Sairio's main concern is the applicability of social network theory within historical variationist analysis, using epistolary prose as the source data. She traces the aforementioned linguistic features across her compiled corpus of the Bluestocking Network to assess the strength of network links and sociolinguistic variables in each informant's participation in the change. Sairio's study is the opposite of Raumolin-Brunberg's (1991), in that she is concerned with language change at the local level and its social significance, but does not account for the role of stylistic variation within the idiolects of her informants. Her thesis is clearly focused upon epistolary prose, and as a result there is untapped potential, particularly within the literary and learned Bluestocking Network, for a broader analysis of multiple genres.

Like Sairio, I am interested in testing the applicability of modern sociolinguistic concepts in the study of historical language change, and

Elizabeth I provides a more challenging example than her eighteenth-century namesake. The Queen's privileged pre-accession position, and unique social position in the post-accession period make her a candidate at the extreme of social norms. Coupled with the distinctive features of Tudor society, Elizabeth provides a real test of the universality of sociolinguistic concepts.

Tim Grant (2010: 512) has remarked that modern-day idiolectal analyses are often centred on 'interesting' individuals. Barbara Johnstone's (2000) analysis of US politician Barbara Johnson is one example. Grant (2010: 512) suggests that this may create an inaccurate representation of the typical traits of an idiolect and the 'average language user'. Although the decision to focus on Elizabeth I is partly motivated by the availability of linguistic data, as well as the potential relationship between her social position and language use, the analysis of individuals at the edge of social norms is a valid test of sociolinguistic concepts. The functionality of sociolinguistics for macro-level historical language change has been largely established (e.g. N&R-B 2003; Nevalainen 2006a). The next step is to see how historical speakers, even those at an extreme end of the social spectrum such as Elizabeth, fit within the general sociolinguistic models of language variation and change.

The processes of macro-level language change are generally realised as an S-CURVE, representing the proportion of a variant within the linguistic community. Nevalainen & Raumolin-Brunberg (2003: 55; also Nevalainen et al. 2011) divide the S-curve into five parts:

- Incipient < 15%
- New and vigorous 15%–35%
- Mid-range 36%–65%
- Nearing completion 66%–85%
- Completed > 85%

Each stage represents the proportion of a variant used within a linguistic community; that is, the average uptake of a form by a number of speakers. Another important area that idiolectal analysis can thus address concerns the participation of a speaker in a change in relation to the remainder of the speech community, and the nature of that speaker's participation with regards to their social characteristics. In linguistic terms, speakers at the vanguard of a language change are known as LEADERS (N&R-B 2003: 21) or EARLY ADOPTERS (Milroy 1992; Chambers 2003: 113). Speakers at the rear of a change showing most reticence are termed LAGGERS (N&R-B 2003: 21), with the remainder classed as MID-RANGE users (Nevalainen et al. 2011). The S-curve provides a neat way of quantifying a speaker's position in a change. However, the relation between various idiolectal components and a speaker's position on the S-curve requires investigation. If a speaker is the leader in one linguistic change, does that mean they will lead all linguistic changes or, alternatively, can an individual be both a leader and a lagger for different changes?

The multi-idiolectal analyses of Raumolin-Brunberg (2005) and Nevalainen et al. (2011) have made important steps towards answering these questions. Both studies implement a quantitative approach to assess how different individuals, represented by correspondence in the CEEC, participate in language change in real time. In Raumolin-Brunberg (2005), the study provides convincing empirical evidence for idiolectal change in adulthood, based on the replacement of the third-person singular verb-ending -*eth* by -*s*. The data available for each individual varies, reflecting the limitations of historical resources, but Raumolin-Brunberg offers insightful analysis for how different individuals participate, or not, in the linguistic change. She relates their linguistic behaviour to social factors (age, gender, social status) and the nature of the variable in their language (categorical or variable). It is relevant to highlight her finding that Queen Elizabeth I has a variable grammar in this case, using both -*s* and -*eth* near equally in letters between 1586–1600.

The investigation of Nevalainen et al. (2011) builds on the earlier study. Their ambitious analysis examines the behaviour of numerous individuals in six linguistic changes in Early Modern English, identifying each speaker's participation as PROGRESSIVE, CONSERVATIVE or IN-BETWEEN. They then consider the social characteristics of those speakers who are leaders and laggers in more than one of the changes. Using the bootstrap method to account for the differing volumes of data representing the individuals in CEEC, the authors find that 'the proportions of progressive and conservative individuals correlated with the course of the changes over time: the longer a process took to run its course, the larger the proportion of in-betweens in mid-course' (Nevalainen et al. 2011: 35). Their findings support their 'progressive pull' hypothesis, which suggests that 'processes of change are propelled by the outnumbering of conservative by progressive individuals throughout their trajectories', despite the majority of individuals in a change representing the in-between category (2011: 6).

Of the 52 individuals with sufficient data across the six linguistic changes, the study found that 33 were categorised as progressive in two changes or more. Conversely, 15 individuals were conservative in two or more changes, with 10 individuals being both progressive and conservative. The majority also showed in-between status in at least one change (2011: 27–28). Their findings highlight 'the variability of individual behaviour', which they suggest may relate to the 'varying social trajectories of the changes' studied (2011: 27). One notable result was the categorisation of all five women speakers in the dataset as progressive users, suggesting that gender may be a significant social factor in the leading of change. This correlates with numerous contemporary sociolinguistic findings where female speakers are more likely to use an incoming prestigious variant (Cheshire 2002: 426), although this does not translate directly to the Early Modern period. As Nevalainen et al. note (2011: 13), women lead changes 'from below' but changes associated with educated domains such as administration, such as negative concord, are led by male speakers. However, the status of gender in their results must be treated with caution, as these five women are not necessarily representative of their social group.

And nowhere is this more apparent than for the findings concerning Queen Elizabeth I. The study suggests that the Queen was the most progressive individual in their dataset, categorised as a leader in five of the six changes. They suggest that Elizabeth's complex biographical experiences and atypical gendered identity offer a plausible basis for her linguistic behaviour:

> Her role [in language change] is not so exceptional after all. Her level of education surpassed that of most contemporary women and, as queen, she had access to language that normally belonged to the male sphere, viz. administration. On the other hand, she was never educated to become the ruler of the country, in other words, to adopt a male social role; her accession only took place after her two siblings, Mary and Edward, had died [...] The combination of female and male identities may provide us with some explanation for Elizabeth's progressiveness; she can be seen leading changes from below, which is typically what women do, but she is also progressive in [negative concord], which has been shown to be led by men in high administrative positions (2011: 28–29).

Their interpretation, which is based on the CEEC correspondence data for Elizabeth, is highly plausible. The study offers an intriguing glimpse of the insight idiolectal analysis can provide into language change as well as the integral role of biographical experience in shaping the language of an individual. However, it also raises further questions in terms of the relationship of Elizabeth's accession—hinted in the above quote—and her linguistic progressiveness. The significance of Elizabeth's early uptake of incoming variants, in relation to her social identity, also warrants further investigation. Moreover, the study focuses only on the CEEC data and thus the significance of style and stylistic variation (i.e. cross-genre) is not explored. Examining how Elizabeth uses variants in different contexts may shed light on their social evaluation and her position as a progressive language user, and provide a more rounded picture of the diffusion of these changes in the Early Modern period.

The authors also make a striking proposition regarding Elizabeth's role in change in her period. They hypothesise that Elizabeth's progressiveness was in fact crucial for the propulsion of linguistic change: 'for a change to spread rapidly in society, it is important that the topmost strata adopt it [...] Elizabeth's central role in her social networks most likely promoted the diffusion of the variant she adopted' (2011: 29). However, this observation somewhat contradicts the authors' other finding that progressive individuals often share social networks. For example, the Bacon brothers and their father are all identified as progressive users (2011: 29). Yet, key individuals in Elizabeth's social network do not share her progressiveness. William Cecil, Lord Burghley and Sir Francis Walsingham are both conservative users, despite their long-standing positions in Elizabeth's Privy Council. The presence of some 'individual who stand alone', versus 'groups, families, and social networks sharing linguistic choices' (2011: 30) is an intriguing and contrary situation, and suggests that a more fine-grained analysis would be beneficial in an attempt to understand why individual speakers, such as Elizabeth, make the linguistic choices they do.

These recent studies are important contributions to idiolectal analysis and historical sociolinguistics, and demonstrate the validity of a corpus-based comparative approach to historical data. However, I propose that the quantitative analysis can be augmented with other analytic techniques, in order to better exploit the scope of (Elizabeth's) idiolectal data. Employing a multi-faceted approach allows us to further test and evaluate the position of the idiolect in the investigation of language variation and change. More specifically, it allows the CEEC trends for Elizabeth to be corroborated across a wider spectrum of linguistic data. Examining the intersection between social and stylistic variation provides us with further, detailed description of her language use and an assessment of its possible impact upon the linguistic preferences of her contemporaries. It thus provides us with a rich basis from which to devise hypotheses and interpretations for the patterns identified in Elizabeth's idiolect, and establish their fit with the current sociolinguistic models of variation and change.

2. The Queen Elizabeth I Corpus (QEIC)

In order to investigate the idiolect of an individual, one of course needs suitable and accessible linguistic data. The following discussion is a brief overview of the composition and rationale behind the electronic Queen Elizabeth I Corpus (henceforth QEIC). A more extensive discussion of the compilation process and a list of the texts included in QEIC can be found in the Appendix (Tables 76–78). The composition of an original corpus, based on the manuscript records and recent edited collections of Elizabeth's works, reflects the need for an electronic resource suitable for comparative analysis on diachronic and stylistic dimensions. The selection of letters by Elizabeth I in CEEC offers a useful precedent, but these texts do not provide enough scope, either diachronically or stylistically, for the purposes of my approach.[4]

In 1925 the historian J. E. Neale wrote a scathing review of Frederick Chamberlain's *The Sayings of Queen Elizabeth* (1923), in which he criticised the unsatisfactory mix of anecdote and hearsay in the book, which he felt offered little sense of the provenance and authenticity of the works (and words) cited (Neale 1925). In all fairness, Chamberlain's work demonstrates the previous difficulties of discriminating between Elizabeth's canonical works and less authentic writing from dispersed and scattered sources. In the last decade, however, multiple modern editions of Elizabeth's works, not only her letters but her more literary works as well, have emerged (Mueller & Marcus 2003; Pryor 2003; May 2004a; Mueller & Scodel 2009a, 2009b).[5] These editions offer a valuable starting point for identifying texts for the electronic corpus, through comparison of the different editorial interpretations and commentary.

The QEIC covers the years 1544–1603, with sub-files for the pre- and post-accession periods. The total word count is c. 78,000. The corpus is comprised of three genres of Elizabeth's writing: correspondence, speeches and translations (see Table 1). The transcriptions are based either on the original manuscript or from an apograph of the original document (see Appendix for a more detailed account of this process). Whilst the corpus does not contain any previously unknown works, it is the first diachronic, electronic collection of Elizabeth's writing that I am aware of, bringing Elizabeth's works in line with macro-level corpora and providing a useful degree of flexibility for computational research techniques.[6]

A key feature of QEIC is the use of modern spelling and punctuation. This reflects the multiple difficulties created by the preservation of original spelling in an electronic corpus. Firstly, the distribution of original spelling in the corpus was inconsistent, as it represented a plurality of systems comprising Elizabeth's, that of contemporary scribes, and also later copyists. This presented a potentially misleading picture about the provenance of the texts. Secondly, original spelling is problematic when

---

[4] Anni Vuorinen (2002) used the CEEC files to compare Elizabeth's letters with those of a small number of male and female contemporaries, looking for evidence of gender differences. Whilst the study was insightful, particularly in its pronoun analysis, it adopted a narrower diachronic and analytic perspective than the one utilised in the present study.

[5] Throughout the study, references to the editors denote editorial comments and specific transcripts in that edition. For references to Elizabeth's writing, I cite the source document in the electronic corpus QEIC.

[6] Despite Elizabeth's historical significance, the number of her extant autograph texts is surprisingly small. Consequently, the pre-accession correspondence is under-represented compared to the post-accession letters (this also reflects the shorter time frame); and the speeches sub-section is much smaller than the other genres. These problems are common to studies working with historical data, what Labov posits as 'the art of making the best use of bad data' (1994: 11), and it is perhaps unrealistic to expect an idiolectal corpus not to encounter such difficulties, even for an individual as well-known as Elizabeth I.

Table 1. Properties of the Queen Elizabeth I Corpus (QEIC). Figures rounded.

	Pre-accession	Post-accession
Correspondence	6200 words	34600 words
Speeches	N/A	5900 words
Translations	22900 words	8300 words
Overall	29000 words	48800 words

using computational concordance programs. As studies using the HC have reported, scholars rarely manage to include all the spelling variants of a word form (Rissanen 1994: 75). Modernising the spelling provides a greater degree of accuracy; a decision that finds further support in the recent modern spelling version of CEEC (Palander-Collin, Juvonen & Hakala 2010).

Nevertheless, original spelling has a certain prestige in historical scholarship. It provides a greater authenticity and 'feel' for the historical text. In linguistic analysis it is arguable that original spelling is even more important, as modernised versions may obscure particular lexical or syntactic elements that are significant for analysis. However, nine of the ten linguistic variables investigated in Part II concentrate on features that remain the same in the transmission from original to modernised versions; e.g. affirmative *do* or the relative markers *who* and *which*. The decision to modernise QEIC is born out of practicality, rather than a lack of interest in Early Modern spelling. Indeed, there is significant potential in a socio-linguistic study of spelling and to pursue this a second, smaller corpus specifically designed for the study of Elizabeth's spelling system is also used. The QEI Spelling Corpus (QEISC) consists of transcripts of autograph correspondence only.[7]

The two formats also enable comparison of forms across corpora (where possible). This adds additional analytical rigor to QEIC, whilst maintaining the practicality of the modernised spelling. Future development, such as encoding the corpus into layers of modern/original features, is desirable. Yet, at present, QEIC and QEISC serve their purpose and can be used with concordance software (AntConc version 2.3.0 was used throughout my analysis) or as a simple text or rich text file.[8]

---

[7] The corpus includes all autograph letters found in QEIC. Because the corpus is used for an experimental sociolinguistic analysis of spelling, I have limited the data to correspondence only.

[8] There is certainly scope for a multi-format edition of the corpus that I envision would allow users access to the different dimensions of the material, such as original spelling, grammatical tagging, palaeographic information and hyperlinks to external evidence. The digitisation of NECTE (allowing user access to acoustic, orthographic, phonetic and grammatical components) is one example of how electronic corpora can be elaborated (see Allen et al. 2007: 16–48).

3. METHODOLOGY

Beatrix Busse suggests that for historical language studies 'it is valid to be more microlinguistically/microstylistically oriented and to investigate the styles of a genre, a person or a situation, and then evaluate these results against a reference corpus' (Busse 2010: 38). This principle underpins the comparative approach used to investigate Elizabeth's idiolect, which was also shown to be profitable in Nevalainen et al.'s (2011) analysis. For each linguistic feature analysed in Part II, the variable is evaluated at an intra-speaker level, documenting the similarities and differences between the pre-accession and post-accession periods, before a comparison is made with macro-level corpora. This approach allows Elizabeth's overall preferences to be established before identifying the points of conformity and deviance with her contemporaries, e.g. with the linguistic preferences of other women or the upper ranks, before evaluating the correlations against our knowledge of Elizabeth's biography and social experiences.

3.1 Macro-level Corpora

The comparative macro-level data used in this study is predominantly drawn from existing published works, which use large corpora compiled for historical sociolinguistic analysis. The majority of studies which offer relevant points of comparison with Elizabeth's idiolect use the Corpus of Early English Correspondence (CEEC): a socially representative, single genre corpus of around 6000 letters, spanning 1410–1681 and incorporating 2.7 millions words (see N&R-B 2003: 43–49). In some chapters, it was necessary to conduct my own analysis of macro-level data. For this, the Parsed Corpus of Early English Correspondence (PCEEC) text version was used. This corpus is slightly smaller than CEEC due to copyright restrictions, and is approximately 2.2 million words with around 4970 letters (see Taylor & Santorini 2006).

Another corpus used in many of the macro-level studies I refer to is the multi-genre Helsinki Corpus, which was designed 'to support the variationist approach to the history of English' (Kytö & Rissanen 1993: 1). The corpus comprises 1.5 million words covering the earliest English documents to 1710, and enables diachronic analysis of linguistic features in various genres including biblical texts, letters and philosophical treatises. The focus is on macro-level patterns rather than stylistic variation in the language of individual speakers. A third resource forming the macro-level baseline is the Corpus of English Dialogues, a collection of texts (1560–1760) representing speech-like written language of around 1.2 million words (see Culpeper & Kytö 2010). Again, the comparative analysis draws on existing studies conducted with the corpus.

3.2 Comparative Analysis

CEEC was developed in the 1990s in order to provide the first socially stratified corpora for historical sociolinguistic analysis. Previous research had concentrated on stylistic variation across genres (including the Helsinki Corpus (HC), largely developed by the same team involved with CEEC). The appreciation of social factors in language change was well established in modern-day sociolinguistics, and it was rightly thought important to develop this focus in historical investigations also. The reasoning behind the development of a single genre corpus to analyse macro-level linguistic change is that it removes (or, more accurately, limits) the interference from other factors known to contribute to variation: the inverse of Raumolin-Brunberg's (1991) decision to use an idiolect to study stylistic variation. By focusing on socially stratified informants participating in the same field of communication, findings can more confidently attribute trends to particular social factors, namely age, gender, domicile, social rank and level of education. The CEEC studies show that such social groups often participate differently in the progression of a linguistic change.

CEEC is comprised solely of correspondence, and the decision to use personal letters as the source genre for a socially stratified corpus has clear merits. Firstly, personal letters typically provide better documentation than other genres about their circumstances of composition, a necessity for sociolinguistic analysis. In correspondence the author, date, recipient, and even location are often recorded. Secondly, letters represent a greater proportion of the social spectrum compared to other genres from the Early Modern period; letter writing as an activity was open to all individuals fortunate enough to have a basic level of literacy.[9] The compilers of CEEC also suggest that personal letters 'share a number of linguistic features with the colloquial spoken idiom' (N&R-B 2003: 43–44). The relevance of this quality follows the established methodology in modern sociolinguistics, which considers every day spoken language as the site 'where the fundamental relations which determine the course of linguistic evolution can be seen most clearly' (Labov 1972: 208).

The clarity and methodological rigor behind CEEC has permitted many 'systematic historical investigations of language changes in their social contexts' (N&R-B 2003: 20). For the starting point of my sociolinguistic analysis of Elizabeth I's idiolect, the baseline provided by CEEC is an obvious choice and follows recent comparative studies of individual speakers that make use of this corpus (e.g. Raumolin-Brunberg 2005, 2006; Nevalainen et al. 2011). From a practical point of view, Elizabeth's correspondence provides the best diachronic representation of her idiolect,

---

[9] Many illiterate individuals are also thought to have used correspondence as a form of communication by enlisting the services of a scribe (see Daybell 2001: 60).

spanning almost 60 years, and CEEC offers a like-for-like genre comparison. The QEIC/CEEC comparison will also allow previous findings relating to Elizabeth's progressiveness in language change to be corroborated, given the larger span of the QEIC correspondence data.

However, the comparative analysis with CEEC is only the first stage of analysis used to explore the QEIC data. Three further comparative approaches are also used to investigate the nuances of Elizabeth's idiolect, reflecting the intention to fully explore the multiple factors—social, interactive, stylistic and systemic—that affect language variation and change, and thus exploit the opportunities presented by idiolectal data for fine-grained analysis. I now discuss each of the four stages in more detail.

3.3 *Social Factors*

In order to assess the role of a social factor in language change, the compilers of CEEC have categorised each informant according to their different social properties. The linguistic usage of informants who share particular social properties (i.e. gender) is then analysed under the different social categories, so that the relevance and role of that factor in the macro-level development of the linguistic change can be established. Investigations of linguistic variation and change in historical periods follow the uniformitarian principle, which proposes that the same forces that act on language use in the present (social, interactive, systemic) were the same in the past. This is a 'necessary working assumption' for the study of historical language and language change (Labov 1994: 23; see also N&R-B 2003: 22).

Queen Elizabeth I is included in CEEC, although with fewer letters than I use in my analysis in Part II, and she too is categorised according to her social characteristics. Her CEEC classification is shown in Table 2.

On the basis of the CEEC classification, we would look for (and expect to find) the greatest likeness between Elizabeth's use of linguistic features and those of the other informants in her social categories; e.g. between Elizabeth's use of feature x and that of the Court, between Elizabeth's use of feature y and that of other women. However, there are problems with the categorisation as it is presented in Table 2, as it gives no indication of the conflicting and contradictory nature of the different attributes that make up Elizabeth's socially unique position. To their credit, the compilers of CEEC acknowledge some of the potential difficulties arising from her classification. Arja Nurmi considers Elizabeth's sex (the basis for categorisation) versus gender role to be the most problematic element. She writes:

> the only person [in CEEC] whose case presents a possible conflict between biological and social reality is Queen Elizabeth I. Her status as a ruler makes her a special case in many respects. In her role as the monarch she is often referred to with masculine-sounding terms

Table 2. CEEC classification of Elizabeth I

Social factor	Elizabeth I
Date of birth	1533
Gender	Female
Social rank	Royalty (no mobility)
Domicile (geographical location)	Court (b. London)
Level of education	Higher (not university)

(e.g. prince) both by others and by herself. Because of her position it could be argued that in a great deal of her daily dealings she has a male gender role rather than a female one. However, as this speculation is difficult to verify in any meaningful way we have included her among the female gender (Nurmi 1999: 35).

I suggest that one meaningful way to determine if Elizabeth's idiolectal preferences are 'more male' or 'more female' is to conduct the analysis proposed here. If the results show that Elizabeth's language coheres with predominantly female trends throughout her life, then the label of 'honorary male' will not extend to Elizabeth's accommodation towards and adherence to the linguistic norms of that social group. Conversely, the 'honorary male' interpretation may be significantly reinforced if Elizabeth's idiolect shows greater comparability with male speakers.

This would be particularly relevant for my first research question if it were found that there was a noticeable shift between the pre-accession and post-accession periods, reflecting Elizabeth's changing social role after her accession. Although the possible distinction between the pre- and post-accession periods is not accommodated for in the CEEC categorisation, the identification of Elizabeth as a progressive user for both male- and female-led changes suggests that her gendered identity may well be a significant factor in her language use (Nevalainen et al. 2011).

One could also note diachronic changes in the assignation of domicile. The compilers of CEEC found it incongruous to assign 'London merchants and courtiers to the same domicile' (Nurmi 1999: 43), and devised the category of 'the Court' to include:

the members of the royal family, courtiers and other high-ranking government officials, many of whom lived in the West End and Westminster [...] keeping apart the Court and London gives us the opportunity of comparing a more prestigious variety with the natural speech of the capital, probably a dialect mixture (N&R-B 2003: 38–40).

The macro-level linguistic evidence suggests that this distinction is justified (e.g. N&R-B 2003: 157–184). However, in the pre-accession period

Elizabeth's contact with other people at the Court depended greatly on her favour or disfavour with the current monarch. After her accession, she moved to occupy and hold its centre. It is possible that Elizabeth's familiarity with, her reaction to, and her social ties within this domicile are far stronger during her reign than in her youth. These examples illustrate the need to consider the social conflicts and diachronic permutations present in Elizabeth's biography, rather than assuming each classification to be continuous and stable.

3.4 *Interactive Factors*

The composition of CEEC from a single genre narrows the analytical focus to social factors. Yet one of the benefits of idiolectal data is the potential to examine other factors involved in language variation and change, such as interactive and stylistic factors. Both of these aspects represent part of the broader category of STYLE, which denotes a speaker's modification (conscious or subconscious) of their language in response and reaction to their communicative context. Coupland (2007: 16) suggests that the concept of genre is so pervasive in society that it is distinguished from subtler, localised processes; genre is at a level of 'cultural salience' and interactive elements are the 'local acts of speaking'.

Dealing with the INTERACTIVE dimension first, researchers using CEEC (Nurmi 1999; N&R-B 2003) have attempted to incorporate this aspect in their analyses, offering REGISTER variation as an additional dimension to the tracing of social factors (age, gender, social rank) in a change. Register variation compensates for the lack of cross-genre stylistic variation, which has been the crux of variationist studies in the past (e.g. Romaine 1980; Dekeyser 1984; Raumolin-Brunberg 1991). Support for register as a factor is found in Romaine's (1982: 157) pioneering sociolinguistic investigation of relative markers in Middle Scots, which carefully documents differences between 'stylistic levels within texts' as well as across different genres.

Consequently, idiolectal analysis also needs to account for any variation within the interactive, localised situations of texts, even if those texts constitute a so-called homogenous genre. The social context of a letter to a close friend upon the birth of their child is undoubtedly going to differ from a letter written to a bank manager, and this will affect the linguistic choices of the writer. CEEC analyses of register variation focus on the relationship between recipient and addressee, categorising the recipient as one of two broad categories: family and non-family. The reasoning is that informants will use less formal language features in letters to family members, and more formal language to more socially distant addressees (Nurmi 1999: 104). The findings of Minna Nevala (2004) show the value of this distinction for the analysis of Early Modern address-forms, for example. However, their methodological approach is problematic for my analysis for two reasons. Firstly, the family/non-family categorisation disregards the possible influence of other interactive elements operating within a letter, such as accommodation. Communication Accommodation Theory (CAT) suggests that individuals modify their language use dynamically (i.e. in a particular communicative scenario, such as a letter) to either converge or diverge with the linguistic preferences of their communicative partner. Peter Garrett's (2010) summary neatly illustrates the potential influence of specific communicative situations on the linguistic choices of a speaker, and consequently highlights the problems of the generalised CEEC approach for an idiolectal study:

> Communication accommodation theory has drawn our attention [...] to the dynamic and interactive nature of communication and our motivations in its process, including effective communication, attitudinal response and our social and personal identities [...] Attitudes and motivations feature not only in our perceptions, evaluations and attributions as we encounter such adjustments and attunements; they are also components of our own communicative competence that underpin, consciously or unconsciously, our mo- ment-to-moment deployment of linguistic [...] resources to achieve our communication goals (Garrett 2010: 120).

Randy C. Bax (2002) demonstrates the significance of CAT for historical linguistics in his analysis of eighteenth-century correspondence between Samuel Johnson and Hester Lynch Thrale, noting points of convergence in semantic content, lexis and syntax. It is plausible that similar interactive elements influence Elizabeth's selection of linguistic variables on a case-by-case basis, and the methodology should allow for this factor.

Secondly, and perhaps more significantly, the family/non-family distinc- tion is difficult to apply to the recipients of Elizabeth's correspondence. The polarised categorisation of recipients (family = nuclear, other and close friends, versus non-family = family servant, other) used for register analysis (N&R-B 2003: 190) presumably provides the most efficient way to assess the relationship between author and recipient in the large amounts of corpus data. However, in the analysis of a socially unique individual such as Elizabeth, the family and non-family distinction is immediately problematic. The relationships we would predict between siblings or with a distant acquaintance are not necessarily applicable in her case. Using address-forms as an example, we can see that the social relationships she had with her recipients are somewhat deviant from the norm. In a letter to her sister, Princess Mary, Elizabeth addresses her sister warmly, as we might expect, and enquires after her health:

(1) To my well beloved sister Mary. Good Sister, as to hear of your sickness is unpleasant to me (27th October 1552, to Mary I, QEIC correspondence).

But only two years later, following Mary's accession, Elizabeth is forced to beg her sister to spare her life, signing at the subscription:

(2) I humbly crave but only one word of answer from your self. Your Highness' most faithful subject that hath been from the beginning, and will be to my end. Elizabeth (17th March 1554, to Mary I, QEIC correspondence).

As another example, in the letters to James VI, King of Scotland, Elizabeth consistently depicts their relationship using sibling terminology, a convention typical of monarchic correspondence. James VI was 33 years her junior, and her godson, and the two never met despite more than 20 years of diplomatic correspondence, in which Elizabeth often pushed the younger King to acquiesce to her demands. Furthermore, Elizabeth authorised the death warrant of his mother, Mary, Queen of Scots, in 1586. Thus, it is not clear how the family or non-family categories relate to this relationship(!). The layers of social convention and personal feeling do not easily transfer to the clear-cut categories.

Overall, the CEEC account of register appears too narrow and limited for an idiolectal study, particularly for the analysis of Queen Elizabeth I. In an attempt to resolve this, my examination of interactive factors endeavours to recognise the different facets involved in the interpersonal dimension of communication. The factors incorporate Elizabeth's relationship with the recipients, but considers them individually rather than categorically, drawing on the historical evidence to interpret Elizabeth's relationship with each recipient at that particular time. Interactive factor analysis also aims to incorporate the function of the letter, as letters written to the same recipient may have different goals. This is particularly relevant to Elizabeth's correspondence given the dramatic events of both the pre- and post-accession period. Lastly, I consider the compositional context (i.e. the speed of composition, existence of drafts), which could also affect the choice of linguistic variants.

3.5 *Stylistic Factors*

The third category incorporates the other dimension of style: genre variation. In modern sociolinguistic study, linguists analyse the properties of different style shifts made by speakers, performed consciously or sub-consciously, to understand the role of variation in communicative contexts and the relationship to language change.[10] The data is often elicited in a

---

[10] Labov (2006: 59) carefully points out that his definition of *style* as the level of 'attention paid to speech' is specific to the 'heuristic device' of his interview methodology, and not 'a claim that this is the way that styles and registers are to be ordered and understood in everyday life', as has sometimes been stated.

sociolinguistic interview or through covert recording, such as Labov's investigation of phonological variation in English speakers in New York (see Labov 2006). In historical language study, elicitation of style data from individual speakers is, of course, not possible, and the focus on different genres may therefore have originated as a proxy for this.

The Helsinki Corpus was developed for the specific purpose of investigating the diachronic development of linguistic features in multiple genres. However, the focus is very much on macro-level patterns rather than stylistic variation in the language of individual speakers. Whilst the compilers of the Helsinki Corpus include sociolinguistic information about the authors, very few authors in the corpus have works included in different genre categories. The sampling technique adopted by the compositors also limits the significance of any idiolectal findings. Elizabeth I, for example, is represented by prose extracts (not autograph) from her translation of Boethius and samples of her correspondence. This is not enough data to establish clear patterns in the Queen's stylistic preferences. Thus, rather than focus on the style shifts in the writing of the same individual(s), the HC shifts the attention away from the speaker and onto the broader cultural conventions of genre. The analyst must presume a level of homogeneity in the letters, prose, or drama written by multiple individuals, bound by shared cultural norms. The macro-level focus requires a compromise in the analytical approach, and one can understand why the team later developed CEEC to address the social dimension of variation and change.

However, Coupland suggests that sociolinguists should analyse genre (stylistic) variation as well as the conventional style-shifting (interactive) variation, because

> [o]ur socialisation into a cultural group's ways of communicating is partly a matter of learning institutional genres—learning how to read them and sometimes learning how to enact them (Coupland 2007: 15).

The significance of genre during Elizabeth's lifetime makes stylistic variation just as important for a study of sixteenth-century language variation as Coupland believes it to be for PDE analysis. In the Early Modern period genres were institutionalised; epistolary prose, for instance, followed specific models (Davis 1965: 237). Thus it is appropriate to investigate stylistic variation in Elizabeth's idiolect across different genres, as well as focussing on the interactive features operating within the different realisations of that genre.

The texts available for Elizabeth I's idiolect cover a range of genres, and this allows me to engage with stylistic variation in a way not attempted (or possible?) in historical macro-level studies. The findings for Elizabeth's idiolect attest to the significance of stylistic variation in the evolution of her idiolect, demonstrating her sensitivity to social conventions and communicative purpose, and offering an important perspective on her status as a progressive language user.

3.6 *Systemic Factors*

The three factors discussed so far address the social and stylistic dimensions. The final factor is systemic. Systemic factors concern the paradigmatic grammatical elements and structures that may promote or demote the linguistic variant. Previous studies, including those conducted within the sociolinguistic paradigm, incorporate systemic elements into an analysis both to assess the interaction with social factors and also to establish if the influence of a systemic element distorts the social data in a significant way, e.g. the influence of phonological context (word-ending) upon the selection of third-person singular verb ending *–eth* or *–s* (Kytö 1993). The factor is particularly important when using small datasets, as the over-representation of a particular systemic context needs to be accommodated into any interpretation of the data (e.g. Raumolin-Brunberg 2005: 48, fn.4). As my findings show, systemic factors are typically intertwined with other factors, with the combinations shaping the distribution of a variant in a text or texts.

3.7 *Linguistic Features*

In selecting the linguistic features for analysis in Elizabeth's idiolect, a number of elements had to be taken into consideration. The first criterion was the availability of existing macro-level comparative material. A key work that has greatly informed and influenced the features studied in QEIC is Nevalainen & Raumolin-Brunberg (2003), a macro-level investigation of 14 morphosyntactic changes using CEEC. Other research using CEEC also bore weight, particularly Nurmi's (1999) extensive analysis of periphrastic *do*.

However, there are limitations on which linguistic features can be considered in Elizabeth's idiolect. Some variables were irrelevant because of the dating of the change: prop-word *one*, for example, mainly develops in the seventeenth century (N&R-B 2003: 64). Other changes were not workable with the available idiolectal data. The number of tokens for prepositional relative *which* vs. adverbial *where*, for instance, was too low for any meaningful discussion at an idiolectal level. Finally, some features have already been extensively analysed in Elizabeth's idiolect, such as third-person singular verb ending *–eth* and *–s* (Lass 1999: 163; Raumolin-Brunberg 2005), and it was considered unnecessary to further duplicate this work. The final selection of linguistic features thus meet the criteria for sufficient data at both the macro- and idiolectal level, and offer a potential contribution to our knowledge of the variable in the Early Modern period.

The first feature discussed in Part II is affirmative declarative *do*. This variant has a curious history in English as the only syntactic context in which *do*-periphrasis failed to generalise in English despite reaching the early stages of the change. Elizabeth's usage is striking and idiosyncratic, socially and stylistically. Affirmative *do* is a distinctive feature of her idiolect, potentially useful for authorial analysis, and revelatory of the different biographical influences on her language. The results also provide diachronic and synchronic detail relevant to our understanding of the variable in a key period of its development. The second analysis considers a related change in EModE. Negative declarative *do* did become standard at the macro-level, yet the analysis reveals surprising similarities between the trends for both types of periphrastic declaratives in Elizabeth's idiolect, suggesting that the development of the forms was inter-connected.

The later chapters are grouped according to Elizabeth's position in the development of the change. Here, the analysis overlaps with the quantitative investigation of Nevalainen et al. (2011). The Queen Elizabeth I Corpus is used to study four linguistic variables that have previously been analysed in Elizabeth's idiolect using CEEC. The first three variables (*ye/you*, first- and second-person possessive determiners, multiple negation vs. single negation) are all linked by Elizabeth's leading position in the uptake of the incoming variant in Nevalainen et al.'s (2011) study. The analysis thus partly seeks to confirm their findings using a larger corpus of correspondence, as well as exploring the other genres contained in QEIC. My methodology and linguistic resources provide an opportunity for a finer-grained analysis with which to explore the social, interactive, systemic and stylistic dimensions of Elizabeth's linguistic leadership, a goal that coheres with my third research question concerning the contribution of idiolectal analysis to historical sociolinguistics. A fourth, original analysis, relative marker *who/which*, completes this section. By discussing these linguistic changes sequentially, I can highlight the similarities and differences in the factors contributing to Elizabeth's progressive uptake and reflect on the role of her accession in the development of each variable.

The other linguistic variable analysed in Part II that is also considered by Nevalainen et al. (2011) is the replacement of relative marker *the which* by *which*. The authors find Elizabeth to be a mid-range user in this change, in contrast to her progressiveness elsewhere. The wider scope of QEIC identifies Elizabeth as a lagger in the user of *(the) which* in specific temporal periods, and I explore the possible factors that may explain this rather unusual trait in her idiolect.

In the penultimate analyses presented in Part II, I discuss in detail two linguistic features whose development shows a clear correlation with Elizabeth's accession: superlative adjectives and *royal we*, and explore the possible causes for this connection. The study concludes with an experimental analysis of Elizabeth's spelling. Expanding the analytical focus of historical sociolinguistics, I explore how spelling can be described and explained using the sociolinguistic methodology applied in the preceding chapters, providing the first systematic account of Elizabeth's spelling system. In Part III, I reflect collectively on the evidence gathered from QEIC exploring its implications for each research question in turn.

PART II

RESULTS AND ANALYSIS

4. AFFIRMATIVE *DO*

The rise and fall of periphrastic *do* in affirmative declaratives has been astutely described as 'a perfectly good change that did not quite make it' (Ihalainen 1983), and consequentially is perhaps 'one of the most researched and most contentious areas of English syntax' (Hope 1994: 11). Affirmative *do* was one of the earliest contexts of English *do*-periphrasis, a syntactic construction now obligatory in negative and interrogative contexts (Rissanen 1999: 239), and in the Early Modern period the variant *do* ((3)) formed part of a bipartite variable in competition with the non-*do* declarative form ((4)). The variable excludes declaratives with modal auxiliaries (*can, could, shall, should,* etc.) or the verbs *be* or *have* in either modal or lexical position.

(3) and yet we **do hope** that you are no partakers of the offence (4th May 1589, to John Norris and Francis Drake, QEIC correspondence).

(4) and therefore I **hope** he will not dare deny you a truth (January 1585, to James VI, QEIC correspondence).

The frequency of affirmative *do* increased during the sixteenth century. However, unlike negative and interrogative contexts, the variant did not progress beyond the incipient stage (c.10%) to become the norm. It instead declined from use, with some studies dating the emergence and decline to a 50-year timeperiod (Ellegård 1953). This period falls within Elizabeth's lifetime. Affirmative *do* has been the focus of many macro-level studies that have attempted to describe and explain the curious failure of the periphrastic variant. As a consequence, there is a good deal of comparative material available. The diachronic and synchronic documentation, and the questions that remain surrounding its demise, provide numerous points to explore from an idiolectal perspective.

It is necessary to raise a methodological point relating to the analysis of this linguistic feature. In previous studies, scholars often present the results using normalised frequencies, e.g. frequency of affirmative *do* per 1000 words. This reflects the difficulties of identifying the non-*do* declarative contexts in large corpora such as CEEC or HC. Nurmi found only minimal differences in a test case of both percentages and normalised frequencies (1999: 53), and considered it sufficient to focus on only *do* tokens in her study. Fortunately, the relatively small size of QEIC makes percentages a feasible option. To calculate the figures, I manually tagged each sub-section of the corpus for all affirmative declarative *do* and non-*do* contexts and then identified and sorted all tokens using the AntConc concordance program. Despite Nurmi's statement to the contrary, discrepancies between the two treatments of the data materialise when the figures from QEIC are placed side-by-side. For example, when analysing the distribution of affirmative *do* by recipient the percentages appear disproportionately high compared to the normalised figures. Catherine Parr, for example, receives letters containing affirmative *do* at an average frequency of 3.2 times per 1000 words—an unremarkable amount in comparison to the overall figure for Elizabeth's correspondence. In percentage terms, however, affirmative *do* accounts for a high 17.6% and thus seems to be far more significant. The difference reveals one of the drawbacks of normalised frequencies in the analysis of affirmative *do*, in that this method cannot convey the proportion of declarative contexts within a text. In the QEIC correspondence, Elizabeth frequently uses modalised sentences instead of the simple or affirmative *do* declarative contexts included in the variable. The normalised figures disguise this dimension of the text, whereas the percentages reveal it. The advances in electronic tagging should help scholars to negotiate this issue in future research. In the following discussion, I use both methods.

4.1 *Results*

In Elizabeth's correspondence, affirmative *do* accounts for 8.4% of all positive declarative contexts; a frequency of 2.6 times per thousand words (Table 3).

Table 3. Frequency of *do* in affirmative declaratives (QEIC correspondence)

	Total (*do* and non-*do*)	% *do*	*Do*/1000 words
PreA	221	15.4	5.4
PostA	1048	6.9	2.1
Overall	1269	8.4	2.6

This overall figure fits the contemporary macro-level frequencies. Nurmi (1999: 108, Table 7.1) reports an average frequency of 2.7 times per 1000 words for sixteenth-century CEEC informants. From this broad perspective, Elizabeth's usage appears to conform to the macro-level norm. However, the diachronic development paints a different picture. The frequencies for the pre-accession correspondence show that Elizabeth used the variant more frequently at this time, at 15.4% or 5.4 times per 1000 words. The figure for the post-accession period reveals a downward trend,

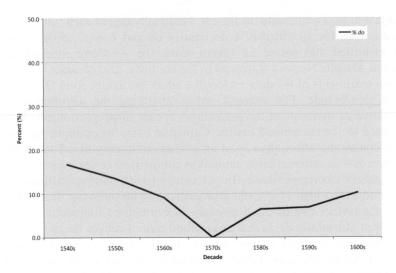

Figure 1: Affirmative *do* (%) by decade (QEIC correspondence)

with affirmative *do* accounting for only 6.9% of contexts, or 2.1 times per 1000 words (p > 0.001).[1]

Breaking the data down further, it is possible to chart the decline by decade. Allowing for error in the 1560s and 1570s due to low token counts, affirmative *do* recedes from 16.7% in the 1540s to 6.4% in the 1580s (p > 0.001). There is a minimal rise to 6.8% in the 1590s, although the difference with the previous decade is not statistically significant.[2] The final three years of Elizabeth's life (1600–1603) may show a slight shift in favour of affirmative *do*, the frequency rising to 10.2%, although again the difference is not statistically significant when compared with either the 1580s or 1590s.

Macro-level studies show a striking contrast with the downward trend in Elizabeth's idiolect, reporting a 'strong quantitative increase of *do*' during the sixteenth century (Stein 1991: 356). Rissanen (1991) and Wischer (2008), using the Helsinki Corpus, and Nurmi (1999) using CEEC, all find that the frequency of affirmative *do* rises across the sixteenth century, with a peak at around 1600. Only after this point does the variant show a decline. Nurmi (1999: 179–182) has suggested that the macro-level decline of affirmative *do* in the early seventeenth century may reflect the increased contact between English and Scots courtiers and councillors following the accession of James I. Affirmative *do* in sixteenth-century Scots English was highly infrequent, and Nurmi hypothesises that the individuals at Court and London accommodated their usage to the dialect of the Scottish nobility.

---

[1] Statistical significance is calculated using the chi-square test. The degree of freedom = 1.
[2] The contrast between the 1540s and 1590s is, however, statistically significant (p > 0.001).

The 1580s marks the start of Elizabeth's correspondence with James VI of Scotland, and it is possible that the decline of *do* in the correspondence may reflect linguistic accommodation on Elizabeth's part towards her Scots-speaking royal addressee. This would indicate an early manifestation of Nurmi's Scottish hypothesis, sharing the same principles of accommodation. I consider this possibility, and the strength of Nurmi's hypothesis in relation to Elizabeth's idiolect, in my analysis of interactive factors.

There is one study that shows an exception to the macro-level upward trend. Ellegård (1953) dates the peak of affirmative *do* (of 10%) to the mid-sixteenth century, with the form showing a fairly rapid and permanent decline from 1550 onwards. Significantly, Ellegård's corpus uses literary texts, and was compiled according to availability of the texts rather than because of their particular properties (e.g. genre or social representativeness). His corpus does not use the controlled criteria of more recent corpora such as CEEC or the HC, and this limits the representativeness of the corpus trends for the macro-level change. Nevertheless, the diachronic trends in Elizabeth's idiolect correlate best with this data: see Figure 2.

The decrease in frequency means that Elizabeth has a different status in the change for the two sub-periods. In the pre-accession period, she can be classed as a leader of the change as the frequency of affirmative *do* is considerably higher in the princess' correspondence than the macro-level norm of that period. Nurmi (1999: 108) records a normalised frequency of 2.4 times per 1000 words in CEEC for 1540–1559. The figure for Elizabeth's correspondence is also higher than the c. 10% peak identified in Ellegård's literary

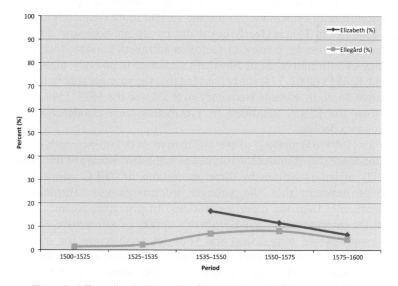

Figure 2: Affirmative *do* (%) in Ellegård (1953) and QEIC correspondence

corpus. In the post-accession period, we find the converse situation, with CEEC recording higher frequencies than Elizabeth's correspondence throughout the decades of her reign. Elizabeth's variable usage could be attributed to two different influences: accommodation to the Scots dialect of James VI, anticipating the 'Scottish hypothesis' of the seventeenth century; or a stylistically sensitive usage of *do* that fits with the more literary texts and authors of the sixteenth century used in Ellegård's corpus. A more detailed analysis of social, interactive and stylistic factors will test these hypotheses.

4.2 *Social Factors*

Having established the diachronic distribution of affirmative *do* in Elizabeth's idiolect and compared it with the macro-level trends, I now assess the role of social factors in the distribution of the variant, in particular to assess if the contrast between the two sub-periods is connected to Elizabeth's accession. The analysis considers four social factors: age, gender, domicile and social rank. Each factor has been previously identified in macro-level analyses as showing different distributional trends for affirmative *do* in the sixteenth century.

Kallel (2002) has proposed that age was a key factor in the uptake of affirmative do during the early to mid-sixteenth century. His analysis of the correspondence written by two generations of the Lisle family (letters dating from 1533–1540) found that the younger generation (b. 1516–1526) used the *do* variant more frequently than the older generation, indicating that the adolescent authors were leaders of this change. Kallel's results suggest that Elizabeth (b. 1533), as one of the younger generations of speakers in the mid-sixteenth century, would also use the variant more frequently than the macro-level norm. This is clearly borne out by the pre-accession data, and thus age appears to be a relevant factor in Elizabeth's usage. Indeed, the frequency of affirmative *do* in Elizabeth's idiolect is possibly higher than expected: Kallel's (2002: 174) study revealed that the younger generation used affirmative *do* at an average frequency of 9.5% for the 1533–1540 period, lower than the 15.4% identified in Elizabeth's correspondence for the following two decades.

Nurmi's (1999: 63) analysis of the affirmative *do* in late sixteenth-century correspondence corroborates the role of age in the distribution of the variant. Her study of letters written by three generations of CEEC informants in the 1590s indicates that the younger informants use affirmative *do* more frequently than the older generations. In principle, Nurmi's results support the interpretation that Elizabeth's uptake of affirmative *do* in the pre-accession period may reflect the youthful predilection for incoming variants. However, Nurmi uses data from a later time period, analysing correspondence from the final two decades of the sixteenth century. In her results, Elizabeth's generation continues to use *do* more frequently than the older generations, with no evidence of a decline. This suggests that Elizabeth's usage should also have remained at a frequency comparable to, if not greater than, her pre-accession usage. Instead, the data shows a downward trend, indicating that other events or experiences of the post-accession period—potentially Elizabeth's accession—resulted in Elizabeth losing her position as linguistic leader in the uptake of this change.

Other social factors may provide some insight into the contrast in Elizabeth's usage in the two sub-periods. In her analysis of affirmative *do*, Nurmi (1999: 172) found gender to be a significant social factor in CEEC. Her results indicated that men used affirmative *do* more frequently than women in the latter half of the sixteenth century, and continued to do so until the mid-seventeenth century. Elizabeth's preferences (2.0 per 1000 words) show a greater correlation with CEEC female informants (2.1 per 1000 words) for the 1580–1599 sub-period. Male informants record a normalised frequency of 3.8 for the same period (Nurmi 1999: 172).

To further examine the comparability between Elizabeth and female informants in the sixteenth century, I have compiled data for the earlier decades using PCEEC (see Table 4). Admittedly, the PCEEC data provides only low token counts, and thus caution is necessary when interpreting the data. However, some reassurance is provided by the fact that the figure for the 1580–1599 period is the same as the CEEC data (see Nurmi 1999: 172).

In the earliest period (1540–1559) Elizabeth's usage is much higher than that of her contemporary female informants, suggesting that her leading position in the change was not typical of her gender. However, for the post-accession decades the correlation is more convincing. For the recalculated data of the 1580–1599 sub-period, Elizabeth's usage (2.0 times per 1000 words) is comparable to that of PCEEC female informants (2.1 per 1000 words). The similarity also extends to the earlier 1560–1579 sub-period. In the previous section, I attributed the low figure of affirmative *do* in these decades to the limitations of the correspondence corpus material. Instead, the drop may reflect a general decline of affirmative *do* in this period amongst female informants, although the token count is very small for both QEIC and PCEEC.

Table 4. Frequency of affirmative *do* (per 1000 words) (PCEEC women informants and QEIC correspondence)

	PCEEC women		Elizabeth	
	Do (n.)	*Do*/1000 words	*Do* (n.)	*Do*/1000 words
1540–1559	5	1.5	34	5.4
1560–1579	4	0.9	1	1
1580–1599	12	2.1	62	2

Table 5. Frequency of affirmative *do* 1580–
1599 by domicile in CEEC (adapted from
Nurmi 1999: 177) and QEIC correspondence:
normalised frequencies per 1000 words

	Do/1000 words
Court	4.3
East Anglia	4.3
London	2.8
North	1.6
Elizabeth	2.0

Female informants provide the best social correlate for Elizabeth's low
use of affirmative *do* in the post-accession period. There is little similarity
between the Queen's preferences and those of other informants in her social
categories. For example, domicile is a significant social factor in the macro-
level distribution of the variant, with East Anglia and the Court showing a
much higher use of the form towards the end of the sixteenth century than
their Northern and London counterparts (Nurmi 1999: 177). Elizabeth uses
affirmative *do* less than half as frequently as her Court-dwelling
contemporaries in the 1580–1599 sub-period; indeed, the relative infrequency of the variant shows a greater resemblance to her London
counterparts (2.8 /1000 words) or the North (1.6 /1000 words).

One possible interpretation is that the high turnover of personnel at the
Court exposed Elizabeth to the dialects of those from further afield, such as
the City of London and migrants from the North (see Keene (2000) for a
discussion of migration patterns for London in the Early Modern period).
Yet, if this were the case, it is curious that the other individuals at the
Court, including Elizabeth's closest courtiers, do not show the same
susceptibility to dialect contact.[3]

---

[3] It is important to note that the Court figure presented in Table 5 includes Elizabeth's CEEC
correspondence for the 1580–1599 sub-period. It is possible that this affects the accuracy of my
comparison with the QEIC correspondence data. One option I have considered is to recalculate
the CEEC data without the CEEC Elizabeth sub-files. For affirmative *do*, I found that this
increases the frequency of the variant for the Court to 4.6 times per 1000 words—a relatively
small amount with minimal effect on the overall trends. Yet adjusting the figures also has its
problems. Doing so deviates from one of the study's central methodological goals—to compare
Elizabeth's idiolectal data with the macro-level baseline; changing the data would create
inconsistencies in the CEEC figures, with some recalculated and some not. One point of using
the results from large corpora is that they represent overall trends, and are not unduly affected
by the preferences of a single individual. Furthermore, I cannot guarantee that
my recalculations exactly match the data used by Nurmi (1999) or that of other studies
(e.g. N & R-B 2003). This causes further problems for future replication of the study's methods
and analysis. Consequently, the practice in this chapter and throughout the study is to present
the CEEC data as found. The difference between the CEEC Elizabeth data and the larger
QEIC should help to ensure the comparisons are reliable.

Overall, the analysis of social factors reveals that age provides the best social explanation for Elizabeth's advanced uptake of affirmative *do* in the pre-accession period. In the post-accession correspondence, female informants provide the most convincing match with her idiolectal preferences. Yet the explanatory scope of these correlates is limited; Elizabeth's pre-accession usage was much higher than the macro-level data would suggest, and, similarly, the dramatic decrease in frequency in the post-accession period bears little resemblance to the diachronic trends for other informants, either male or female. The data provides no clear evidence that the switch from a leading position to a low usage correlates with Elizabeth's accession, although the distinctiveness of her preferences at different timeperiods may well provide a useful feature for authorship analysis.

4.3 *Systemic Factors*

The next stage of analysis is to investigate the role of systemic factors in Elizabeth's use of affirmative *do*. Regardless of the debates over the initial origin of *do*-periphrasis (see Wischer 2008 for a concise overview), linguists have reached a consensus that periphrastic *do* has most likely 'always been a feature of spoken language' (Rissanen 1987: 103). Over the course of the sixteenth century, as the variant was increasing in frequency in most genres (but cf. Ellegård 1953), affirmative *do* diversified into different functions in spoken and written modes. This has led some linguists to grant preference to 'sometimes one, sometimes another set of factors' in their analysis of affirmative *do* (Rissanen 1999: 241).

Under the banner of systemic factors, the analysis considers syntactic and lexical contexts that are attested to promote affirmative *do* in EModE. These have a tangible connection to 'writing and planned speech in the rhetorical vein', and hence represent more literary and formal modes of writing (Rissanen 1999: 241). The subsequent section on interactive factors investigates a separate type of affirmative *do* called DISCURSIVE FOREGROUNDING *DO*, which is defined by 'the repetition of *do*-construction in rapid succession' to highlight and emphasise that passage of text (Rissanen 1999: 243). Discursive foregrounding *do* tends to occur in formal spoken mode texts to add intensity and emphasis and often to flag-up points of an argument or debate—hence the decision to analyse it separately in the section concerned with localised, context-specific interactive features.[4]

---

[4] Wischer (2008: 144) does not make an explicit distinction between written and discursive foregrounding *do*, but instead appears to subsume the two under the description 'a stylistic device in formal texts'. My account follows Rissanen's categorisation (1991, 1999) as my results suggest that Elizabeth does make a distinction between formal, spoken discursive foregrounding and literary, rhetorical uses.

The role of affirmative *do* in 'writing and planned speech in the rhetorical vein' (Rissanen 1999: 241) encompasses two elements. Firstly, the periphrasis provides semantic or syntactic clarification by identifying the verb in a clause—what Smith terms 'a tracking device' (1996: 160). This function was a necessary consequence of the rapid syntactic and lexical developments in sixteenth-century English, which led to a greater level of ambiguity in clause components (Nevalainen 1991: 308; Rissanen 1999: 242; Wischer 2008: 146–147). For example, affirmative *do* can be used to divide complex verb groups (i.e. with verb-initial adverbials) into more explicit components, separating the grammatical and semantic elements (Rissanen 1999: 242). It has also been suggested (Samuels 1972: 174; Wischer 2008: 146) that affirmative *do* collocates with Romance verbs (new borrowings) to disambiguate and flag up the verb in an utterance. Smith (1996: 160) and Samuels (1972: 174) further suggest that *do* occurs with Germanic strong verbs to mark tense, as the previous vocalic distinction had been lost in the Great Vowel Shift. However, this context has little significance in Elizabeth's idiolect.

The second role of affirmative *do* in written and literary (con)texts reflects the stylistic ideals of the sixteenth century. For example, the lengthening function of the periphrasis can add weight to a short verb phrase, either in final position or to those situated within weighty clauses. Rissanen (1999: 241) suggests that this function occurs in texts 'produced by writers or speakers conscious of stylistic demands'. The periphrasis can also provide a contrastive function, emphasising one part of a coordinate clause over another (Wischer 2008: 148).

In the previous macro-level studies (e.g. Wischer 2008), systemic factors are typically analysed according to the distribution of affirmative *do* across the different contexts, rather than by calculating the percentage of *do* from the overall figures of *do* and non-*do* in 'x' context. Like the use of normalised frequencies for the diachronic trends, the representation of *do* in this way is a necessary shortcut because of the problems of identifying declaratives in large macro-level corpora. One benefit of the idiolectal study is that the smaller corpus enables the systemic data to be presented using both methods, allowing an assessment of the conventional *do*-only approach.

In the analysis of Elizabeth's correspondence, I consider four syntactic contexts that are attested to promote affirmative *do* at the macro-level. Each has a discernable influence upon her practice: adverbials between the subject and the lexical verb ((5)); clause-final verb position ((6)); inversion of subject with a component of the verb phrase ((7)); and an intervening clause between subject and verb ((8)).

(5) you **do forthwith cause** him to be sent back hither (4th May 1589, to John Norris and Francis Drake, QEIC correspondence).

(6) as in other things **I do understand** (28th January 1549, to Edward Seymour, QEIC correspondence).

(7) **so do I see** by his overture that (4th July 1602, to James VI, QEIC correspondence).

(8) **she (being called from sin to repentance) doth** faithfully hope to be saved (31st December 1544, to Catherine Parr, QEIC correspondence).

In the QEIC correspondence, 58.5% of affirmative *do* tokens occur in one of the four syntactic contexts. There is a slight increase between the pre- and post-accession periods (55.9% to 59.7%), although this is not statistically significant. The distribution between the four syntactic contexts is not equal (see Table 6). When treated using the conventional method, i.e. calculating the percentage of *do* tokens only in each context, intervening material accounts for the highest proportion (30.2% of the *do* tokens), with adverbials also high (14.2%), offering clear systemic characteristics for Elizabeth's use of the variant.

Table 7 shows the recalculated data as the percentage of *do* in the total *do* and non-*do* tokens. Firstly, the figures reinforce the significance of these syntactic contexts in Elizabeth's idiolect and, by extension, the attested significance in macro-level accounts. The percentage of *do* in all four syntactic contexts is far higher than in the tokens classified without a context, which amount to only 4.3% of tokens. The difference between each syntactic context and the non-systemic declaratives is statistically significant ($p > 0.001$). However, the distribution also shows differences

Table 6. Affirmative *do* in syntactic contexts (%), *do* tokens only (QEIC correspondence)

	Do tokens (n.)	% overall
Adverbial	15	14.2
Verb final	6	5.7
Inversion	9	8.5
Intervening clause	32	30.2
No context	44	41.5
Total	106	

Table 7. Affirmative *do* in syntactic contexts (%) out of *do*/non-*do* (QEIC correspondence)

	Do and non-*do* (n.)	% *do*
Adverbial	73	20.5
Verb final	31	19.4
Inversion	19	47.4
Intervening material	124	25.8
No context	1022	4.3
Total	1269	

Table 8. Affirmative *do* in syntactic contexts (%) out of *do*/non-*do* (QEIC correspondence, pre- and post-accession periods)

Context	Pre-accession correspondence		Post-accession correspondence	
	Do and non-*do* (n.)	% *do*	*Do* and non-*do* (n.)	% *do*
Adverbial	15	40.0	58	15.5
Verb final	8	25	23	17.4
Inversion	6	83.3	13	30.8
Intervening material	19	31.6	105	24.8
Second person	0	0	0	0
No context	173	8.7	849	3.4
Total	221		1048	

in the ranking and the implied importance of the contexts in Elizabeth's idiolect. Inversion, in particular, contrasts considerably with the *do*-only data. In Table 6 it accounts for only 8.5% of all affirmative *do* forms. However, out of all the inverted declaratives in QEIC correspondence, affirmative *do* occurs in almost half of them (47.4%). Clauses with intervening material are thus ranked second in this treatment of the data. Verb-final contexts show a frequency of around 20%, which also contrasts with the low percentage for the *do*-only figures.

The figures also reveal that the influence of the syntactic contexts changes over time (see Table 8). For example, 83.3% of inverted contexts contain *do* in the pre-accession period, compared with only 30.8% in the post-accession period (allowing for a low token count). The other syntactic contexts also show a decrease over time, although the figures are not statistically significant. It is also important to note that the no-context declaratives also decrease over time, from 8.7% to 3.4% (p > 0.01). I investigate this dimension, and its relation to discursive foregrounding *do*, when considering interactive factors.

The quantitative figures for the syntactic contexts can only tell half the story. Qualitative analysis helps to illustrate the connection between the contexts and the literary and rhetorical associations attested in the literature, and reveals that even though the decline in percentages between periods is not significant for all contexts there is a discernable shift in how Elizabeth uses each syntactic construction, perhaps reflecting the different influences and purposes of her correspondence either side of her accession. For example, the pre-accession instances of intervening material show signs of careful construction incorporating rhetorical devices, with Elizabeth using parentheses ((9), and also (8)), or using *comparatio* ((10))[5]:

---

[5] Peacham (1593: 156–157) defines *comparatio* as those forms of speech 'which do tend to most especially to amplifie or diminish by form of comparison'.

(9) how she (beholding and contempling what she is) **doth** perceive (June 1544, to Catherine Parr, QEIC correspondence).

(10) that as a good father that loves his child dearly **doth** punish him sharply, So God favouring your Majesty (21st April 1552, to Edward VI, QEIC correspondence).

It is worth noting here that *do* occurs in a main clause following separation from the subject by a subordinate clause. Samuels (1972: 174) suggests that this is a promoting factor during the Early Modern period, with the periphrasis flagging up the main verb. However, analysis of Elizabeth's *do* data shows this context accounts for 15% of tokens (16 of 106), suggesting that its influence in Elizabeth's idiolect is minimal. In the case of example (10), for instance, the emphatic nature of the rhetorical device contributes to the promotion of *do* as much as (if not more than) the syntactic construction. By contrast, the intervening material contexts in the post-accession corpus reflect an increase in conjoined clauses with a shared elliptical subject, a construction typical of less literary composition. Wischer (2008: 147) has observed a similar propensity for affirmative *do* in such clauses in her analysis of the HC, citing examples from trials, diaries and sermons (i.e. spoken-mode genres).

(11) but I doubt not but your answer to his treasonable letter will make him and such like know that you not only hate the treason **but do owe** as much to the traitor (May 1593, to James VI, QEIC correspondence).

(12) I will not willingly call you in question for such warnings if the greatness of the cause may not compel me thereunto. **And do entreat** you to think that if any accident so befall you as either secrecy or speed shall be necessary (4th July 1602, to James VI, QEIC correspondence).

Thus, for this particular context we can see a shift in the use of *do* from rhetorical contexts to contexts where *do* aids comprehension. Both properties are recognised in the outline of affirmative *do* presented at the beginning of this section, but the chronology suggests that there may have been a shift in Elizabeth's stylistic valuation of the variant over time to less literary contexts. The contrast suggests a possible connection to her accession, and also offers a qualitative dimension for this feature from the perspective of authorship assessment.

The distribution of *do* in inverted contexts shows a similar change. In the pre-accession data, affirmative *do* occurs in over 80% of inverted declaratives, falling to around one third in the post-accession period. This quantitative decrease is apparently connected to the stylistic context of the inversion. In the pre-accession period, the examples have a self-conscious, rhetorical quality to them, as in (13), where Elizabeth aligns herself with the testimony of Augustine. In the post-accession examples, inverted *do* occurs after clause-initial adverbs (*yet, so, now*) and foregrounds a shift in topic ((14)) or indicates a contrastive element ((15)). The non-*do* inverted declaratives ((16)) show a comparable function in the post-accession period:

(13) For **now do I say** with Saint Austin (21st April 1552, to Edward VI, QEIC correspondence).

(14) **Now do I remember** your Cumber to read such scribbled Lines (16th March 1593, to James VI, QEIC correspondence).

(15) You would none of such a league as myself should not be one, **so do I see** by his overture that himself doth (4th July 1602, to James VI, QEIC correspondence).

(16) My dear brother, never were there yet prince nor meaner wight to whose grateful turns I did not correspond in keeping them in memory to their avail and my own honour. **So trust I** that you will not doubt but that your last letters by Fowles and the Duke are so acceptably taken (1st December 1601, to James VI, QEIC correspondence).

Wischer (2008: 250) states that 'many scholars have rightly argued that *do* is more likely used if there is an adverb before the lexical verb'; a claim she supports using her own analysis of the proportion of *do* in this context in the HC. As Table 8 shows, the context may be statistically significant but it is not a defining factor in Elizabeth's use of affirmative *do*. Many more adverbial clauses occur in the QEIC correspondence without periphrasis, a finding that suggests this context may be somewhat exaggerated in the conventional accounts. In Elizabeth's idiolect, there is also a clear distinction between the pre- and post-accession adverbial contexts. In the earlier letters, *do* occurs in expressions of deference, working alongside the adverbial to intensify or emphasise the utterance, such as a request ((17)):

(17) With my hearty commendations I **do most heartily** desire you to further the Desires of my last letters (29th October 1555, to William Paulet, QEIC correspondence).

In the post-accession period, the adverbial contexts containing *do* express demands, rather than deference, although the combination with the adverb again links to intensification or emphasis ((18), (19)). This function of the syntactic context again fits with the contrast in Elizabeth's social status before and after her accession, and possibly reflects the different type of letters she wrote as Princess and as Queen. However, the presence of non-*do* adverbials with a similar function ((20)) means that the change in function over time cannot fully explain the decline of *do* seen in this context in the later period.

(18) We **do therefore** charge and command you forthwith (15th April 1589, to Robert Devereux, QEIC correspondence).

(19) all dilatory excuse set apart you **do forthwith** cause him to be sent hither (4th May 1589, to John Norris and Francis Drake, QEIC correspondence).

(20) And if Essex be now come into the company of the fleet we **straightly** charge you (4th May 1589, to John Norris and Francis Drake, QEIC correspondence).

The verb-final contexts also show differences between the pre- and post-accession examples. In the pre-accession correspondence, the two examples occur in letters to Edward Seymour, and refer to Elizabeth's mental state. Rissanen (1999: 241) suggests that affirmative *do* helped to lengthen short final-verbs, reflecting the stylistic ideals of the period. However, in the given example it appears more likely that *do* combines with the final verb to emphasise and intensify Elizabeth's statement:

(21) My lord, these are the Articles which I **do remember** (January 1549, to Edward Seymour, QEIC correspondence).

In the post-accession period, similar examples occur without affirmative *do*:

(22) The whole world that be spectators both what princes do and what they suffer (March 1597, to James VI, QEIC correspondence).

There are more ambiguous examples of *do* + final verb in the post-accession correspondence. The two instances occur in the final line of the letter's main body before the subscription. They resemble the rhetorical device *correctio*, often used as a climactic expression, with the conjunction providing a contrastive element[6]:

(23) Thus I finish to trouble you but **do** rest (January 1586, to James VI, QEIC correspondence).

Wischer (2008: 148) identifies similar contrastive uses of *do* in the HC, although she does not mention any epistolary-specific formula of this kind in her data. In the non-*do* data, verb-final *correctio* also occurs, although not as part of the closing formula:

---

[6] George Puttenham (1589/2007: 223) describes *correctio* (Gk. *metanoia*) as the figure whereby 'we seeme to call in our worde again and put in another fitter for the purpose [...] the speaker seemeth to reforme that which was said amisse'. *Correctio* appears in other guises in Elizabeth's correspondence, such as the explicit use of negators to self-correct and mark contrast: 'Who of judgment that deemed me not simple could suppose that any answers you have writ me should satisfy, **nay**, enter into the opinion of one not void of four senses, leaving out the fifth?' (22nd December 1593, to James VI, QEIC correspondence).

(24) But finish this reason with justice which no man may reproach but every creature **laud** (19th May 1589, to James VI, QEIC correspondence).

Overall, the analysis of the four syntactic contexts reveals that Elizabeth's use of affirmative *do* is influenced by elements relating to comprehension and to more explicitly rhetorical expressions. The diachronic perspective suggests that the latter decreased over time, and this partly explains the decline in *do* seen in the overall trend of her correspondence. The idiolectal data corresponds to macro-level literature, in terms of the influence of the syntactic contexts, but the methodology indicates that the order of importance, based on *do* tokens only, may be less accurate than anticipated.

In addition to syntactic factors, lexical properties have also been identified as influential in the selection of affirmative *do*. Samuels (1972: 174) suggests that Latinate neologisms promote affirmative *do* during the sixteenth century, prompted by a need for semantic clarification of the tense and word class of the new, often specialist, borrowings. Wischer (2008: 146) suggests that affirmative *do* also circumvents the difficulties of incorporating the loanwords into the English inflectional paradigm; her documentation of HC data suggests that Romance borrowings are in the majority in her *do*-data, although unfortunately she does not provide specific figures.

In the QEIC correspondence data, 49% of the verbs modified by affirmative *do* are of Latinate origin and 6.6% are first attested in the sixteenth century (based on the dating given in the OED Online) with Elizabeth's usage often corresponding closely to the year of first citation. For example, *sentinel* is first attested in 1593 in a work by Thomas Nashe, the same year as Elizabeth's letter to James VI:

(25) who divers nights **did sentinel** their acts (16th March 1593, to James VI, QEIC correspondence).

However, the low proportion of recent borrowings in the data suggests that this systemic factor plays only a marginal role in Elizabeth's idiolectal preferences. A number of contemporary loanwords also occur in non-*do* declaratives, suggesting that she was untroubled by their Latinate origins:

(26) I fear you may fail in an heresy, which I hereby **do conjure** you from (3rd December 1600, to Charles Blount, QEIC correspondence).
(27) I **conjure** you, even for the worth that you prize yourself at (25th November 1591, to James VI, QEIC correspondence).

This may reflect the influence of Elizabeth's high level of education, which would make her familiar with Latinate lexis, as well as the recipients of her letters who largely shared her familiarity with Latin and Greek. Interestingly, Nevalainen (1991: 308) found that neologisms had little impact on the distribution of affirmative *do* in sixteenth- and seventeenth-century liturgical prose—texts also written by individuals with a Humanist education. Overall, the majority of Latinate verbs collocating with affirmative *do* in QEIC date from the Middle English period and were not neologisms in Elizabeth's lifetime. The syntactic contexts—with their affiliation to rhetorical devices and ease of comprehension—would appear to be the more significant systemic factor in her use of affirmative *do*.

4.4 *Interactive Factors*

The macro-level studies suggest that the analysis of interactive factors for affirmative *do* should focus on Elizabeth's relationship with the addressee. Using the broad classification of 'family' and 'non-family', Nurmi's macro-level analysis of the CEEC data showed that affirmative *do* was more common in letters written to family members in the first half of the sixteenth century. In the latter half of the century, the correlations shift with the form more typical of letters to non-family members. In interpreting these trends, she suggests that there was an early association between colloquial language and the use of affirmative *do* before a re-evaluation made it 'acceptable, or even fashionable, in more formal language' (Nurmi 1999: 105).

However, as noted in the introduction, the family/non-family categorisation used in CEEC is problematic when dealing with an individual as socially unique as Elizabeth I. Table 9 thus shows the distribution of *do* in QEIC correspondence by individual recipient, and avoids any sweeping generalisations about their relationship with Elizabeth. The first eight addressees (of 33 in QEIC) receiving the greatest proportion of affirmative *do* are included, whereas recipients who receive only one letter in the corpus are omitted.

The top-ranked recipient is Robert Devereux, Earl of Essex, represented by letters from the 1580s and 1590s. The next three individuals in the table all date from the pre-accession period, which suggests that Elizabeth's high

Table 9. Affirmative *do* (%) by recipient (QEIC correspondence)

	Period	Total *do*/non-*do*	% *do*	*Do*/1000 words
Robert Devereux	PostA	6	33.3	6.2
Edward VI	PreA	30	23.3	7.3
Catherine Parr	PreA	17	17.6	3.2
Edward Seymour	PreA	113	16.8	7.8
Charles Blount	PostA	15	13.3	4.4
Robert Dudley	PostA	17	11.8	3.0
James VI	PostA	866	6.7	2
Mary I	PreA	52	5.8	2

use of affirmative *do* in this period was a broad idiolectal trait, rather than specific to a particular individual or letter. The results counter Nurmi's macro-level observation that family recipients were more likely to receive affirmative *do* in the early to mid-part of the century, as the recipients here represent both categories. The recipients of the post-accession period shown in the table are also a mix of family and non-family. All had an enduring relationship with Elizabeth, but this is not a particularly useful trend as other recipients with a similar claim, e.g. her secretaries William Cecil and Francis Walsingham, are absent. The mix of recipients also shows no fit with the CEEC trend that suggests that affirmative *do* may have been re-evaluated as a more formal linguistic feature at an interactive level (Nurmi 1999: 105).

In the CEEC data, the level of affirmative *do* declines from around 1600—much later than the decrease in Elizabeth's correspondence. Nurmi's (1999: 179) 'frivolous theory' to explain this dip cites the change in personnel at the Court, with the Scottish nobility moving with James VI (now James I) to London after Elizabeth's death. Affirmative *do* was far less established in Middle Scots that in EModE with a frequency of 0.54 times per 1000 words in the period 1570–1640 in the Helsinki Corpus of Older Scots (HCOS). Nurmi suggests that the new high-ranking Scottish individuals influenced the linguistic fashions in the Court and the wider area. As I speculate above, one explanation for the dip in affirmative *do* during the post-accession period could be the letters to James VI in the QEIC correspondence, which account for 60 of 94 letters. It is possible that Elizabeth modified her preferences in order to converge towards the Scottish king. However, the frequency of affirmative *do* in the letters to James VI and in letters to the other recipients in the post-accession corpus is very similar: 6.7% for the Scottish king and 7.8% in letters to other recipients, offering no support for the accommodation hypothesis. We might expect Elizabeth to be sensitive to the linguistic preferences of her Scottish counterpart, given the diplomatic nature of their correspondence; however the data suggests that the cause for the decline in *do* in Elizabeth's idiolect has another source.

Closer examination reveals that the variation in the frequency of affirmative *do* can be traced on a letter-by-letter basis as well as by recipient. A letter written in December 1601 to James VI has a frequency of affirmative *do* of 7.2 times per 1000 words. The next letter to James VI in the QEIC correspondence, composed 3rd February 1602, contains no instances of affirmative *do* at all. The variation suggests that recipients receiving letters containing high levels of affirmative *do* may share letters of a similar subject-matter or purpose, making it the functional and contextual aspects of the text, not solely the recipient, which influences the selection of affirmative *do* in Elizabeth's idiolect. Whilst the scale of CEEC may foreground these elements in the family/non-family categorisation, an idiolectal analysis requires a more refined and qualitative approach.

I previously referred to a function of affirmative *do* characterised by repetition across a passage of text, and distinguishable from the instances triggered by comprehension purposes or rhetorical styling. Rissanen defines discursive foregrounding *do* as:

> a marker of argumentative expression which aims at influencing the audience's views and opinions. *Do* in itself is not necessarily emphatic, but it adds to the intensity and emphasis of the utterance (Rissanen 1999: 240).

Discursive foregrounding *do* is the main function of the form in the early to mid-sixteenth century. In the HC, this function contributed to the high frequency of *do* in trial records and sermons (1500–1570), genres representative of formal speech (Rissanen 1999: 240). The rhetorical functions of affirmative *do* develop later in the century, although the broad timeframes of the HC make a more precise timing difficult. Rissanen's examples of discursive foregrounding *do* from the HC typically show four or five near-sequential examples of *do* which he defines as a "cluster", the characteristic property that differentiates discursive *do* from other functions (Rissanen 1991: 325, 1999: 240).

In the analysis of systemic factors I found that syntactic contexts accounted for 58.5% of the *do*-tokens identified in the QEIC correspondence. However, given that correspondence is typically positioned towards the spoken end of the spectrum, it is plausible that the remaining 41.5% of the tokens with no clear systemic motivation may arise from the discursive use of affirmative *do*, more closely affiliated with spoken modes (c.f. Rissanen 1991: 331). A discursive use of affirmative *do* would also explain the variable frequencies of affirmative *do* identified in the recipient data and even across individual letters. It may also explain the decline of *do* in Elizabeth's correspondence between the pre- and post-accession periods.

To ascertain if Elizabeth uses affirmative *do* discursively, I have examined the 10 letters in the corpus with the highest frequency of the variant, as it seems probable that these texts are most likely to show clearest evidence of clusters. Because of the low token counts, they are ranked by normalised frequency of *do* rather than percentage with the normalised frequency of simple (non-*do*) contexts included for comparison. If a letter does contain clusters, then a careful consideration of the interactive properties (recipient, function and compositional context) should help us to understand Elizabeth's usage, and potentially the changes over time.

The letter with the highest frequency of *do* dates from the pre-accession period and was written to Edward Seymour during the Seymour affair (1549) in Elizabeth's adolescence. Other letters from the same series rank

Table 10. Individual letters with highest frequency of affirmative *do* (QEIC correspondence)

Date	Addressee	Total *do*/ non-*do*	*Do*/1000 words	Non-*do*/ 1000 words
1549, 6th February	Edward Seymour	10	20.8	31.3
1549, January	Edward Seymour	14	12.8	46.8
1555, 29th October	William Paulet	4	11.4	11.4
1589, 15th April	Robert Devereux	3	10.6	5.3
1552, 21st April	Edward VI	8	9.1	15.2
1553, March	Edward VI	11	8.2	37.0
1585, January	James VI	11	7.8	34.9
1549, 21st Feburary	Edward Seymour	28	7.7	35.6
1597, March	James VI	16	7.6	33.1
1593, 16th March	James VI	23	7.6	36.0

second and eighth in the table. Closer examination suggests that affirmative *do* occurs in clusters typical of the discursive foregrounding function, shown in the following extracts:

(28) My lord, these are the Articles which I **do** remember; that both she and the Cofferer talked with me of; and if there be any more behind, which I have not declared as yet, I shall most heartily desire your Lordship and the rest of the Council, not to think that I **do** willingly conceal them, but that I have indeed forgotten them. For if I **did** know them, and did not declare them, I were wonderfully and above all the rest to be rebuked (January 1549, to Edward Seymour, QEIC correspondence).

(29) And whereas I **do** understand that you **do** take in evil part the letters that I **did** write unto your Lordship I am very sorry that you should take them so (21st February 1549, to Edward Seymour, QEIC correspondence).

(30) and whereas your Grace **doth** will me to credit Master Tyrwhitt I have done so, and will do so as long as he willeth me (as he doth not) to nothing but to that which is for mine honour, and honesty, and even as I said to him, and **did** write to your Lordship, so I **do** write now again that when there **doth** any more things happen in my mind which I have forgotten I assure your Grace I will declare them most willingly (6th February 1549, to Edward Seymour, QEIC correspondence).

The content and context of these examples compares favourably with the trial records of Sir Nicholas Throckmorton, a document that is often used as a representative example of discursive foregrounding *do* in the literature (e.g. Rissanen 1999: 240; Nevalainen 2006b: 109). Throckmorton's trial

occurred in 1554, five years after Elizabeth wrote the letters to Edward
Seymour, and Rissanen's description of the role of *do* in the records can be
applied to the Seymour extracts with little alteration:

> Some of the instances [...] show the marks of [syntactic] factors [...]
> But, essentially, the clustering of periphrastic *do* in this extract of
> intensive dialogue seems determined by factors typical of spoken
> discourse: the clustering of *do* marks the importance of the action
> [...] narrated by Throckmorton (Rissanen 1991: 326).

In the Seymour letters, Elizabeth defends herself against the accusation
that she conspired to marry Thomas Seymour. The texts contain extensive
narration alongside professions of innocence. (28) was taken from the
autograph conclusion to Elizabeth's statement, documented by her
interrogator Sir Robert Tyrwhitt. Whilst the collocation with systemic
conditioning factors is undeniable (verb-final and adverbial contexts), the
cluster occurs as she asserts the truthfulness of her statement and appeals
directly to Edward Seymour, Lord Protector, who would read the
confession. In (29), the cluster heightens the apology that follows, with
negligible systemic contexts. In (30), the tone of desperation and frustration
is clear, Elizabeth providing a detailed and rather repetitive description of
her actions peppered with affirmative *do* before concluding with a
superlative expression of assurance: 'I will declare them most willingly'.
The date of these letters and Throckmorton's trial indicates that Elizabeth
was potentially an early adopter of the variant in this function.

Overall, the letters to Seymour provide the clearest examples of discursive
foregrounding *do*, and illustrate how this function of *do* can be isolated
from, as well as overlap with, the systemic factors discussed in the previous
section. It is significant that these letters date from the pre-accession period,
when Elizabeth's usage of affirmative *do* was at its highest level.

Discursive clusters contribute significantly to the frequency of *do* in the
pre-accession period, found in three letters with the highest proportion of
do in the corpus. However, there are definite exceptions, and possible
patterns, to this pre-accession trend. Firstly, Elizabeth does not always use
discursive foregrounding *do* where we might expect. The "Tide" letter to
Mary I has a comparable purpose to the Seymour letters, yet contains only
one instance of affirmative *do* (1.6 times per 1000 words). Non-*do*
declaratives occur 40 times per 1000 words, indicating many potential
contexts. It is not presently clear why this is the case.

A second point relates to Nurmi's observation regarding family and non-
family recipients. Whilst the overall frequencies showed no comparable
distribution in the QEIC correspondence, the presence or absence of
discursive *do* may in fact make Elizabeth's relationship with the recipient a
relevant distinction in the pre-accession period. In the ranking of individual
letters, the pre-accession correspondence is represented by one family

recipient (Edward VI; there are no letters to Mary I) and two non-family recipients. From one perspective, this indicates that Elizabeth may have used different discursive and stylistic techniques when writing to her sister compared to her brother, and reaffirms the belief that the generalisation of 'family' and 'non-family' categories is problematic. However, the letters to Edward VI also differ in the function of *do* compared to the other pre-accession letters included in Table 10 (i.e. the letters to non-family recipients).

In Elizabeth's letters to her brother and King, there is minimal evidence of discursive clustering. Instead, affirmative *do* occurs predominantly in the systemic contexts typical of written modes:

(31) What cause I had of sorry when I heard first of your Majesty's sickness all men might guess, but none but my self could feel, which to declare were or might seem a point of flattery and therefore to write it I omit [...] For now **do** I say with Saint Austin that a disease is to be counted no sickness that shall cause a better health when it is past than was assured afore it came [...] Moreover I consider that as a good father that loves his child dearly **doth** punish him sharply, so God favouring your Majesty greatly hath chastened you straightly, and as a father doth it for the further good of his child, so hath God prepared this for the better health of your grace (21st April 1552, to Edward VI, QEIC correspondence).

The first instance of *do* occurs in an adverb-initial context preceding a citation from Augustine. The use of third-party opinions or facts to support an argument was a popular rhetorical device of the sixteenth century, known as testimony. The latter two instances of affirmative *do* occur in analogical structures (as ... so), forms of *comparatio*. Perry (1990: 66) has previously observed that Elizabeth's letters to Edward are often more akin to exercises in composition, and the location of affirmative *do* in these letters thus indicates a connection with expressions associated with Classical rhetoric.

Elizabeth's use of affirmative *do* in the pre-accession period thus clearly incorporates both the discursive function, associated with spoken texts, and the syntactic contexts typical of more literary styles. The finding illustrates that even at a young age Elizabeth was aware of and utilised the two functions of *do*. We could attribute this partly to her rigorous early schooling, which ensured familiarity with classical models and rhetorical ideals; her religious education may have exposed her to the discursive function. The presence of both functions helps to explain the high frequency of affirmative *do* in this period of the correspondence. The perceivable difference in letters to family (rhetorical and comprehension-motivated *do*) and non-family (discursive foregrounding *do*) is interesting, and most likely reflects the type of letter Elizabeth had to write to these recipients, based on the immediate context and the social conventions of the period. The absence of discursive foregrounding *do* in the "Tide" letter to Mary I, therefore, may reflect the conflict between the type of letter Elizabeth would write to a family member and the letter's purpose; perhaps she did not consider discursive foregrounding *do* to be stylistically appropriate. Unfortunately, Nurmi does not discriminate between the different functions of *do*, so it is not possible to see if the division identified in Elizabeth's pre-accession correspondence is typical of a macro-level trend.

In the post-accession letters, the examples of discursive foregrounding *do* are less explicit. Of the four letters from the later period, the text to Robert Devereux, Earl of Essex has the highest frequency of affirmative *do* (10.6 times per 1000 words), five times that of the post-accession average (2.1 per 1000 words). The frequency of *do* is even more significant when compared with the low number of non-*do* contexts in the letter (5.3 times per 1000 words). However, in terms of individual tokens, affirmative *do* accounts for only two of the three declarative contexts in this letter, stretching Rissanen's definition of a cluster. However the presence of the variant in the majority of contexts (regardless of actual quantity) justifies its description as discursive foregrounding *do*, particularly in light of the letter's short length. In the letter to Devereux, affirmative *do* occurs in a series of emphatic and intensive statements. The content reflects the change in Elizabeth's status between the pre- and post-accession period, as she expresses her disapproval of Devereux's actions and orders him to return to Court:

(32) [W]e gave directions to some of our Privy Council to let you know our express pleasure for your immediate repair hither; which you have not performed as your duty **doth** bind you, increasing greatly thereby your former offence and undutiful behaviour in departing in such sort without our privity, having so special office of attendance and charge near our person. We **do** therefore charge and command you forthwith, upon receipt of these our letters, all excuses and delays set apart, to make your present and immediate repair unto us (15th April 1589, to Robert Devereux, QEIC correspondence).

The other three letters from the post-accession period are addressed to James VI, and have a similar frequency of affirmative *do* (7.6–7.8 times per 1000 words). The function of *do* in these letters is mixed. Some contain short near-sequential uses of *do* that fit Rissanen's definition of clustering:

(33) And therefore **do** require that a question may, upon allegiance, be demanded by your self of the Master Gray, whether he knoweth not the price of my blood which should be spilled by bloody hand of a

murderer which some of your near a kin **did** grant (January 1585, to James VI, QEIC correspondence).

However, other instances of affirmative *do* in the letters to James VI have no apparent discursive function and instead are attributable to localised systemic triggers, such as inversion:

(34) **Now do** I remember your cumber to read (16th March 1593, to James VI, QEIC correspondence).

The evidence for the post-accession correspondence indicates that Elizabeth's use of affirmative *do* narrows and becomes less explicit in this period. It occurs in shorter clusters and seems more likely to occur in isolated instances triggered by systemic factors. The letter to Devereux is an unusual example. By comparison, the pre-accession examples appear calculated and deliberate, both in terms of their frequency in the discursive clusters and in the precise placement in points of rhetorical expression. This suggests that the form may have had a high profile in Elizabeth's adolescent idiolect that lessened over time, contributing to or reflecting the decline of the form.

4.5 *Stylistic Factors*

The final stage of analysis investigates the role of stylistic factors in Elizabeth's usage of affirmative *do*, expanding the analysis of her correspondence to consider other genres representing more literary modes. In his discussion of affirmative *do* in the HC, Rissanen (1991: 322) observes that early instances of discursive affirmative *do* are typically located in formal genres; for instance the variant occurs far more frequently in trial records and sermons than dramatic comedies. He points out that this finding does not contradict the association between discursive *do* and spoken modes, as "'spoken" is not synonymous with "colloquial'". The correlation between systemic factors and literary written texts also locates affirmative *do* at the formal end of the spectrum, with early examples found in educational treatises such as Ascham's *The Schoolmaster*.

Affirmative *do* is less frequent in less formal written-mode texts, such as narrative fiction—a fact Rissanen (1991: 328) attributes to the authors' lesser concern for 'stylistic ambition' in these texts. The peak of affirmative *do* at the end of the sixteenth century is thus attributed to the discursive and systemic functions spreading from their original formal contexts to more informal genres, such as private correspondence and dramatic dialogue (Rissanen 1991: 328–329).

Dieter Stein suggests that the decline of affirmative *do* began in the more formal genres, even as the variant was on the rise elsewhere. He suggests that *do* was associated with the 'courtly ideal of life-style', and that as this ideal fell from popularity in the last quarter of the sixteenth century, the associated linguistic features declined as well (Stein 1991: 361). It appears that affirmative *do* was re-evaluated stylistically by style-conscious authors. Stein's dating of the re-evaluation correlates with the decline seen in Elizabeth's idiolect, and offers a possible explanation for contrast between her pre- and post-accession usage. The results in Table 11 show that the frequency of affirmative *do* correlates with the formality of each genre in Elizabeth's idiolect. In both the pre- and post-accession periods, the translations show the highest frequency of affirmative *do*, and correspondence the least. In the post-accession period, the parliamentary speeches occupy mid-position. This indicates that the formality of the text is relevant to Elizabeth's idiolectal preferences, even when the overall frequency of *do* differs between timeperiods.

Stein (1991: 361) suggests that the mixed corpus of literary texts used by Ellegård to provide the diachronic macro-level trends obfuscates the range and variation attributable to stylistic variation, arising from the 'contemporary stylistic ideals' that Stein proposes are present within the different literary texts. The cross-genre variation within Elizabeth's idiolect certainly reinforces Stein's point; combining the average of these genres, for example, would hide the considerable range in frequencies. It is not clear if Stein was thinking of idiolectal variation specifically when he made his critique, but the QEIC data demonstrate the ability of idiolectal stylistic analysis to provide a clear picture of the intersection between style and linguistic variation.

The percentage of affirmative *do* in the pre-accession translations is the highest of all genres in this sub-period (55.1%) and in Elizabeth's writing overall (excluding the letters with minimal tokens). The normalised frequency (19.3 times per 1000 words) testifies to the frequency of the variant, and the impact is not lessened when the translations are treated individually (see Appendix, Table 62); for instance, the translation of Calvin, written in 1545, contains almost twice as many affirmative *do* clauses (22.9 per 1000 words) as simple clauses (12.5 per 1000 words). By comparison, the proportion of *do* in the later translations is much lower, offering a more dramatic demonstration of the decline of affirmative *do*

Table 11. Affirmative *do* in QEIC correspondence, speeches and translations

	Total *do*/non-*do*	% *do*	*Do*/1000 words
PreA correspondence	221	15.4	5.4
PostA correspondence	1048	6.9	2.1
Speeches	160	8.8	2.3
PreA translations	805	55	19.3
PostA translations	432	12	6.3

seen in Elizabeth's correspondence.[7] In contrast with the frequency of affirmative *do*, the number of simple contexts in Boethius (60.8 per 1000 words) is particularly high, suggesting that Elizabeth felt little need for affirmative *do* in her 1593 translation.

In the analysis of Elizabeth's correspondence certain syntactic contexts appeared to promote the variant, prompted by the demands of comprehension or rhetorical and literary ideals. Her translations are more literary texts, and the greater frequency of *do* in this genre, compared to her correspondence, suggests that the same syntactic factors should be relevant, if not more so than in her correspondence. For the translation analysis, a fifth syntactic context, second-person verb endings ((35)), is included. There were no examples of this context in Elizabeth's correspondence, as the second-person pronoun *you*, rather than *thou*, is the dominant form.

(35) **Thou** didst pray for me (1544, Navarre, QEIC translations).

Surprisingly, only a third of the *do* tokens occur in syntactic contexts in the pre-accession translations when calculated using *do*-tokens only. The distribution of periphrasis across the five contexts is fairly even with intervening material accounting for the greatest proportion (12.2%). The distribution counters the hypothesis that syntactic contexts would play a significant role in the high frequency of affirmative *do* in this genre due to the association with comprehension and rhetorical ideals.

However, calculating the percentage of *do* from the *do* and non-*do* data reveals that *do* is in fact the dominant form in syntactic contexts in the pre-accession translations, thus demonstrating the incomplete picture created using *do*-only analysis of syntactic features (see Appendix, Tables 63 and 64). Using both methods reveals that *do* is prominent in both syntactic contexts and other declarative contexts. For example, 82.6% of inverted contexts take *do* and 79.5% of adverbial contexts also occur with periphrasis. Only in verb-final contexts does declarative *do* account for less than half of the tokens, at 25%. The role of *do* in these contexts is thus more pronounced than in the correspondence from the same period (see Figure 3).

The majority of declarative *do* tokens occur in the no context category—67.5% of *do*-only tokens and 52.6% of *do* and non-*do* declaratives. Following Rissanen's (1991: 331) thinking, the number of non-conditioned contexts in the pre-accession translations may be attributable to discursive foregrounding *do*—a function already identified in the near-contemporary correspondence with Edward Seymour. The following extract is typical of the

---

[7] The difference between the pre- and post-accession translations is highly significant (p > 0.001). The same p-value applies to the post-accession translations and correspondence.

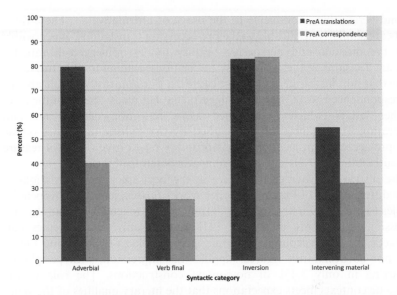

Figure 3: Affirmative *do* (%) in syntactic contexts out of *do*/non-*do* tokens (QEIC pre-accession translations and correspondence)

tone, subject and prevalence of affirmative *do* in the pre-accession translations:

(36) And indeed we may see, through how many vain illusions the superstition **doth** make with God, when it **doth** think to please him. For they **do** take almost only the things the which he himself **doth** testify that he careth not for them: and they **do** neglect those that he hath ordained, and declared to be acceptable unto him, or else they **do** reject them openly. Therefore all those which **doth** setteth up religions, or ceremonies invented of their own minds for to honour God, **do** worship but their own dreams (1545, Calvin, QEIC translations).

Affirmative *do* occurs in every declarative context in this short extract, a patterning perhaps best described as continuous, rather than as a cluster. One possible interpretation of this fascinating distribution is that it represents analogous usage. Smith (1996: 160) suggests that in some cases *do* was self-replicating, the use of the variant prompting a subsequent example. Interestingly, Smith's example of this phenomenon is taken from the Authorised Version of the Bible, and the overlap in genre (religious prose) may offer one explanation for the frequency of *do* in the translations.

However, other generic dimensions of affirmative *do* may also be relevant. Rissanen (1991: 328) notes that sermons by Latimer and Fisher are characterised by their 'strong' argument, personal discourse and second-person bias, conducive to the usage of affirmative *do*. These three traits are similarly applicable to the pre-accession translations. It is possible that the didactic and persuasive oratory model influenced Elizabeth's stylistic decisions in these two early translations, leading to an effusive use of *do* that dominates the declarative contexts. The contrast with Elizabeth's correspondence is striking, and it suggests that her ready uptake of the form in her letters—which I explained as a reflection of her age and generation—is enhanced and magnified by the stylistic properties of the two pre-accession translations. This property may prove a helpful feature for authorship analysis in manuscripts attributed to this period.

The distribution of declarative *do* in the post-accession translations is very different from Elizabeth's earlier works in this genre (see Appendix, Tables 65 and 66). Firstly, the overall frequency is much lower than the pre-accession translations, at around 12%. The *do*-only data indicates that syntactic contexts account for the majority of tokens (84.6%) and the *do* and non-*do* declarative figures support this impression, with periphrasis occurring in only 3.4% of no-context constructions. The role of the syntactic contexts meets expectations that the literary qualities of the genre would trigger *do* for reasons of rhetoric and comprehension.

Clause-final verbs account for the majority of *do*-tokens (55.8%); in part a reflection of the verse sections in Elizabeth's translation of Boethius. Elizabeth shares her usage of affirmative *do* as a metrical filler with many other writers of verse during this period. Indeed, it is a function that outlasts many others, found until at least the eighteenth century. Beal (2004: 73) suggests that 'despite being stigmatized [...] the semantically empty syllable as a line filler was too convenient to resist', and notes its use in Duncan's (1789) translation of Boethius, as well as verse by Wordsworth. The difference between the pre- and post-accession translations for this context is statistically significant (p > 0.001). Examples are also found in the prose sections of Boethius ((37)) and in Cicero ((38)):

(37) And with what bounds the great heaven/thou guidest, the stable earth **do** [sic.] steady (1593, Boethius, QEIC translations).

(38) So it follows that either none **doth** live (1592, Cicero, QEIC translations).

The lower frequency of declarative *do* and the dominance of syntactic contexts in the data indicate that Elizabeth's reticent use of affirmative *do* is comparable to the trends in her post-accession correspondence (see Figure 4). In the translations, declarative *do* accounts for a greater percentage of tokens in the syntactic contexts than the equivalent contexts in the correspondence. This suggests that Elizabeth's use of periphrastic *do* in the more literary genre was limited to a narrow set of preferred contexts. Only

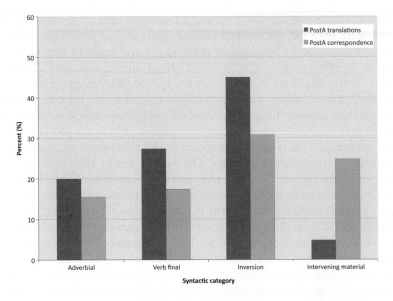

Figure 4: Affirmative *do* (%) in syntactic contexts out of *do*/non-*do* (QEIC post-accession
translations and correspondence)

intervening material—the context typical of spoken language—occurs more
frequently in the correspondence.

The persistence of affirmative *do* in systemic contexts and the near-
complete loss of discursive *do* in the post-accession translations compares
favourably with the progression of the macro-level decline. Studies
(Rissanen 1991; Wischer 2008) show that the variant declined first in
spoken-mode contexts, in which discursive *do* was most prominent. This
was possibly due to the regularisation of *do* in negatives and questions that
contradicted the sporadic, discursive function of the affirmative form,
alongside the stylistic re-evaluation proposed by Stein (1991). The variant
prevailed longer in written modes due to the connection with syntactic
factors and elucidation of meaning (Rissanen 1991: 328–329). The findings
from Elizabeth's speeches and translations re-affirm these macro-level
distributive trends. However, Rissanen's analysis of the HC dates the
recession to the seventeenth century, and Elizabeth's stylistic preference
anticipates the decline by over 20 years.

The frequency and distribution of affirmative *do* in the translations is an
exaggerated rendering of the patterns seen in Elizabeth's correspondence.
Earlier, I noted that the diachronic trends in her letters showed a plausible
correlation with the trends from Ellegård's literary corpus. His corpus,
comprised of literary texts by male authors, suggests that affirmative
do declined first in texts most concerned with literary and stylistic

expression. In the pre-accession period, Elizabeth's uptake of affirmative *do* was higher than the macro-level average; there is thus precedent for her post-accession usage to be similarly pre-emptive and lead the decline that began in literary genres. The intersection of diachronic and stylistic variation at the idiolectal level, interpreted against the background of the macro-level trends, offers some persuasive evidence for how Elizabeth understood the socio-stylistic function of affirmative *do* over the course of her lifetime.

The final genre in QEIC to be considered in this analysis of affirmative *do* is Elizabeth's parliamentary speeches. The overall rate of affirmative *do*, at 8.8%, is slightly higher than the post-accession correspondence (6.9%), although the difference is not statistically significant. Based on the *do*-only tokens, syntactic contexts account for the majority of occurrences (78.6%), and the *do* and non-*do* data emphatically corroborates this trend, with only 2.6% *do* in no-context declaratives. The prominence of the syntactic contexts shows a greater resemblance to the translations than the post-accession correspondence, which may reflect the formality of the genre and the concern for the rhetorical ideals associated with oration. The low token counts unfortunately mean that the percentages for each context in the *do*/non-*do* data are less reliable than for the other genres (see Appendix, Tables 67 and 68). Nevertheless, the following extract exemplifies the complex syntax and high register lexis typical of Elizabeth's speeches, and the role of affirmative *do* within the discourse. The example shows affirmative *do* in an inverted position, occurring in an adverbially modified verb phrase. This particular context meets Stein's (1991: 359) parameters for a syntactic pattern motivated by 'the intensity content' of the utterance, an instance where the discursive and systemic properties coincide in the use of *do*:

(39) And whatever any prince may merit of their subjects for their approved testimony of their unfeigned sincerity, either by governing justly, void of all partiality or sufferance of any injuries done even to the poorest, that **do** I assuredly promise inviolably to perform for requital of your so many deserts (12th November 1586, QEIC speeches).

The blend of properties associated with spoken and written modes, including the overlap of systemic and semantic (emphatic) properties of affirmative *do*, reflects the confluence of rhetorical models and the spoken mode of the genre. It is interesting that the speeches show no evidence of discursive clustering. The lack of this function re-affirms the nature of the decline in affirmative *do* seen in her post-accession correspondence, with *do* primarily restricted to systemic, conditioned contexts. Allowing for the limited number of *do* tokens, there is no discernable difference in distribution between the speeches from the 1560s and the 1580s.

4.6 *Summary*

Affirmative declarative *do* has been described as 'a perfectly good change that did not quite make it' (Ihalainen 1983), a description based on the macro-level development of the form during the sixteenth century. The analysis of the variant in Elizabeth's idiolect has shed light on the possible motivating factors for the rise and subsequent decline. Her use of affirmative *do* can be considered progressive in the pre-accession period, offering corroborative evidence for Nevalainen et al.'s (2011) identification of Elizabeth as a leader of linguistic change. However, rather than progressing to completion, the variant becomes marginal and disfavoured in her post-accession writing; in one sense, the decline can also be considered progressive, pre-empting the macro-level trend identified in CEEC by several decades (Nurmi 1999).

Social factors provide only partial explanation for the distribution seen in Elizabeth's idiolect. In the pre-accession, her youth is the most likely candidate to explain the trend, with little correlation identified with other social groups. Social correlates for the post-accession period are also in short supply. CEEC female informants appeared to offer the best fit with Elizabeth's preferences, but the low frequencies of the data and the difference in the overall diachronic trends raise questions about the significance of the correlation. It is possible that Elizabeth's post-accession circumstances cause her to re-assess her linguistic preferences, and accommodate to the gentlewomen around her. Yet I am not aware of any evidence that suggests other female writers modify their usage across different genres as Elizabeth does.

Instead, the downward trend of affirmative *do* more plausibly relates to the stylistic associations of the form. Elizabeth's correspondence correlates with the trends seen in Ellegård's literary corpus, and the severity of the decline in the more formal genre (translations) further supports this patterning. Her usage of affirmative *do*, in both periods, is attuned to the stylistic significance of the form. The discursive function in the Seymour letters, the systemic clarifications in the letters to Edward VI, and the combination of elements in the pre-accession translations indicates that the variant was highly salient in her youth. From a diachronic perspective, the decline of the form in the post-accession period can be recognised as a continuation of her earlier stylistic sensitivity. The plurality of stylistic functions in her early writing suggests that any changes in the value of the variant would be foregrounded for Elizabeth, offering an explanation for the restriction of *do* to mainly conditioned contexts (particularly in the more formal genres) in the post-accession period. As a result, Elizabeth's usage anticipates the later trends of her contemporaries; CEEC and the HC show that the form only began to decline after 1600 (Nurmi 1999; Wischer 2008). Her stylistic sensitivity may also explain why the change is perceptible in Elizabeth's correspondence as well as her more literary work, contrasting with the macro-level genres. The change is a persuasive example of the role of stylistic variation in the process of language change, and illustrates the benefit of using an idiolect as the source data for historical language analysis.

The stylistic profile suggests that somebody introduced or exposed Elizabeth to the particular functions of affirmative *do* from an early age, perhaps during her early education or—given the discursive function—through her early experience of religious prose, such as sermons. We know that she spent a good deal of time with her stepmother Catherine Parr in the 1540s, a woman who was pious and learned, and was held in great respect by the young princess (Demers 2005: 103). The time Elizabeth spent in Parr's household corresponds with the most prominent examples of affirmative *do* in the pre-accession corpus, identified in the two translations and the letters (written soon after Parr's death) of the Seymour affair. Elizabeth's governess, Kat Ashley, is also a possible candidate. Although her level of learning is debated, the testimonies collected in the wake of the Seymour affair (see Haynes 1740) suggest that discursive *do* was a high frequency feature of Ashley's writing (Evans 2012). The strong social ties between Elizabeth and these women offer a plausible scenario for the transmission of stylistic associations and linguistic preferences to the young Princess.

In the post-accession period, contact with many of the authors represented in Ellegård's all-male corpus at the Court may have influenced the decline of the form in Elizabeth's language. Further analysis of the preferences of other individuals at the Elizabethan Court across a multi-genre corpus would help to contextualise the social elements of her linguistic preferences during this time.

Finally, I do not believe we can ascribe the change in Elizabeth's preferences directly to her accession. The evidence in Elizabeth's writing suggests that she was aware of and concerned with the stylistic significance of *do* throughout her life. Significantly, her leading position in the change—anticipating both the rise and the fall of the variant—is consistent in both periods.

5. NEGATIVE DO

The distributional trends and functional characteristics of affirmative *do* in Elizabeth's idiolect offer a convincing testament to the value of idiolectal analysis for our understanding of the relationship between Elizabeth's biography and language use, as a feature for authorship analysis, and for our understanding of the factors motivating the 'failure' of the change. Periphrastic *do* in negative declarative contexts is therefore an intriguing companion piece to the previous analysis, as negative *do* successfully became the dominant variant in English unlike its affirmative counterpart.

First attested in the late fourteenth century, negative *do* (*do* + *not* + verb) was the rising variant throughout the Early Modern period ((40)), reaching almost 40% in the mid-sixteenth century (Ellegård 1953: 161). It was in competition with the established finite verb + *not* construction that had emerged following the demise of *ne* in Middle English ((41)). A third alternative, pre-verbal *not*, also developed during the Early Modern period although this variant appears to have been restricted to colloquial contexts (Rissanen 1999: 271).[8] The movement from post-verbal *not* to negative *do* + *not* is typically treated as a binary variable, and this is the stance adopted here:

(40) bridleless colts **do not know** their rider's hand (5th November 1566, QEIC speeches).

(41) you **know not** how to use it (4th May 1589, to John Norris, QEIC correspondence).

The early stages of this change are contemporary with the emergence of affirmative declarative *do*. Some studies suggest that the development of both forms is connected; for instance Nurmi (1999: 179) finds a similar decline in both types of *do* in CEEC at the start of the seventeenth century. She suggests that the trend reflects the prestigious influence of Scots English, which uses periphrastic *do* far less frequently, in the period following the accession of James I. Rissanen (1999: 271) identifies similar discursive functions for both forms in literature of the sixteenth century. My investigation of negative *do* considers the factors relevant to Elizabeth's language, and aims to establish if there is any evidence of a relationship between the two forms at an idiolectal level.

In order to make reliable comparisons between Elizabeth's language and the social information from CEEC, I follow Nurmi's (1999) methodology. This has become something of a standard, and is used by other studies including Kallel (2002), Warner (2005) and Culpeper & Kytö (2010). I identified all negative declaratives in QEIC with the negator *not* using the AntConc concordance program, and classified each construction as negative *do* or non-*do* accordingly. Declaratives containing other sentential negators (e.g. *never*) were excluded, along with declaratives containing auxiliary and lexical *be* and *have*, modal auxiliaries and 'marginal'

---

[8] *Not* + verb occurs once in the QEIC correspondence, in a pre-accession letter to Mary I: 'and all for that they have heard false report and **not hearken** to the truth known' (17th March 1554, to Mary I, QEIC correspondence). The single example indicates that this variant was highly marginal in Elizabeth's idiolect, and justifies the treatment of negative *do* as a bipartite variable.

Table 12. Negative declarative *do* and non-*do* (QEIC correspondence)

	Total *do*/non-*do*	% *do*	*Do*/1000 words	Non-*do*/1000 words
Prea	15	20.0	0.5	1.9
PostA	119	11.8	0.4	3.0
Overall	134	12.7	0.4	2.9

auxiliaries (*dare*, *need* and *ought to*). Using this method, it is notable that the token counts for negative declaratives are considerably lower than the affirmative declaratives discussed in the previous chapter. This is somewhat surprising. Before sorting the data, I identified 552 instances of negator *not* in the QEIC correspondence, yet only 134 qualify for the negative declarative variable. The contrast between the number of negator tokens and declarative contexts suggests that non-*do*/negative-*do* finite verb constructions may not have been Elizabeth's preferred negation strategy. Therefore caution is necessary when discussing the distributional trends in Elizabeth's usage.

5.1 *Results*

Negative *do* shows a downward trend in the QEIC correspondence (Table 12). Accounting for 20% constructions in the pre-accession period, the frequency falls to 11.8% in the post-accession period—a decline that parallels Elizabeth's use of affirmative *do*.[9] And, as with that variant, the idiolectal pattern contrasts with the macro-level trend. In CEEC (Nurmi 1999: 148, adapted from Table 9.3) there is an overall rise in the use of negative declarative *do* during the Early Modern period, from 20.6% in 1540–1559 to 25.7% in 1580–1599, and resulting in standardisation by the end of the eighteenth century.

The percentage of negative *do* in Elizabeth's pre-accession correspondence fits closely with the 20.6% identified in CEEC for the same period (Nurmi 1999: 148), placing Elizabeth within the mid-range users at the new and rigorous stage of the change. Her conformity in the early period is somewhat surprising. Kallel's (2002) analysis of the Lisle family correspondence (1533–1540) examines the uptake of negative *do* and finds that the younger generation (b. 1516–1626) use negative *do* more frequently than the older generation. More specifically, the three younger children (aged 12 and under) use negative *do*, with the older adolescent children preferring the non-*do* form. Kallel's results imply that Elizabeth would also use negative *do* more frequently than the older generations. However, this appears not to

---

[9] The difference between the pre- and post-accession period is not statistically significant.

have been the case, with her usage conforming to the average. The result also contrasts with Elizabeth's uptake of affirmative declarative *do* where she was a leader of the change during this period.

In the post-accession period, negative *do* declines from 20% to 11.8% in Elizabeth's correspondence, in contrast to CEEC which shows a steady rise and reaches 25.7% by the 1580–1600 period.[10] More specifically, informants from Elizabeth's generation participate in this increasing use of negative *do*, with an average frequency of 31.3% by the latter decades of the sixteenth century for those born 1520–1539 (Nurmi 1999: 173). Closer examination shows that Elizabeth's usage fluctuates across the post-accession period. The decline in the post-accession period is predominantly caused by correspondence written in the 1580s, with negative *do* accounting for 3.4% or 0.15 times per 1000 words. The figure for the 1590s, which has a similar number of tokens, shows an increase in the frequency of negative *do* to 16.1% or 0.5 times per 1000 words, and the difference between the two decades is statistically significant ($p > 0.5$). These figures suggest the decline is best characterised as a 'dip', rather than an overall downward trend. In addition, although the token count for the 1600–1603 period is too low to make any general conclusions, a further increase to 1.0 per 1000 words fits with the upward momentum. The dating of the 'dip' suggests that the differences between the pre- and post-accession periods are unlikely to relate directly to Elizabeth's accession.

In the macro-level data, there is no comparable decline during this period. To find evidence of a dip, we must look at the seventeenth-century CEEC data, where the frequency of negative *do* falls from 25.7% to 15.2% at the start of the century, before the variant re-initiates its ascent to become the dominant form (Nurmi 1999: 148). Nurmi (1999: 179) has previously explained the dip with her Scottish hypothesis. It is possible that the decline of negative *do* in Elizabeth's correspondence anticipates this later drop because she accommodated to the preferences of James VI, although the analysis of affirmative *do* found no evidence to support a theory of accommodation. Examining the influence of different social and stylistic factors may offer further insight into the trend for negative *do* in Elizabeth's idiolect.

5.2 *Systemic Factors*

It is first necessary to establish the role of systemic factors, to establish whether *do*-inhibiting contexts are over-represented in the material, given the relatively small dataset. Previous studies have found that certain lexical

[10] The difference between Elizabeth and CEEC in the 1580–1599 sub-period is statistically highly significant ($p > 0.001$).

verbs lagged behind other predicates in the uptake of negative *do*. Ellegård (1953) identified verbs in his literary corpus that displayed this behaviour, referred to collectively as the *know*-group: *know, boot, care, doubt, mistake, trow, fear, skill* and *list*. In the CEEC, Nurmi (1999: 150) found *know* and *doubt* to be significant in her analysis, with the other verb forms highly infrequent in, or absent from, her material.

In the pre-accession QEIC data, there are no *know*-group verbs present in the negative declarative data. The figure for this period thus represents the main-group verbs. In the post-accession data, three know-group verbs are present: *fear, know* and *doubt*. Re-classification into two groups suggests a lag in *know*-group frequency, at 3.2% *do* (n = 1), although the distribution is not statistically significant. The infrequency of *know*-group verbs indicates that the low percentage of negative *do* is not caused by the over-representation of *do*-limiting contexts. Henceforth, the figures for Elizabeth refer to the overall frequency of negative *do*, with no distinction between *know*-group and other verbs.

5.3 *Social Factors*

The investigation of social factors concentrates primarily on the post-accession period. This is due in part to the better representation of social groups in CEEC for the latter decades of the sixteenth century (Nurmi 1999), but also to the potential insight the analysis may provide into the downward dip identified in Elizabeth's correspondence.

The first social category to consider is gender (Table 13). In the CEEC 1580–1599 sub-period, men use negative *do* more frequently than women (Nurmi 1999: 153). Elizabeth's usage is lower than both genders, but is closer in number to female informants.[11] This echoes the similarity found between female informants and Elizabeth's use of affirmative *do* in the same period. However, the strength of the comparison for negative *do* is less convincing; the percentage for Elizabeth is almost half that for female informants in CEEC, and without knowledge of the connection with affirmative *do* it would be reasonable to assert that Elizabeth uses negative *do* at a frequency that shows little similarity to either gender.

Elizabeth's deviant usage in the post-accession period is also clear when compared with other social groups. Education level shows minimal fit; her usage is lower than the 26.1% for informants with a high level of education (Elizabeth's biographical social group) and much lower than informants with minimal education (30.3%) (Nurmi 1999: 156–157) (p > 0.001). There is a similar lack of correlation between Elizabeth (9.6%) and her domicile group, the Court (32.7%). The difference is statistically significant

---

[11] The difference between Elizabeth and male CEEC informants is statistically highly significant (p > 0.001); the distribution between Elizabeth and female informants is not.

Table 13. Negative *do* (%), Elizabeth (QEIC correspondence) and CEEC male and female informants (adapted from Nurmi 1999: 153)

	Elizabeth (%)	CEEC men (%)	CEEC women (%)
1580–1599	9.6	26.9	16
1600–1619	–	14	17

(p > 0.001). The discord is unexpected, based on the historical evidence of Elizabeth's centrality at the Court, and the role of social ties in promoting language change. It does compare with Elizabeth's use of affirmative declarative *do*, however, which shows similar atypical properties in this period.

Overall, the expected social groups shows minimal fit with Elizabeth's low use of negative *do* in the post-accession period, suggesting that the developmental trends seen in her correspondence may be idiosyncratic. Furthermore, the contrast with the conformity of her pre-accession correspondence indicates that different factors may have operated on Elizabeth's idiolect to change her preferences from conformative to deviant. There is currently nothing to suggest that this relates specifically to her accession.

5.4 *Interactive Factors*

The trends for negative *do* in the QEIC correspondence show intriguing variation across the represented decades. Due to the relatively small size of the corpus, it is feasible that the different recipients, topics and composition contexts may contribute to the diachronic distribution.

The pre-accession letters show a rate of *do* (20%) that matches the macro-level trends in CEEC. However, the variant is not equally distributed throughout the pre-accession QEIC correspondence, but instead is constrained to two letters written to Edward Seymour, Lord Protector during the Seymour affair:

(42) For if I did know them, and **did not** declare them, I were wonderfully and above all the rest to be rebuked (c. January 1549, to Edward Seymour, QEIC correspondence).

(43) And to say that which I knew of my self I **did not** think should have displeased the council or your Grace (21st February 1549, to Edward Seymour, QEIC correspondence).

(44) to the which thing I **do not** see that your Grace has made any direct answer at this time (21st February 1549, to Edward Seymour, QEIC correspondence).

By comparison, there is only one non-*do* construction in the same group of letters. Interestingly, this occurs in a section of reported writing (with the negator and object inverted):

(45) so she writ that she **thought it not** best for fear of suspicion (28th January 1549, to Edward Seymour, QEIC correspondence).

The presence of negative *do* in the letters to Seymour, and no other pre-accession recipients, is potentially significant. The same letter group contained a higher frequency of affirmative *do* than other letters in the pre-accession period, identified as discursive foregrounding *do*, a particular type of affirmative periphrasis used to highlight a particular section of text and emphasise or intensify the content. Negative *do* in the Seymour letters may show a comparable function. Rissanen (1999: 246) suggests that an emphatic role was a likely early promoting factor for *do*-periphrasis in negative constructions, and Culpeper & Kytö's (2010: 195–197) analysis of the CED identifies a similar role in spoken-mode genres. Linguists have also speculated that the affirmative variant helped to promote periphrasis in negative contexts (Rissanen 1999: 271), a hypothesis that may find support in (42). As a third point, Culpeper & Kytö (2010: 195–197) observe that negative *do* operates as a cohesive marker in contemporary trial records and depositions to link topics, reflecting the greater interactive properties of these genres. The examples from the Seymour letters are highly compatible with all three suggestions. In the letters, Elizabeth is pleading her case and responding to a series of questions or accusations addressed to her in an earlier letter or encounter (e.g. (44)). What is not seen in these letters is any evidence that Elizabeth used negative *do* for more literary or rhetorical purposes, a function identified in the affirmative *do* data.

In the post-accession corpus, James VI is the main recipient of letters containing negative *do*, at a frequency of 14.9%. Only one other recipient, Robert Devereux, receives a letter containing negative *do*, and it is difficult to assess if this restricted distribution between recipients is due to interactive factors or simply reflects the greater representation of James VI in the corpus. The chronological distribution of negative *do* indicates that it may be the latter. Of the 13 tokens of negative *do* in letters to James VI, only two occur in the 1580s. The majority occur in letters written after 1590, and the difference is statistically significant ($p > 0.5$). If Elizabeth was using *do* differently by recipient then we might expect it to be distributed more evenly in the letters to James VI, rather than correlating with the overall diachronic trends. The recipient patterns also provide counter-evidence for the hypothesis that Elizabeth moderated her usage of negative *do* to accommodate to James VI, in anticipation of the macro-level effect described by Nurmi's Scottish hypothesis (1999: 179).

The negative *do* constructions in the post-accession letters show some resemblance to the examples seen in the Seymour letters. There is no clear evidence of a cohesive function, but more convincing instances of intensification and emphasis. Examples (46) and (47) are introduced by Elizabeth's opinion (*assure*, *vow*) of the negated action, followed by an *if*-statement. Negative *do* could be seen to intensify the contrastive statement, a function already identified for affirmative *do* in the post-accession correspondence. Yet, similar properties are also present in the non-*do* constructions, indicating only a minor influence.

(46) I assure you if I **did not trust** your words I should esteem but at small Value your Writings (May 1586, to James VI, QEIC correspondence).

(47) I Vow if you **do not rake** it to the bottom you will verify What many a Wise man hath (Viewing your proceedings) judged of your guiltiness of your own Wrack (January 1593, to James VI, QEIC correspondence).

(48) Your excuse will play the boiteux If you **make not** sure work with the likely men to do it (August 1588, to James VI, QEIC correspondence).

(49) I pray God he be so well handled as he may Confess all his Knowledge in the Spanish Conspiracy and that you **use not** this man as slightly as you have done the Ringleaders of this treason (January 1593, to James VI, QEIC correspondence).

(50) although I **do not doubt** as now I do perceive that you should think them now overstale (January 1586, to James VI, QEIC correspondence).

Example (50) is of particular interest here, as it occurs with a *know*-group verb (*doubt*). The presence of negative *do* in this context may be connected to the instance of affirmative declarative *do* that follows. This is further evidence in support of the hypothesis that the two forms were connected in Elizabeth's idiolect.

Unlike affirmative *do*, which persisted in particular contexts during this period, the post-accession correspondence provides no definite evidence that Elizabeth made a distinction between negative *do* and post-verbal *not* according to interactive factors. The discursive functions identified in the Seymour letters are less evident in her post-accession correspondence.

5.5 *Stylistic Factors*

The final stage of analysis considers the potential influence of stylistic variation. I have been unable to satisfactorily explain why Elizabeth's use of the variant fails to conform to the macro-level norm in the post-accession correspondence using social, systemic and interactive factors. However, there is one macro-level resource yet to be mentioned—Ellegård's (1953) literary corpus. In the analysis of affirmative *do*, this corpus showed best fit with Elizabeth's usage despite the dating of the rise and fall occurring earlier than the findings of more recent computerised investigations. In the case of negative *do*, Ellegård's literary corpus again provides the best match for the trends in Elizabeth's correspondence. This suggests that stylistic variation is a significant factor in her use of negative *do* as well as for affirmative contexts.

The significance of stylistic variation for this variant is not limited to Elizabeth's idiolect, but is also a key factor in the macro-level studies development of negative *do* during the Early Modern period. Anthony Warner, working with Ellegård's corpus, suggests that the 'dramatic collapse' (2005: 258) in the final decades of the sixteenth century is attributable to a stylistic re-evaluation of the variable. Warner divides Ellegård's corpus into texts of greater and lesser lexical complexity, a classification based on the 'informational density' and 'exact informational content' of a text. Warner establishes the level of complexity in the corpus using two components: type-token ratio and the average word length. A high ratio and high average word length indicate a text with a high lexical complexity; these are typically texts at the more formal and written (literary) end of the spectrum. A low ratio and low average word length are typical of less formal and spoken texts (Warner 2005: 260).

Warner finds a distinctive correlation between lexical complexity and the rate of negative *do*. In the early to mid-sixteenth century, texts with higher lexical complexity (i.e. those with more 'literary' attributes) contain a

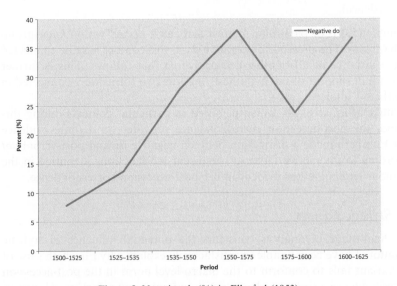

Figure 5: Negative *do* (%) in Ellegård (1953)

greater frequency of *do* than contemporary low complexity texts. However, in the final decades of the sixteenth century the rate of *do* plummets in the texts with high lexical complexity. Warner interprets the decline as evidence of a radical re-evaluation of the negative *do* in texts most concerned with style. By contrast, texts of low lexical complexity show a slow but steady rise in the rate of *do* from sixteenth-century levels, indicating that the construction was unaffected at the more vernacular or colloquial end of the spectrum (Warner 2005: 264–266). The size of the drop in Ellegård's graph is due to the number of texts of high lexical complexity in this period.

Spoken and written mode genres show a similar pattern. In the HC, Nurmi finds a higher frequency of negative *do* in genres representing the written mode, e.g. law, handbooks, science, treatises, sermons and histories, for the sub-period 1500–1570. In the final decades of the sixteenth century there is a shift, and spoken genres including 'autobiography, comedy, diary, fiction, private letters, and trial proceedings' show a higher frequency of *do* than the more written genres from 1570–1640 (Nurmi 1999: 146). The decline of *do* in the written mode genres in the HC fits the dip Warner identifies in texts of greater lexical complexity in Ellegård's corpus. Warner (2005: 264–265) suggests that the spoken/written division represents the same stylistic distribution as his measurement of lexical complexity. Consequently, categories of stylistic variation are here referred to using the HC classification of spoken and written modes, which proved useful in the analysis of affirmative *do*, but considered broadly synonymous with low and high lexical complexities respectively.

The dip in Elizabeth's correspondence in the final decades of the sixteenth century thus corresponds to that seen in the Ellegård corpus. By examining the other genres in QEIC, it should be possible to identify if the dip is connected to the re-evaluation of *do*. If Elizabeth follows the macro-level literary trends, we would expect the frequency of negative *do* to be highest in her pre-accession translations, as the most written and literary genre of this period. In the post-accession period, evidence of stylistic re-evaluation should manifest a drop in frequency across all genres, but with the greatest difference in the translations. As the most literary genre, this is where the stylistic pressures would be most acute.

The figures in Table 14 confirm these hypotheses and provide persuasive evidence that the trends in Elizabeth's post-accession writing are a consequence of her awareness of, and response to, the stylistic re-evaluation of negative *do*. The frequency of negative *do* is very high in the pre-accession translations: 72.9%, or 1.9 times per 1000 words. This is the highest level of negative *do* identified in any of Elizabeth's writings, dwarfing the frequency identified in her pre-accession correspondence (the difference is statistically significant: p > 0.001).

In the pre-accession translations, it is significant that many of the negative constructions co-occur with affirmative declarative *do*, offering further

Table 14. Frequency of negative *do* (QEIC correspondence, speeches and translations)

	Total *do*/non-*do*	% negative *do*	*Do*/1000 words
PreA correspondence	15	20.0	0.5
PostA correspondence	119	11.8	0.4
Speeches	19	15.8	0.5
PreA translations	59	72.9	1.9
PostA translations	27	3.7	0.1

evidence that the forms are interrelated in Elizabeth's idiolect. In the data, negative *do* functions as a marker of contrast (*comparatio*), and as a metrical filler for prosodic purposes:

(51) And in this place we do principally sin in two manners: the first is that poor men for to seek the truth of God, **doth not overpass** their nature as it was convenient, but doth measure high highness according to the rudeness of their wits, and they **do not comprehend** him such as he doth declare himself unto us, but do imagine him to be such as they have invented in their own brains (1545, Calvin, QEIC translations).

Overall, it seems likely that the high frequency of negative *do* is a consequence of Elizabeth's attempt to recreate contemporary literary styles in these earnest and precocious compositions. Their mid-sixteenth century dating marks the point just before negative *do* underwent stylistic re-evaluation and so we can expect the variant to have been prominent in formal literary contexts during Elizabeth's youth and early education.

Elizabeth wrote the post-accession translations approximately two decades after the supposed re-evaluation around 1575. The frequency of negative *do*, at 3.7%, is much lower in these texts than the pre-accession translations (p > 0.001). The token counts are fairly low, with an overall total of 27 negative declaratives. There is only one token of negative *do*, found in Cicero, with no examples in Boethius. The figures suggest that Elizabeth considered negative *do* unnecessary or inappropriate for these literary texts.

(52) Which all, if I **did not confess** to be so great (1592, Cicero, QEIC translation).

(53) But he won who **kindled not** his hate with his fortune but covered it with his mercy, nor judged not worthy death (1592, Cicero, QEIC translation).

The translation data suggest that Elizabeth did participate in the stylistic evaluation of negative *do* in the mid- to late sixteenth century. However, the macro-level analyses suggest that the re-evaluation only applied to texts at the more written and literary end of the spectrum in the sixteenth century. How can we be certain that the low level of negative *do* in Elizabeth's correspondence is a consequence of the same process? Firstly, the CEEC data suggests that the re-evaluation of negative *do* also had implications for this genre. The drop seen in the early seventeenth century is evidence of the permeation of the stylistic evaluation—'a social psychological fact'—moving from the more explicit, literary and public contexts represented by Ellegård's corpus to less formal, socially representative texts of CEEC (Warner 2005: 271). In sociolinguistic terms, this represents a 'change from above'. Unlike many of her contemporaries, Elizabeth applies the stylistic re-evaluation across her writings and thus anticipates the trend in correspondence that occurs some 20 years later. The same explanation was proposed for the decline of affirmative *do* in QEIC; the parallel evidence for both declarative *do* forms provides additional support for this interpretation.

Interestingly, the slight upward trend seen in the 1590s correspondence also aligns with the rise shown in Ellegård's results, suggesting that Elizabeth was acutely aware of the stylistic trends attached to negative *do*. This is a remarkable property of her language use and provides insight into her engagement with the literary fashions. Her presence at the Court, the domicile most concerned with prestigious linguistic forms, and the source of much Elizabethan literature, provides biographical evidence to contextualise the trend. Indeed, the strength of the re-evaluation in her correspondence, which pre-dates the change in CEEC, suggests she adopted the stylistic change at a very early stage. It could cautiously be suggested that Elizabeth was not merely adopting these trends, but helping to set and establish them.

An alternative interpretation of the rise seen in Elizabeth's 1590s correspondence is that it correlates with the general increase of negative *do* seen in spoken-mode texts at the macro-level, e.g. CEEC correspondence (Nurmi 1999: 147), CED trials and depositions (Culpeper & Kytö 2010: 195), because Elizabeth's correspondence became more informal over time. A more detailed analysis of the lexical complexity of Elizabeth's correspondence, following Warner's (2005) methodology, would help to indicate which is the better explanation. It may be that both explanations are applicable.

The frequency of negative *do* in the parliamentary speeches (15.8%, or 0.5 times per 1000 words) is slightly higher than in the post-accession correspondence (11.8%, or 0.4 times per 1000 words), although the difference is not statistically significant. Given that the speeches represent the years 1563–1586, we might expect the figure to mirror the frequency of the 1580s correspondence (3.4%), suggesting this genre shows less of a decline. The distribution of tokens across the six speeches is fairly uneven, with the majority occurring in speeches from 1586. For the earlier decades, only the 1566 speech contains negative declarative constructions, with one token of each variant. It is therefore not possible to say, with the present data, if Elizabeth used *do* more frequently in her earlier speeches.

Treating the speech data collectively, the function of *do* seems relatively stable and this can explain the lesser dip. As the following examples indicate, Elizabeth uses negative *do* to create cohesion in her speeches and to intensify her expression. These functions are similar to those previously identified in the Seymour letters, as well as in spoken mode genres more generally (Culpeper & Kytö 2010: 195–197). In (54), negative *do* collocates with a *know*-group verb, which could indicate that Elizabeth was more inclined to use the variant in the 1560s—before the stylistic re-evaluation—than in the later decades:

(54) I marvel not much that bridleless colts **do not know** their rider's hand (5th November 1566, QEIC speeches).

In an example from the 1580s, the extra syllable provided by periphrastic *do* appears to reinforce the negation and provides a necessary contrast with the extensive coordinate negation (*nor*) of the preceding text. This example occurs at the point where Elizabeth avoids giving a direct answer to the request that she allow the execution of Mary, Queen of Scots. Again, affirmative *do* occurs in close proximity to the negative form:

(55) I am not so void of judgement as not to see mine own peril, nor yet so ignorant as not to know it were in nature a foolish course to cherish a sword to cut mine own throat, nor so careless as not to weigh that my life daily is in hazard; but this I do consider: that many a man would put his life in danger for the safeguard of a king. **I do not say** that so will I, but I pray you think that I have thought upon it (24th November 1586, QEIC speeches).

The instances of negative *do* in Elizabeth's parliamentary speeches may therefore be motivated by the demands of formal oration. The macro-level data from the CED showed no decline or dip in the formal spoken genres during the Early Modern period (Culpeper & Kytö 2010: 195–197), suggesting they were exempt from the literary re-evaluation identified by Warner (2005). One possible interpretation is that the level of *do* found in the parliamentary speeches is lower than the macro-level frequencies of CEEC and CED data because Elizabeth is suppressing her use of the construction in non-discursive contexts, in line with the re-evaluation seen in her translations and correspondence, but continuing to use it for discursive functions. Unfortunately, the low token counts for the speeches prevent any definitive conclusions.

5.6 *Summary*

The QEIC data indicates that Elizabeth was a mid-range user of negative declarative *do* during the pre-accession period, based on a comparison between her correspondence and the macro-level data in CEEC. The result differs from the finding that Elizabeth was a leader in the change for affirmative *do*, which was at a similar macro-level stage (new and vigorous) in the period. It seems probable that this reflects the smaller range of functions for negative *do* than the affirmative form in her idiolect. In her correspondence, negative *do* is used to intensify and add cohesion to the text, but there is no evidence of a more literary or rhetorical usage. From being an average user, Elizabeth leads the dip in the latter half of the sixteenth century. There is no indication that the changes over time relate directly to her accession. Instead, an explanation can be found in the broader socio-historical context, with Elizabeth participating in the stylistic re-evaluation of the form.

Affirmative and negative *do* appear to be linked in Elizabeth's idiolect, with the dip in both variants showing a comparable stylistic sensitivity. The recent macro-level studies give no indication that the trends in Elizabeth's correspondence would fit best with Ellegård's literary corpus. Yet the similarities between Elizabeth's idiolectal preferences and the macro-level data for the all-male literary corpus are striking. This is best shown by combining the results from the different genres in QEIC to create an overall figure—replicating, to a greater degree, the mixed (literary) genres used in Ellegård's data. For both contexts, Elizabeth's usage parallels Ellegård's findings for the later decades. The similarity for affirmative *do* is most striking. For negative *do*, the low token counts—even when using the whole of QEIC—cause problems for the middle period (1550–1575), but Elizabeth's idiolect shows the same downward trend as the literary corpus.

The contexts of use for negative *do* and affirmative *do* are similar in Elizabeth's idiolect. Although some macro-level studies suggest that the two variants influenced and promoted the other in EModE (e.g. Nurmi 1999; Rissanen 1999), other analyses have preferred to treat the two variants as distinct and independent forms. Wischer's (2008: 139) investigation of the demise of affirmative *do*, for example, makes only a passing reference to the negative context. The QEIC data provides persuasive evidence that the development of the two contexts were intertwined, at least in Elizabeth's idiolect, and warrants further investigation in speaker data for the sixteenth century.

As the final point in the analysis of *do*-periphrasis, I wish to reflect on Nurmi's Scottish hypothesis. There was little evidence to suggest that the decline of affirmative *do* in Elizabeth's correspondence was a result of accommodation with James VI. The findings for negative *do* provide an even stronger case against the accommodation hypothesis, with James VI

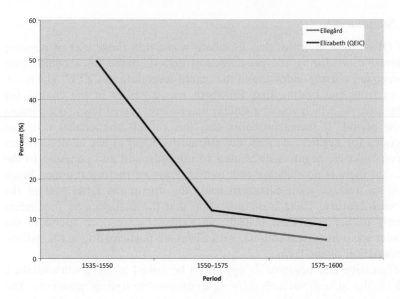

Figure 6: Affirmative *do* (%) in Ellegård (1953) and QEIC (all genres)

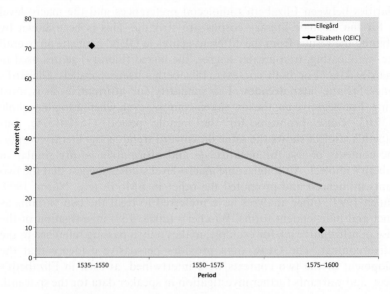

Figure 7: Negative *do* (%) in Ellegård (1953) and QEIC (all genres)

the main recipient of negative *do* in the post-accession period. Stylistic variation provides a more convincing explanation for the decline in QEIC. Whilst this does not disprove Nurmi's hypothesis, it is somewhat jarring that Elizabeth anticipates the later macro-level trend, but for reasons seemingly unconnected to those stated by the Scottish hypothesis. What seems more likely is that Elizabeth was at the leading edge of the stylistic re-evaluation of periphrastic *do* and implemented the change across her writing from the 1580s onwards. By the time the stylistic re-evaluation had begun to filter through to the mid-range—i.e., the main bulk of informants in CEEC—the Scots had arrived at the Court. The infrequency of periphrasis in their dialect may have reinforced the stylistic re-evaluation currently underway in EModE. The idiolectal data does not invalidate the Scottish hypothesis, but suggests that the accession of James VI was merely one element in a larger change that had begun earlier in the sixteenth century amongst those most concerned with style: a group including Elizabeth I.

6. THE REPLACEMENT OF YE BY YOU

In the fifteenth century, the second-person pronoun was marked for case: *ye* was the subject form ((56)) and *you* the object ((57)), although the forms show variation as early as the fourteenth century, with *you* replacing *ye* in subject position ((58)).

(56) **Ye** shall commonly see (1544, Navarre, QEIC translations).
(57) I will send **you** word of them (January 1549, to Edward Seymour, QEIC correspondence).
(58) **You** shall find that few princes will agree (November 1585, to James VI, QEIC correspondence).

Over the course of the fifteenth century, the generalisation of *you* to both positions became more frequent. The situation in the sixteenth century is one of considerable variation, with the forms occurring in both subject and object position (Lass 1999: 154). The analysis of Elizabeth's idiolect follows the methodology used by N&R-B (2003) to collect the macro-level data in CEEC, and focuses on the variation of subject-position pronouns only. All instances of the forms *ye* and *you* in subject position in QEIC were identified using the AntConc concordance program, with accusative and infinitive clauses (e.g. I pray ye/you do something) excluded from the dataset, as N&R-B (2003: 61) found these contexts to be 'sites of confusion'. The methodology does not limit the appreciation of the *ye/you* variable in Elizabeth's idiolect, as *ye* does not occur in object position in QEIC.

6.1 *Results*

The results for *ye/you* in the QEIC correspondence are shown in Table 15. *You* is the generalised form in subject position in Elizabeth's idiolect, with the change complete in the pre-accession period. There is no indication that

Table 15. Second-person pronoun forms *(ye/you)*, subject position only (% *You*) (QEIC correspondence)

	Total *ye* and *you*	% *you*
Pre-accession correspondence	28	100
Post-accession correspondence	405	99.8

this linguistic change was influenced by her accession, or indeed that there was even a process of change over the course of her life. The correspondence results suggest that Elizabeth adopted the incoming variant from childhood.

Elizabeth's uptake of *you* in the pre-accession period contrasts considerably with the macro-level figures. Although *you* generalised very quickly, taking only 80 years (1480–1560) to progress from incipient to complete stages of a change, the macro-level real-time data shows that *you* accounted for 37% of forms in subject position in the 1520–1559 sub-period; i.e. the mid-range stage. It then rose to 96% in 1560–1599 when the change completed (figures adapted from N&R-B 2003: 60, 218). The difference in Elizabeth's uptake and the CEEC figures is statistically significant for both periods (p > 0.001). This trend thus corresponds with that of the CEEC data examined by Nevalainen et al. (2011), who also found Queen Elizabeth to use subject *you* more frequently than many of her contemporaries.

6.2 Social Factors

The first social factor that appears relevant to Elizabeth's participation in the change is her age. It is likely that her youth during the early stages of the change in the mid-sixteenth century encouraged her rapid acquisition of *you* in subject position, in contrast to the older generations. The CEEC data shows generational patterns in the progression of the change. In the 1520–1539 period, Elizabeth's father Henry VIII (b. 1491) uses *you* 52.6% of the time, whereas the older Thomas Wolsey (b. 1473) does not use *you* at all (N&R-B 2003: 101–103). The CEEC sub-file for Elizabeth clearly shows Elizabeth to be a leader in the change; she is one of the youngest informants in their dataset for the period 1540–1559, and one of the few to use *you* exclusively at this time (N&R-B 2003: 96). There is thus persuasive evidence that age is a factor in Elizabeth's leading uptake of *you*.

However, citing age as the sole factor for Elizabeth's linguistic leadership is unsatisfactory. As N&R-B (2003: 96) acknowledge of their CEEC results, 'there is no unfailing correspondence between the age of an informant and his or her choice of variant', although they fail to expand on the relevance of this statement to Elizabeth in particular. However, the CEEC results illustrate their point clearly. In the 1540–1559 sub-period, Henry VIII uses *you* 80% of the time. Yet his contemporary in generation, Thomas Cromwell (b. c. 1485) does not participate in the change at all and continues to use *ye* in subject position (N&R-B 2003: 102). The patterns exemplify a principle of sociolinguistics, that a speaker's linguistic choices arise from multiple, intersecting factors (Bayley 2002: 118). Thus, the role of other social factors in the change, as well as other linguistic factors, may offer further insight into Elizabeth's leading position.

A second social category that appears relevant to Elizabeth's linguistic behaviour is gender, particularly when considering the biographical evidence from her early childhood. In CEEC, women lead the uptake of *you* throughout the sixteenth century. In the 1540–1559 sub-period, women use subject *you* 75% of the time, whereas male informants show a lower usage of 53.1% (Nevalainen 2000: 54). The near-complete stage of the change in the language of female informants offers a better match with Elizabeth's pre-accession idiolect. The strength of the correlation increases if the prominent role of women as Elizabeth's companions and educators in her formative years is taken into account (Borman 2009: 44–61, 99–126). Examples (59)–(61) show the use of *ye/you* by several women connected to Elizabeth's childhood, taken from PCEEC:

(59) I knowe not wether **ye** be aparaphryser or not, yf **ye** be lerned in that syence yt ys possyble **ye** may of one worde make ahole sentence (Catherine Parr, 1547; Origin2, 152).

(60) I parceyv strange newes concernyng a sewte **you** have in hande to the Quene for maryage (Mary Tudor I, 1547; Origin2, 150).

(61) Wherein as **you** shall doo that which to youre honor, truthe, and dutie aperteyneth, so shall we remember the same unto you and yours accordingly (Jane Grey, 1553; Origin2, 185).

The macro-level trends for social rank and domicile support the hypothesis. In the 1520–1559 sub-period, the upper-ranks use subject *you* around 40% of the time, a figure much lower than the pre-accession frequency in QEIC (N&R-B 2003: 142). This figure counts male informants only. Likewise, the generalisation of *you* is at the mid-range stage at the Court for the same period (1520–1559) (N&R-B 2003: 171–172). In social terms, Elizabeth's age and gender provide the best correlates for her leading uptake of *you* in the pre-accession period.

Familial connections may also be relevant. The CEEC data showed that Henry VIII uses *you* 80% of the time in the period 1540–1559; a progressive frequency that is even more striking given his death in 1547. Elizabeth's sister, Mary, represented in (60), also appears to prefer *you*. Catherine Parr, on the other hand, appears to use *ye* in subject position ((59)). The biographical accounts suggest that Elizabeth had much greater contact with

Table 16. *You* (%) out of *ye/you*, subject position only (QEIC)

	Total (*ye/you*)	% *you*
PreA correspondence	28	100
PostA correspondence	405	99.8
Speeches	27	100
PreA translations	5	0
PostA translations	34	100

Parr in the 1540s than she did with her father or sister, living in the Queen's (later Queen Dowager's) household until 1548. Perry (1990: 25) suggests Elizabeth's contact with her father was most likely in official contexts, such as listening to his speeches. Whilst this may have influenced Elizabeth's political ideologies, it is less clear if it explains her uptake of *you*.

In the post-accession period, the change completes across the macro-level, and Elizabeth's usage is now the norm.

6.3 *Stylistic Factors*

In his discussion of EModE morphology, Lass (1999: 154) notes that one effect of the generalisation of *you* was the restriction of *ye* to 'special registers'.[12] The evidence of *ye/you* in Elizabeth's idiolect has so far been drawn from her correspondence, one of the less formal genres in QEIC. Lass's comments suggest that Elizabeth may show stylistic sensitivity in her use of the variable. To investigate this hypothesis, Table 16 shows the findings for *ye/you* in the three genres in QEIC.

Predominantly, the figures match the trends in the correspondence. In the post-accession period, the parliamentary speeches and translations contain 100 percent *you* in subject position, suggesting that *ye* lacked even a specialist stylistic function in Elizabeth's post-accession idiolect.

However, the results of the pre-accession translations do not follow the trends seen in the contemporary correspondence. Instead, *ye* occurs five times and *you* not at all in subject position. An explanation lies in the pronominal system Elizabeth uses in these texts, seemingly adopting the second-person pronominal system of ME rather than the Early Modern system found in her correspondence. Second-person *thou/thee* are the main second-person pronouns in the pre-accession translations, with over 250 tokens, and are used to refer to singular persons. Subject *ye* and object *you* refer to plural referents, see ((62)), explaining why *ye/you* occurs comparatively infrequently in these works.

---

[12] I take 'special registers' to mean high register, literary genres such as religious prose.

(62) Wherefore the apostle doth teach us, that such an opinion that we have of God which is uncertain and without order, is ignorance of God. In the time (said he) that **ye** did not know God, **ye** did serve unto those which naturally be no Gods (1545, Calvin, QEIC translation).

The results could indicate that Elizabeth's idiolect changed from the archaic ME system to the EModE system in only a couple of years. However, this seems unlikely. The macro-level data shows that, in the 1520–1559 sub-period, one third of the informants studied show variable grammars, i.e. use both *ye* and *you* in subject position (N&R-B 2003: 92–93). Given the generalised status of *you* in Elizabeth's pre-accession correspondence, it is improbable that she would change her usage from the old to the new system so rapidly without leaving any evidence of the transitional stage. Unfortunately, there are no comparative forms from the years when the translations were written (1544 and 1545) in the correspondence corpus. The 1544 letter written to preface Elizabeth's translation of Navarre contains only object-position *you*.

Instead, the distribution of second-person pronouns in the pre-accession translations is more likely evidence of stylistic variation. The pre-accession translations are pious, formal works, designed to display Elizabeth's scholarly abilities (Teague 2000: 33). Whilst they may not exemplify the 'special register' to which Lass refers (1999: 154), the conscious utilisation of the older pronominal system for these works suggests that the advanced stage of the generalisation of *you* in Elizabeth's idiolect made the second-person pronoun forms stylistically significant in more formal, literary genres. In the post-accession translations, this aspect is no longer apparent, with *you* generalised throughout.[13]

6.4 *Interactive and Systemic Factors*

Under interactive and systemic factors, the final analytical step focuses on the single example of *ye* in the post-accession correspondence, which is located in an autograph postscript to a scribal letter:

(63) Though **you** have some tainted sheep among your flock, let not that serve for excuse for the rest. We trust you are so carefully regarded

---

[13] In the post-accession translations, the frequency of *thou* is also much lower than the earlier compositions. When viewed alongside the data for *ye/you*, it seems probable that Elizabeth changed her stylistic evaluation of the pronominal paradigm from a numerical to a socially structured system. The dominance of polite *you* in the translations, for example, fits with the social significance of the pronoun seen in the late sixteenth century amongst the upper ranks (Lass 1999: 152–153). Unfortunately, the low frequency of *thou* in Elizabeth's correspondence and speeches (the more interactive genres in QEIC) means I am unable to pursue this feature of her idiolect further. See Nevala (2004) for a discussion of *thou/you* in CEEC.

as naught shall be left for your excuses, but either **ye** lack heart or want will, for of fear we will not make mention as that our soul abhors (October 1593, to Edward Norris, QEIC correspondence).

The tone of the postscript is both affectionate and instructive. Elizabeth addresses Edward Norris as 'Ned', and warns him to keep a close eye on the men ('sheep') in his service. Yet, there is little at an interactive level that would explain why Elizabeth would use *ye* in this letter, rather than in other letters of a similar tone and function. In addition, whilst the form occurs in subject position, the addressee is singular, not plural, and therefore is not compatible with the ME system she uses in the pre-accession translations.

A better explanation for *ye* may be systemic. In addition to subject *ye*, EModE also contained a weakened (unstressed) form of *you*, also spelled < ye > and a probable cause of confusion between the two pronominal case forms (Lass 1999: 154). In the example above, *ye* occurs in a weak position, with stress most likely falling on the second syllable of 'either' and the verbs 'lack' and 'want'. This implies that the pronoun may reflect Elizabeth's pronunciation of the weak form of *you* rather than a true instance of nominative *ye*.

6.5 *Summary*

QEIC reveals that Elizabeth was a leader in the replacement of subject *ye* by *you*, with the change complete in the pre-accession period, corroborating the findings of CEEC-based studies (N&R-B 2003; Nevalainen et al. 2011). Elizabeth's young age, and her contact with female speakers who also led the change, are the most convincing social correlates. The link with a familial 'lect' is also possible, based on the uptake of Henry VIII and Mary I, although this is more problematic when the biographical details are considered. Stylistic influences were notable in Elizabeth's pre-accession translations, and it may be that her stylistic sensitivity to the variant was heightened by the advanced stage of the change in her more informal or vernacular writings, which lead to the decision to use the ME pronominal paradigm in the pre-accession translations. The significance of stylistic variation in Elizabeth's idiolect and its relationship with her position in a linguistic change will be seen again in the chapters that follow.

As a change, there is no evidence of a correlation with Elizabeth's accession. Subject *you* is a characteristic feature of her idiolect throughout her lifetime. As a result, her progressiveness offers a potentially valuable feature for authorship analysis, especially since many of her close contemporaries at the Court such as William Cecil and Francis Walsingham are conservative users (Nevalainen et al. 2011: 31). The presence of *ye* in a number of signed scribal letters from the post-accession period thus raises questions about the extent of Elizabeth's involvement in the composition of these texts. For instance, a famous letter to George and Elizabeth Talbot, Earl and Countess of Shrewsbury, in which Elizabeth thanks them for their previous hospitality towards the Earl of Leicester, contains a now suspect line: 'And therefore **ye** may assure yourselves [...] as so well deserving creditors as **ye** are shall never have cause to think **ye** have met with an unthankful debtor' (May 2004a: 150).

Finally, the idiolectal analysis of *ye/you* demonstrates the benefits of a synchronic/diachronic intersection, revealing both the rapidity of the change, the plausible influence of multiple social factors, and the significance of stylistic purposes in Elizabeth's selection of incoming and outgoing forms.

7. First- and second-person possessive determiners

Towards the end of the fifteenth century, the replacement of the long (*n*-forms) first- and second-person singular possessive determiners (*mine* and *thine*) with the short (*n*-less) forms (*my* and *thy*) was underway. The progression of the change was greatly influenced by the phonological context. The switch to *my* and *thy* was complete in consonant-initial contexts ((64)) by 1500 (N&R-B 2003: 62), but the change progressed slower in other environments with the long forms 'preferred before vowel-initial nouns' ((65) and (66)), and to a lesser extent initial- < h >, during the sixteenth century ((67) and (68)) (Lass 1999: 147).

(64) the order of **my** writing (31st December 1544, to Catherine Parr, QEIC correspondence).

(65) **mine** estate of health (1548, to Edward Seymour, QEIC correspondence).

(66) against me or **my** estate (4th July 1602, to James VI, QEIC correspondence).

(67) **mine** honour, and honesty (28th January 1549, to Edward Seymour, QEIC correspondence).

(68) it is true upon **my** honour (January/February 1585, to James VI, QEIC correspondence).

Because the influence of phonological environment is so significant in the macro-level trends, this systemic factor is incorporated into my overall treatment of Elizabeth's idiolectal data. To account for the different rates of change, the tokens are split into three categories: vowel-initial, < h >-initial and *own* (a word-specific category). Each category is considered both independently and collectively, in order to make like-for-like comparisons with the different combinations of categories used in baseline studies.[14] As expected, Elizabeth uses *my/thy* categorically in consonant-initial contexts and thus this environment is excluded from the analysis. The approach to phonological categories differs from the collective, quantitative evidence used by Nevalainen et al. (2011), which finds Elizabeth to be an overall progressive user in this change. As will be seen, the refinement of the data reveals interesting nuances in Elizabeth's usage, and sheds further light on the complexities involved in the uptake of a change by an individual speaker, and the relation to macro-level developments.

In Elizabeth's correspondence there are very few second-person possessive determiners, and so the few tokens of *thy/thine* are discussed separately and qualitatively. The quantitative and general discussion concentrates on the first-person forms in the QEIC correspondence. Schendl (1997: 179) reports similar difficulties when collecting second-person pronoun data in his multi-genre corpus study. Nevalainen et al. (2011) report no such difficulties, which may reflect their use of a boot-strapping method in calculating their data.

7.1 *Results*

The results for Elizabeth's correspondence (Table 17) indicate that her uptake of *my* was at an advanced stage in two of the three phonological contexts. In vocalic and <h>-initial contexts, the frequency of *my* is around 85% in the pre-accession correspondence, meeting the threshold for a completed change. In the post-accession correspondence, the figures reach 100%.[15] Only the lexis-specific context *own* shows a slower uptake. Here, *my* accounts for only one of the seven tokens in the pre-accession period (14.3%), placing it at the earliest 'incipient' stage of the change. This rises to the 'nearing completion' stage in the post-accession period, with a rapid shift to 63.2% (12 of the 19 tokens).[16] In two of the three contexts, therefore, there is no evidence of a linguistic shift connected to Elizabeth's accession. The increase of *my* in *own* contexts in the post-accession period more likely reflects the general progression of the change in her idiolect.

Overall, the increase in *n*-less variants identified in Elizabeth's correspondence fits with the diachronic macro-level trends in CEEC and the results for Elizabeth presented in Nevalainen et al. (2011). The pattern of

---

[14] N&R-B (2003) present the CEEC real-time data for each environment individually, before grouping vowel-initial and *own* contexts together to discuss the different social factors. Unfortunately, this does not always allow for the best evaluation of Elizabeth's preferences.
[15] The difference between the pre- and post-accession figures for <h>-initial and *own* contexts is significant (p > 0.5) and vocalic contexts are very significant (p > 0.01).
[16] No other lexis-specific contexts appear to be relevant in Elizabeth's idiolect.

Table 17. *my* (%) out of *my/mine* in three phonological contexts (QEIC correspondence)

	Total: vocalic	% *my* - vocalic	Total: <h>	% *my* - <h>	Total: own	% *my* - *own*
PreA	7	85.7	8	87.5	7	14.3
PostA	68	100.0	31	100.0	19	63.2
Overall	75	98.7	39	97.4	26	50.0

Table 18. *my/thy* (%) in three contexts (CEEC)–adapted from N&R-B (2003: 218)

	% *my/thy*: vocalic	% *my/thy*: <h>	% *my/thy*: *own*
1500–1539	36	82	12
1540–1579	70	99	36
1580–1619	93	–	60

diffusion across the three contexts also coheres to the macro-level trends, with <h>-initial contexts at the most advanced stage, vocalic contexts second-most advanced, and *own* contexts lagging behind.

The CEEC data uses sub-periods that do not match the QEIC pre- and post-accession division, but the nature of the token distribution in Elizabeth's correspondence means that the same figures can be used for comparison. In the vocalic contexts Elizabeth's usage is ahead of the curve, whereas in <h>-initial contexts she is behind (although well within the completed stage of the change). It is in *own* contexts that Elizabeth's usage stands out, appearing to lag behind the CEEC norm in the 1540–1579 period (Table 18).

The deviant trend for the *own* phonological context highlights a potential difference between the QEIC correspondence data and macro-level CEEC data. In Elizabeth's letters, *mine* is spelled fully in <h>-initial and vocalic contexts. In *own* environments in the correspondence, however, she does not modify the determiner form. Instead, she alters the adjective, e.g. <my none> and <my own>. Modernised transcripts of Elizabeth's pre-accession correspondence render <my none> as 'mine own' (e.g. letter to Edward Seymour, 1549 in May 2004a: 108). The logic behind the editorial decision is understandable for the intended readership. However, the OED recognises *nown* (<none>) as a distinct and contemporary alternative to *own*, originally derived through meta-analysis in the fourteenth century (OED Online). Examples from Elizabeth's correspondence are included in the dictionary's citations for the entry.

The definition suggests that incorporating 'my none' into the *own* category for a comparison with CEEC is a questionable decision, if in fact Elizabeth distinguished between *own* and *nown* as two separate adjective forms.[17] However, treating *nown* as a distinct context to *own* makes it difficult to calculate the figures for the variable in a reliable way. Whilst a good number of the tokens are taken from manuscripts from which I have made direct transcriptions, others in the corpus are based on modern editions of the correspondence and it is difficult to determine if they too follow May's editorial approach.

As I later show with examples from PCEEC, the CEEC data includes *own* and *nown*, although it appears that the CEEC-based studies (N&R-B 2003; Nevalainen et al. 2011) do not distinguish between the two adjectives. Therefore, the present analysis will continue to treat the examples of < my none > as comparable with the long form < mine own > . The possibility of a distinction between adjective forms in Elizabeth's idiolect may well explain the lag in this context compared to other phonological environments, and this is reflected in the discussion.

Another point to be addressed in the initial analysis is the evidence for second-person possessive determiners. The five tokens of *thy/thine* all occur in one letter, addressed to Elizabeth's godson John Harington. The letter is very short and was enclosed with a copy of the 1576 Parliamentary speech. The note is one of only three letters in QEIC to contain *thou* second-person forms, rather than *you*. The lack of tokens is, unfortunately, a common problem when working with historical data. The polite second-person pronoun *you* was the conventional address-form in Early Modern correspondence, and *thou/thy/thine* was less common, particularly in letters by royalty (Lass 1999: 149; Nevala 2004: 170).

(69) Boy Jack, I have made a clerk write fair my poor words for **thine** use, as it cannot be such striplings have entrance into Parliament Assemblies as yet. Ponder them in **thy** hours of leisure and play with them till they enter **thine** understanding, so shalt thou hereafter perchance find some good fruits hereof when **thy** godmother is out of remembrance, and I do this because **thy** father was ready to serve and love us in trouble and thrall (March 1576, to John Harington, QEIC correspondence).

The six tokens show the same distributional pattern as the figures for *my/ mine*. *Thine* occurs only in vowel-initial contexts, with *thy* found in consonant-initial and < h > -initial environments. There are no examples of *own*.

---

[17] Wiggins (2011) reports that *nown* is used as pet name in the correspondence between Bess of Hardwick and George Talbot, Earl of Shrewsbury. It is feasible that this is a derivative usage of the meta-analysed adjective, given its personal reference and sense of possession.

7.2 *Social Factors*

CEEC data suggests that gender, social rank and domicile all played a part in the diffusion of the *n*-less variants from the late fifteenth century onwards, indicating that social factors may help to explain the patterns in Elizabeth's idiolect. As noted above, the CEEC data combines vocalic and *own* contexts when calculating the influence of the different social factors, and excludes < h > -initial environments from discussion. For comparison, I have re-calculated Elizabeth's idiolectal data in the same way (see Table 19). Admittedly, combining these two contexts in an analysis of Elizabeth's idiolect is less than ideal, as the uptake of *my* is far more advanced in the vocalic environment (100% in the 1580–1619 sub-period) than in *own* contexts (62.5%).

At the macro-level, women lead the uptake of *n*-less variants throughout the sixteenth century—what N&R-B (2003: 119) refer to as a 'systematic gender advantage'. Based on the combined results in Table 19, it appears that Elizabeth's usage correlates more closely with male informants (50%) for the 1540–1579 period rather than female informants, who use *my/thy* 60% of the time. However, the difference between vocalic and *own* contexts is important here. Examination of PCEEC shows that < my none > occurs only once in the letters of sixteenth-century female informants, in a letter penned by the elderly Anne Gresham in 1582:

(70) so that I mey in goy **my nown** (Anne Gresham, 1582; Bacon, II, 197).

By contrast, *nown* occurs in letters by three different male informants in PCEEC. The majority of examples occur in the correspondence of Robert Dudley, Earl of Leicester. This finding is interesting from a biographical perspective, as Dudley was Elizabeth's contemporary and a childhood friend before he assumed his position at the Court ((71)). In a cursory examination of sixteenth-century letters in other collections, *my nown* also occurs in the letters of Thomas Howard, Duke of Norfolk, written in the 1570s (see Murdin 1759: 169–170).

(71) as one that desyreth no name but **my none** name (Robert Dudley, 1586; Leycest, 94).

Table 19. *my* (%): vocalic and *own* contexts combined (QEIC correspondence)

Period	% *my* - vocalic and *own* contexts
1540–1579	52.9
1580–1619	92.9

< mine own > is by far the more common construction in the letters of both male and female informants in PCEEC, including a letter by Elizabeth's sister, Mary I. This suggests that Elizabeth's use of < my none > is fairly unusual and lends further support to the hypothesis for her distinct conceptualisation of this environment.

Proceeding on the assumption that female informants led the change in both phonological contexts, Elizabeth's high uptake of *my* in vocalic contexts (85.7%) correlates most closely with this gender. Her usage is well above the CEEC average of 70% for the 1540–1579 period and thus presumably in-line with the progressive uptake of female informants. As I also hypothesised in the analysis of *ye/you*, Elizabeth's contact with her early caregivers is a plausible explanation for Elizabeth's exposure to, and subsequent uptake of, *n*-less variants. The domicile information further supports the hypothesis. At the Court (1540–1579) the change has only just entered the mid-range stage (> 35%) (N&R-B 2003: 180), showing little similarity with Elizabeth.

The social group data suggests that the change was instigated during Elizabeth's early childhood, when her exposure to female caregivers was greatest. As a change from below, *my/thy* did not gain ground in more learned circles until the end of the sixteenth century. The more peripheral position of women at the Court, such as those involved with Elizabeth's household, suggests a plausible channel through which the forms could enter Elizabeth's repertoire. Her youth may also have enhanced her receptivity to the form. Yet it is difficult to explain quite how Elizabeth came to use the adjective form *nown*, which most likely contributes to the significant lag in the *own* context compared to her progressive usage in the vocalic and < h >-initial environments; although the presence of the form in the letters of Robert Dudley suggests a potential connection to local networks, distinct from the larger domicile groups in CEEC.

7.3 *Stylistic Factors*

In his discussion of the change in EModE, Schendl (1997) suggests that the influence of non-systemic factors (i.e. factors other than phonological environment) was negligible in the first half of the sixteenth century, with the variants becoming stylistically significant only in the later decades. Analysing the multiple genres in the HC alongside a self-compiled supplement, he suggests that the long forms 'were the stylistically unmarked forms before vowels' in the early sixteenth century, with no clear patterns of use according to the formality of the genre (Schendl 1997: 185). His analysis of genres written in the latter-half of the century, by contrast, shows a clear gradation across the formal to less formal genres, with the latter containing the greater proportion of *n*-less variants (Schendl 1997: 182). Evidence from private correspondence leads him to propose that vowel-initial short forms 'acquired a stylistic marking as informal' in the final decades of the sixteenth century (1997: 187). His corpus includes a small number of letters between Elizabeth I and James VI, and his stylistic interpretation leads him to suggest that the presence of vowel-initial *my/thy* in these letters is 'surprising' (1997: 186). He was presumably unaware of the advanced stage of the change in Elizabeth's idiolect as a whole (excepting < own/nown >), and the dominance of vocalic *n*-less variants in her earliest correspondence.

The stratification of the change in the macro-level CEEC data discussed above provides further support for Schendl's hypothesis. Whilst the data provides no direct insight into the stylistic and interactive associations of the variable, the progression of the change from below and the delayed uptake of the Court suggests that *my/thy* forms did not acquire the prestigious associations that would have caused them to supplant *mine/thine* more rapidly. The preservation of the long forms in poetic styles as a 'conscious archaism' in LModE texts (Schendl 1997: 180; see also Lass 1999: 147) is a further sign that the change progressed more slowly in formal and literary genres.

The results for the three genres in QEIC are shown in Table 20. The translations contain first- and second-person possessive determiners and both forms are included in the figures. The speeches, as with Elizabeth's correspondence, contain only first-person forms.

Although token frequencies are low, the cross-genre comparison suggests stylistic variation is present in both the pre- and post-accession periods. The pre-accession translations contain a slightly higher proportion of *n*-forms than the contemporary correspondence (the data for this genre is taken from the 1544 text, as the 1545 work contains no tokens). There are two properties of note in the pre-accession translation, each of which contrasts with the pre-accession correspondence. Firstly, *my* occurs in vocalic contexts much less frequently in this genre (30%) than in the contemporary letters (85.7%); a property that may be stylistically motivated.

Secondly, in the 1544 manuscript Elizabeth uses *own*, e.g. < myne own > , rather than the *nown* form identified in her correspondence, and the *n*-form *mine* occurs twice in this context. There were no examples of *mine own* (only *my nown/own*) in the correspondence. This provides further evidence for the argument that *own* and *nown* were distinct forms in her idiolect.

Table 20. First- and second-person *n*-less possessive determiners (%), vocalic and *own* contexts combined (QEIC).

	Total (*n*- and *n*-less forms)	% *my*
PreA correspondence	14	50
PostA correspondence	87	92
Speeches	24	20.8
PreA translations	31	41.9 (including *thy*)
PostA translations	10	90 (including *thy*)

(72) satisfy **mine** ignorance and fault (1544, Navarre, QEIC translations).
(73) through **mine own** ill will (1544, Navarre, QEIC translations).
(74) by **my own** fault (1544, Navarre, QEIC translations).

The difference between the two pre-accession genres suggests stylistic variation. The higher frequency of *n*-forms in vocalic contexts and the use of *mine own* in the translation are compatible with the macro-level trends connecting *n*-forms to more formal genres. In the analysis of *ye/you*, Elizabeth used the ME pronoun system in the pre-accession translations. It is plausible that the possessive determiners reflect a similar stylistic shift, in order to create a more literary and formal style—one perhaps appropriate to the religious subject. As a loosely comparable genre, Schendl (1997: 182) found that *n*-variants were the dominant form in the bible (based on samples in the HC) throughout the sixteenth century.

In the post-accession translations, the stylistic variation is less pronounced. There is only one example of an *n*-form, second-person *thine* in an *own* context ((75)). In the other nine tokens, the *n*-less variants occur in vocalic and *own* contexts, including an example of *nown* ((76)).

(75) All they that were, either have perished by their stubbornness or were saved by thy mercy. So it follows that either none doth live, or they that breathe be won **thine own** (Cicero, 1592, QEIC translations).
(76) It ill becomes Philosophy to leave alone an innocent's way. Shall I dread **my nown** blame (Boethius, 1593, QEIC translations).

Schendl hypothesises that the stylistic association between the *n*-forms and more formal texts strengthened in the latter-half of the sixteenth century. In Elizabeth's translation, the hypothesis shows a better fit with her practice in the earlier decades.

The frequency of *n*-variants in Elizabeth's post-accession speeches suggests a different trend, with *my* accounting for only 20.8% of forms in vocalic and *own* environments.[18]

(77) for **mine own** life (24th November 1586, QEIC speeches).
(78) the trust of **mine assured** strength (1576, QEIC speeches).

It is plausible that the influence of phonological context is greater in the oratorical genre, where articulation and prosody are foregrounded, than in written communication, leading to the reduction in *n*-less forms. Scribal interference is also a possibility. The only autograph example occurs in the 1567 speech ('my admonitions' (1567, QEIC speeches)), while the remaining examples of vocalic and *own* contexts survive as apographs only, one in the 1576 speech and two from 1586. As a result, it is difficult to make any

---

[18] The difference between the speeches and the post-accession correspondence is statistically significant (p > 0.001).

definitive statements about Elizabeth's practice in her speeches based on the present data.

Overall, the comparison of the correspondence and translations suggests that stylistic variation is a relevant factor in Elizabeth's use of the variable in the pre-accession period, with the older *n*-variant forms more likely to occur in more formal genres. The correlation is less apparent in the post-accession period, although there may be some stylistic patterning in the speeches. Consequently, Elizabeth can be identified as a stylistic leader of the change, as well as a linguistic leader in the conventional quantitative sense. Whilst I concur with Schendl (1997: 189, fn.5) that period divisions are necessarily fuzzy, the difference between the pre-accession translations and correspondence suggests that Elizabeth anticipated the stylistic associations of the *n*-variant, which Schendl dates to the latter-half of the sixteenth century, comparable with her anticipation of other stylistic trends such as affirmative and negative *do*.

7.4 *Interactive Factors*

The correspondence data shows little evidence that the *n*-forms pattern by recipient or by function. Elizabeth uses *n*-forms in both address forms and within the main body of the letter to individuals of various social standing:

(79) to stand in **my nown** wit (21st February 1549, to Edward Seymour, QEIC correspondence).

(80) Scribbled with **my own** wracked hand this 23 day of July (1563, to Nicholas Throckmorton, QEIC correspondence).

(81) I am that prince that never can endure a menace at **my enemy's** hand (May 1594, to James VI, QEIC correspondence).

(82) **Mine own** Crow (1597, to Lady Margaret Norris, QEIC correspondence).

In sum, interactive factors have little explanatory power and it is plausible that the greater informality of the correspondence reduces the level of stylistic markedness attached to the variants at the other end of the formality spectrum. Coupled with the advanced stage of the change in her idiolect, this leaves little scope for local, interactive significance. The low profile of the variable would explain why she makes little distinction in her letters to James VI or any other recipient (cf. Schendl 1997).

7.5 *Summary*

The QEIC data offers a complex picture of the *n*- and *n*-less variants in Elizabeth's idiolect, indicating that the quantitative identification of

Elizabeth's progressiveness (e.g. Nevalainen et al. 2011), whilst accurate, hides a range of variation and potential influences that act upon the individual speaker. In <h>-initial and vocalic contexts, the change is well developed, placing Elizabeth amongst the leaders of the change in the pre- and post-accession periods. There is no evidence that the accession affected her preferences for the variable. Age and gender were key social correlates that, when combined with biographical evidence, create a plausible scenario between Elizabeth and her caregivers to explain the early and rapid adoption of the *n*-less variant (*my*). Stylistically, the data also indicates that Elizabeth was a leader in attaching stylistic significance to the long *n*-variant, with different patterns found in her pre-accession correspondence and translations. The results illustrate how the focused data of an idiolectal analysis can highlight the range of aspects involved in linguistic variation and in turn expound the trends identified at the macro-level.

The merits of the multi-factored approach also emerge in the analysis of the complexities of the *own* context, with the *own* and *nown* forms in Elizabeth's writing both intriguing and methodologically problematic. Of the three contexts, *own* clearly lagged behind in her idiolect, a ranking that correlates with the macro-level norm. However, I am not convinced that the CEEC category corresponds to Elizabeth's usage. The presence of <mine own> in the 1544 translations, versus <my none> and <my own> in the pre-accession correspondence, may simply be a spelling curiosity—a by-product of Elizabeth's youth and the greater inconsistency of her spelling at this time. Yet, when considered alongside the results for pre-vocalic contexts in the translations, which show a greater frequency of *n*-variants than the contemporary correspondence, there is persuasive evidence that she conceptualised the two forms of the adjective *own* differently and distinctly. If so, then the data in fact represents a two-part change. Firstly, the switch from *mine* to *my*—a change that is largely complete in the pre-accession period and accords with the other contexts, making Elizabeth a clear leader of the change. Secondly, the more idiosyncratic shift from *nown* to *own*, a slower process that lasts into the post-accession period. There is no indication that the shift correlates with her accession, with *nown* found as late as the 1590s.

This is a minor, arguably innocuous, component of Elizabeth's idiolect, but it is difficult to explain (working on the premise that the Queen did distinguish between the adjective forms). The presence of *nown* in the letters of Robert Dudley, Earl of Leicester is an intriguing coincidence, given the biographical history, and suggests that local networks may have significant influence upon Elizabeth's linguistic preferences. I have unfortunately been unable to access the original manuscripts penned by Elizabeth's early tutors, such as Roger Ascham's letters, to clarify if similar evidence can be identified, and as I have already outlined, the modernised spelling in published editions hides the evidence of the original spelling.[19] (This is a good example of the differences between publications produced for literary and historical research and the standard required for linguistic analysis.) Should further autograph manuscripts become available, this would be an interesting element to pursue. Nevertheless, the evidence of *own* and *nown*, as well as other trends connected to the variable, offer some distinctive linguistic features that may prove valuable for authorship analysis.

8. MULTIPLE NEGATION VS. SINGLE NEGATION

Multiple negation denotes two or more negators co-occurring in the same sentential negative structure. In single negation, the secondary negators are replaced with 'non-assertive indefinites' (*any, ever*) (Nevalainen 2000: 49). The methodology used to investigate the variable in QEIC follows the narrow criteria used in previous macro-level studies (e.g. Nevalainen 2000, 2006c; Kallel 2007) and focuses on the negative clauses only where non-assertive forms are possible. To give an example, the following quotation ((83)) from Elizabeth's 1545 translation uses multiple negation (*no + never*). The same structure as non-assertive single negation is shown below ((84)) (*no + ever*):

(83) **no** man did **never** tremble more miserably (1545, Calvin, QEIC translations).
(84) **no** man did **ever** tremble more miserably (modified).

Using the AntConc concordance program, all negative constructions containing *not + no, none, nor, neither, never, ne* and the non-assertive forms *anybody, -one, -thing, -where* and *ever* were identified. A construction is classed as one example of either multiple or single negation, regardless of the number of negators or non-assertive forms present; thus (83) is one token of multiple negation. This follows the method established in previous investigations, e.g. N&R-B (2003) and Nevalainen et al. (2011).

8.1 *Results*

The QEIC correspondence contains a low number of multiple and single negation constructions, with 67 examples identified overall: 12 constructions for the pre-accession period and 55 for the post-accession period. This limits the statistical significance of the data. It is difficult to determine if the token count reflects a property of Elizabeth's idiolect (i.e. she preferred other negation strategies) or a broader symptom of Early Modern

---

[19] In his English letters, Ascham uses <mine own> (e.g. Giles 1864: 21, 23, 47, 101) and less frequently <my own> (e.g. 1864: 47), although the modernised spelling may disguise *own* and *nown* variation.

correspondence. Nevalainen (2000, 2006c) makes no mention of quantitative limitations in CEEC, and Kallel (2007), whose study focuses on the correspondence of the upper-ranks, does not provide the word-counts for his corpus. Recall, however, the related discrepancy between the number of *not* tokens in QEIC correspondence and quantity of data for the negative *do* variable.

Nevertheless, the results for QEIC correspondence suggest that multiple negation is a marginal construction in Elizabeth's idiolect, with just one construction in the pre-accession correspondence (0.16 times per 1000 words) and four constructions in the post-accession letters (0.11 times per 1000 words). Elizabeth thus shows a clear preference for single negation. The 90% + frequency indicates the change had reached the completion stage (> 85%) in her pre-accession idiolect and remained stable throughout her life.

The completion of the change in the pre-accession period marks out Elizabeth's usage from many of her contemporaries with the frequency of single negation at 70.8% and 'nearing completion' in CEEC (1540–1579) (Table 21). The progressiveness seen in the QEIC correspondence supports the findings of Nevalainen et al. (2011), who identified single negation as the fifth of six variables studied in which Elizabeth was a leader of a change. The degree of Elizabeth's progressiveness appears quite striking when compared against the CEEC macro-level trend. Results from a different correspondence corpus (Kallel 2007), which collects letters written by the upper-ranks (but not royalty), shows a less striking contrast with Elizabeth's usage (Table 22).

Table 21. Single Negation (%) in QEIC correspondence and CEEC (adapted from N&R-B 2003: 221)

	1500–1539	1540–1579	1580–1619
CEEC	52.3%	70.8%	88.7%
Elizabeth	–	92.9%	92.5%

Table 22. Single Negation (%) in QEIC correspondence and Kallel's self-compiled corpus (adapted from Kallel 2007: 33–34)

	1525–1549	1550–1574	1575–1599
Kallel corpus	51%	95.7%	98%
Elizabeth	90%	100%	93.6%

By the end of the century, the continued spread and diffusion of the variant at the macro-level means that Elizabeth's usage is more comparable with her contemporaries. Interestingly, the macro-level studies by Nevalainen and Kallel differ in the date of the change's completion. Kallel's (2007: 32–34) letter corpus shows that multiple negation is all but obsolete by the 1590s, whereas the uptake of single negation is somewhat slower in CEEC. Based on the descriptions of both corpora, it seems likely that Kallel's selection of correspondence by educated, male writers skews his data towards those informants who led the change, unlike the more representative composition of CEEC. I address this aspect and the relevance to Elizabeth's idiolect below.

In this change, as in the previous chapters, there is no evidence that she modified her usage in response to her accession.

8.2 *Systemic Factors*

Macro-level studies have shown that clause complexity affects the rate of the change from multiple to single negation. Distinguishing between noncoordinate and coordinate constructions, e.g. *not...neither/nor*, Nevalainen (2000: 50) and Kallel (2007: 33–34) find that coordinate constructions lag behind the noncoordinate forms. Because of the low token counts for QEIC, it is possible that either noncoordinate or coordinate structures are over-represented and consequently skew the representation of Elizabeth's overall preferences. Recalculating the correspondence results into noncoordinate and coordinate structures reveals that coordinate constructions are more likely to use multiple negation (21.1% compared to 2.1%; p > 0.01—see Appendix, Table 69). The greater proportion of noncoordinate structures may thus have some influence on the overall percentage, but not unduly so. Kallel's macro-level corpus data (2007), which has a comparable time span to QEIC, suggests that the lag in coordinate structures in Elizabeth's idiolect accords with the macro-level trends (see Appendix, Table 70). This is a notable correlation: the progression of the change at a systemic level shows the same patterning in her correspondence as at the macro-level, despite the greater rapidity of the change in her idiolect.

Kallel (2007: 46–47) proposes that the switch from multiple negation to single negation was driven by semantic ambiguity. He suggests that double negators underwent lexical re-analysis in the Early Modern period, resulting in two concurrent denotations in multiple negative constructions: either (a) a single negative meaning or (b) a double negation. The new status of the second negator, which could now operate independently as well as part of the sentential negation, required clarification, leading to the introduction of non-assertive pronouns. The lag identified in coordinate constructions may reflect a lesser ambiguity of these structures compared to noncoordinate configurations. This offers a persuasive explanation for the different distribution of the structures in Elizabeth's idiolect, despite the progressiveness of the change overall.

The multiple negation coordinate constructions in the QEIC correspondence show an intriguing consistency in form. The collocate *nor never* occurs in three of the four post-accession constructions, possibly used as an intensifying expression. Rissanen (1999: 271) notes that *never* was a common means of emphatic negation in EModE.

(85) trust I pray you **never** a Conqueror With trust of his kindness **nor never** reign precario more (16th March 1593, to James VI, QEIC correspondence).

The repetition suggests that the construction may have had a semi-fossilised or idiomatic status in Elizabeth's idiolect, which would limit the salience of any semantic ambiguity. At the same time, the restriction of multiple negation to predominantly formulaic contexts provides further proof of the advanced stage of the change in her idiolect.

8.3 *Social Factors*

Elizabeth's high usage of single negation in the pre-accession period indicates that she was a leader in this linguistic change. The results corroborate both the CEEC-based findings of Nevalainen et al. (2011) for this particular variable, and their suggestion that progressiveness is a dominant characteristic of Elizabeth's idiolect.

For single negation, age is a likely contributing social factor to Elizabeth's rapid uptake. The macro-level CEEC data (N&R-B 2003: 221) indicates that, overall, the change was at the nearing completion stage in the period 1540–1579, with the majority of informants showing a preference for single negation. Elizabeth, as the part of the younger generation, would be most receptive to the incoming form. The significance of age in this change fits with other linguistic variables analysed in her idiolect that emerged at a similar time.

Yet, evidence from the macro-level indicates that age is not the only relevant social factor in Elizabeth's usage. I have already outlined Kallel's hypothesis for a language-internal motivation for the decline of multiple negation, and showed the systemic variation in Elizabeth's idiolect that corroborates his proposal. The sociolinguistic studies indicate that single negation was a change from above, and entered through the upper-ranks of society. This does not disprove Kallel's hypothesis, but rather shows the social dimension of the change. Rissanen's (2000) study of the HC found that fifteenth-century statutes contain some of the earliest and most frequent examples of non-assertive negation compared to other genres, e.g.: 'Provided that this acte be **not** available to **eny** person for **any** entre syn the first day of this present parliament' (c. 1490, cited in Rissanen 2000: 122). The language of statutes is characterised by its concern for accuracy, non-ambiguous reference and clarity (Rissanen 2000: 125). According to Kallel's hypothesis, it would be in texts such as statutes where we would first expect to see signs that semantic imprecision was a concern.

The social implications of the stylistic development emerge in the social groups involved in the composition of such texts. In their discussion of CEEC data, N&R-B (2003: 145–146; also Nevalainen 2006c: 263) observe that the fifteenth-century figures show the upper-ranks to be the clear leaders of the change. By the decades of Elizabeth's childhood, the leading position of the upper ranks has been surpassed by another social group: social aspirers (see Table 23). Social aspirers are the speaker group consistently found to be most aware of linguistic connotations (Chambers 2003: 103–105), and N&R-B (2003: 152) suggest that single negation developed prestigious social significance by the mid-sixteenth century due to the early association with the upper-ranks and official genres such as statutes, thus explaining social aspirers' leading position in the change.

Being from the upper-ranks of Tudor society, we would expect Elizabeth's uptake in the pre-accession period to correlate with non-professional informants. However, comparison shows that her uptake of single negation differs from these groups and instead there is a greater similarity between Elizabeth (92%) and social aspirers (80%).

The definition of social aspirer used by the CEEC corpus—an individual who climbed two ranks or more (Nurmi 1999: 42)—is an inaccurate description of Elizabeth's situation in the pre-accession period. Whilst her position in relation to the succession varied, her social rank did not change. One interpretation of the social rank data is that Elizabeth's contact with the upper-ranking male informants, as part of her social group, introduced her to the incoming variant, with her age consequently boosting the progression of the change in her idiolect. Yet, an argument can also be made that the intrinsic values concerning language and its social significance were relevant to the young princess, particularly the emphasis placed upon her education to become 'as learned as possible' (Somerset

Table 23. Single Negation (%) (QEIC correspondence) and CEEC social ranks (male informants only) adapted from Nevalainen (2006c: 263)

	1520–1559	1560–1599
Elizabeth	92%	94%
CEEC: Nonprofessional upper ranks	46%	90%
CEEC: Professional upper ranks	41%	82%
CEEC: Social aspirers	80%	98%

1991: 15). As a member of the younger generation at Court, it is possible that Elizabeth's uptake of single negation was spurred by her awareness of the form's prestigious associations, which led her not only to adopt the variant used by her learned superiors, but to surpass them in frequency. In sociolinguistic terms this phenomenon is recognised as hypercorrection: the 'overzealous' uptake of a variant in 'a sociolect that is not native to [the speaker]' (Chamber 2003: 64). (The fit of this concept with Elizabeth's idiolect is considered in more detail in Part III.)

Elizabeth's educators, as learned men from the universities, offer a plausible scenario for her exposure to the prestigious and learned associations of the form in childhood. Her rigorous schooling in Latin, a language where multiple negation is not a valid construction, may also have influenced her usage. By the 1560–1599 period, the change to single negation is nearly complete across the upper ranks, making Elizabeth's usage comparable with all three groups.[20]

Considering the role of gender, the macro-level trends show men leading the change. For example, in the 1580–1610 sub-period, single negation accounts for 80% of examples used by female informants in CEEC, and 91% of examples for male informants (Nevalainen 2000: 54). Elizabeth shows a better fit with male informants. The correlation potentially reflects the similarity in educational opportunities between the upper-ranking males and Elizabeth, as opposed to her female contemporaries, which would expose the former to the prestigious associations of single negation.

This interpretation is supported by the similarity between Elizabeth and the preferences of her domicile, the Court. Nevalainen (2000: 50) reports that informants at the Court were at the forefront of the change throughout the sixteenth century, although she does not provide specific figures. In order to provide some quantitative data for comparison, I have calculated the frequency of single negation in the PCEEC sub-files for three men close to Elizabeth at the Court: William Cecil, Francis Walsingham and Robert Dudley. As well as meeting the criteria for leaders of the change—located at Court, highly educated and from the upper ranks—these men are also Elizabeth's (near) contemporaries in generation: William Cecil b. 1520, Walsingham b. 1532 and Dudley b. 1532/3. Thus, the data provides a generational comparison with Elizabeth as well as a comparison for social rank and domicile factors. The similarity between the four idiolects is apparent. Only Walsingham lags behind in his uptake of the variant, and it seems likely that the trend arises from an over-representation of coordinate constructions in his correspondence: the context that does not promote single negation as readily as noncoordinate constructions.

---

[20] The CEEC data confirms my suspicions that Kallel's (2007) dating reflects the bias towards the upper-ranks in his corpus material. Using the CEEC upper-ranks only, the figures for the two studies are much closer.

Table 24. Single negation (%) 1580–1599
(QEIC correspondence and PCEEC sub-files)

	Total	% single negation
Elizabeth	47	93.6
William Cecil	28	96.4
Francis Walsingham	11	81.8
Robert Dudley	29	96.5

In Nevalainen et al. (2011: 32), the authors find Cecil and Walsingham to be, on the whole, far more conservative in their linguistic preferences than the queen. It is plausible that the status of single negation, as a feature of administrative documents and a change from above, can explain their comparable uptake with Elizabeth in the final decades of the sixteenth century. Nevalainen et al. (2011: 32) observe that '[t]he fact that several people combined progressiveness with conservatism seems to reflect the various social trajectories of the ongoing changes'. What is interesting in regard to Elizabeth, when compared to her contemporaries at Court, is her sensitivity to and participation in changes across the social spectrum. For single negation, Elizabeth's post-accession usage correlates with the usage of others of her social rank and domicile, and—by implication—her level of education.

8.4 Stylistic Factors

The decline of multiple negation has traditionally been viewed as a prestige issue. Seventeenth and eighteenth century prescriptive grammarians condemned the form because of the lack of a comparable construction in Latin and its apparent illogical meaning (i.e. two negatives = positive) (Kallel 2007: 27). However, studies of Early Modern English suggest that the dating of the change largely precedes these prescriptive criticisms. Richard Ingham's (2008: 123) proposal that the uptake of single negation 'may embody natural language change rather than prescriptivist pressure' is highly plausible.

However, this does not preclude the possibility of prestige factoring into the progression of the change after its initiation by other processes. The sociolinguistic data indicates that the emergence of single negation was a change 'from above', and the form potentially acquired prestige through its association with particular social groups and genres. The rapid uptake by social aspirers in the mid-sixteenth century supports this hypothesis. If Elizabeth also considered single negation to be the prestigious construction, as suggested by the completion of the change in her pre-accession correspondence, then the frequency of single negation should be similar in all genres in the pre- and post-accession periods.

As shown in Table 25, the results for the pre-accession translations do not support this hypothesis. Multiple negation is more frequent than we might expect with single negation accounting for only 55.2% of constructions. Interestingly, the majority of constructions containing multiple negation in the pre-accession translations are noncoordinate constructions, whereas multiple negation only occurred in coordinate constructions in the correspondence. The presence of multiple negation in the context that did not lag in the adoption of single negation grants the results for the pre-accession translations additional import.

The figures could indicate that single negation was not as established in Elizabeth's early idiolect as initially thought. Yet, if the figure is representative of her overall preferences, the distribution suggests she changed her preferences to the incoming construction in the space of four or five years (1544–1549). It is difficult to correlate this with the biographical information. The social categories analysis suggests that Elizabeth's education greatly influenced her uptake of single negation, through her knowledge of Latin and exposure to the linguistic preferences of her educators. This education was well underway by the time the translations were composed; Sir John Cheke, William Grindal and Roger Ascham had all tutored Elizabeth by the end of 1545—the year the second translation was completed. Thus, we would expect their influence to emerge in these texts.

The figures may instead show stylistic variation. One explanation for the greater frequency of multiple negation is the influence of the translations' original language upon Elizabeth's chosen constructions. Both texts were translated from French, a language that uses two-part negators (e.g. *ne ... pas*). The texts show occasional lexical and syntactic traces of their French heritage. In the translation of Calvin, for example, there are 10 instances of the French conjunction *et*, and there is also continued debate about the level of involvement of Jean Bellemain, Elizabeth's French tutor, in the production of the two works (Mueller & Scodel 2009: 25). Another possibility is that, as with other linguistic features in these texts, Elizabeth

Table 25. Single negation (%) (QEIC correspondence, speeches and translations)

	Total	% single negation
PreA correspondence	12	91.7
PostA correspondence	55	92.7
Speeches	6	83.3
PreA translations	29	55.2
PostA translations	6	66.7

deliberately used multiple negation to create an archaic tone in the work, perhaps appropriate to the formal and pious subject matter.[21] This interpretation is not without problems, however, as it is difficult to fit this stylistic choice with the theory that Elizabeth's uptake of single negation was influenced by the variant's contemporary prestige.

A third explanation is that Elizabeth uses multiple negation as an emphatic device, appropriate for the didactic and pious topics addressed in the translations. Rissanen (1999: 272) notes that the combination *not none* was used emphatically in written texts, prior to its replacement by the non-assertive construction *not any*, and a possible emphatic multiple structure in Elizabeth's use of *nor never* has already been identified. Examples from the pre-accession translations show similarities, often co-occurring with other emphatic markers such as affirmative *do*:

(86) There was **never no** man that did see (1544, Navarre, QEIC translations).

(87) nevertheless **no** man did **never** tremble more miserably at every time (1545, Calvin, QEIC translations).

Translation was a highly valued activity during the sixteenth century, particularly for women, and the young Elizabeth was displaying her precocious academic abilities in creating the works for her stepmother Catherine Parr (see Trill (1996) for a discussion of Early Modern female translation). Thus, I am inclined to view the frequency of multiple negation as stylistic variation, rather than indicative of the general progression of the change in her idiolect in the 1540s.

The results for the post-accession translations suggest that stylistic variation is also relevant to Elizabeth's later writing. The token count for these texts is low, but nevertheless there is a difference in the distribution of single and multiple negation between the two translations. The four tokens of single negation occur in the prose translations of Cicero, such as example (88), and the two tokens of multiple negation are found in Boethius. The presence of the Middle English negator *ne*, which had largely fallen out of use by the end of the sixteenth century (Rissanen 1999: 270), in Boethius suggests that multiple negation may be stylistically motivated in this text; certainly, there are no other examples of the form in QEIC.

(88) as **no** age shall **ever** be so far (1592, Cicero, QEIC translations).

(89) Hope though **naught ne** fear (1593, Boethius, QEIC translations).

Pemberton (1899: xiv) notes that Elizabeth uses archaic lexis in her version of Boethius, including 'ancient' terms not found in Chaucer's fourteenth-

---

[21] For instance, multiple negation occurs more frequently in formal genres than less formal genres in the ME period (Iyeiri 1998: 138).

century translation. The presence of multiple negation, particularly with *ne*, fits the archaic style Pemberton observes. By contrast, the Cicero prose uses negators typical of Elizabeth's contemporary speeches and correspondence, perhaps indicative of different stylistic goals.

Stylistic variation is less evident in the parliamentary speeches. The frequency of single negation is 83.3%, similar to the post-accession correspondence, although based on a small number of tokens. The single token of multiple negation occurs in a coordinate construction, the context that promoted the variant in Elizabeth's letters. The construction is another example of *nor never*, the negator combination seen in her contemporary correspondence.

8.5 *Summary*

The replacement of multiple negation with single negation provides another context in which Elizabeth is a linguistic leader, with the change completed in her idiolect in the pre-accession period. The results from QEIC support the CEEC-based analysis (Nevalainen et al. 2011), which also found Elizabeth to be a progressive user in this change. The QEIC data also offers further insight into the factors that contribute to Elizabeth's uptake and enriches our understanding of the social and stylistic dimensions of single negation in sixteenth-century English.

The rapid uptake indicates that Elizabeth's accession had no discernable influence on her use of single or multiple negation. Instead, the analysis suggests that her education contributed to the promotion of the form in her idiolect. This can best explain the correlation with others of her rank and domicile, and the contrast with the female majority of CEEC who lagged behind in the change; women who largely did not share the same educational opportunities as Elizabeth. Education may also explain the stylistic variation in the pre-accession religious translations, and in the later translation of Boethius.

When compared to the other linguistic features discussed so far, it is becoming clear that the same factors do not necessarily contribute to Elizabeth's leading position in a change. The social factors promoting single negation such as Elizabeth's education contrast with the hypothesised role of her female caregivers in the uptake of subject-position *you* and first- and second-person possessive determiners. The idiolectal analysis gives a more detailed picture of the relationship between Elizabeth's contradictory social position and her experiences and her language use, as outlined at the start of this study (see also Nevalainen et al. 2011: 28–29). Furthermore, the consistent and often striking evidence for stylistic variation in the linguistic features analysed so far suggests that this may be an integral factor in explaining Elizabeth's progressiveness.

As a final point, Elizabeth's early uptake of single negation may prove useful for authorship attribution studies for works dated to the pre-accession period. In later documents, the nature of the change as one 'from above' may entail that, for manuscripts associated with the Court (such as official correspondence), it is more difficult to use this feature to discriminate between Elizabeth's language and that of her Courtiers and secretaries.

9. ANIMACY AND RELATIVE MARKER: *WHO/WHICH*

The personalisation of the English WH- RELATIVE SYSTEM is another change that occurred over the course of Elizabeth's lifetime, and offers a further opportunity to investigate her participation in morphosyntactic language change. Over the course of the Early Modern period, the choice of *wh-* relative markers (*who, which* and *whom*) was increasingly influenced by the animate status of the antecedent. In subject position, the relative marker *who* began to replace *which* with animate antecedents. Relative *who* is first attested in 1426 in the Paston Letters, located in the closing formulae with reference to God, before expanding to occur in non-formulaic contexts with animate antecedents of both divine and non-divine status in the sixteenth century (Rissanen 1999: 294–295). The "dehumanisation" of *which* took longer, and *who* and *which* co-occurred with animate antecedents well into the seventeenth century in Standard English (Dekeyser 1984: 71–72; Rissanen 1999: 294; Adamson 2007). The object form *whom* has a different developmental history to *who*, occurring in English from the ME period, and is much better established as a marker of animacy in the sixteenth century (Rissanen 1999: 293). This change has not, to my knowledge, been previously studied in Elizabeth's idiolect, and the results should provide a useful complement to the previous analyses, offering an indication of the extent to which Elizabeth's linguistic behaviour can be classed as progressive, as well as further insight into the factors that helped to shape her idiolectal preferences.

9.1 *Results*

The analysis of animacy focuses primarily on subject-position relative markers *(the) which* and *who* as these forms show the greatest variation at the macro-level and, as shall be seen, at the micro-level also. The results indicate that the association of *who* with animate referents, which includes divine and spiritual beings as well as humans singular and plural, is well

Table 26. Animate *who (%)* out of *who/which* (QEIC correspondence)

	Total (*who/which*)	% *who*
Pre-accession correspondence	4	100%
Post-accession correspondence	51	92.2%

established in Elizabeth's idiolect throughout her life. Taken as a proportion of both markers with animate antecedents, *who* accounts for 100% of tokens in the pre-accession period (admittedly with a low token count) and 92.2% in the post-accession period.

In CEEC, subject-position *who* accounts for 59% of animate antecedents taking *who* or *which* in the first half of the sixteenth century (N&R-B 2002: 112). This figure rises to 76% percent in the 1560–1599 period (N&R-B 2002: 118). Comparing these results with those from the QEIC correspondence, Elizabeth is at the head of the change in both periods, with the difference in latter period statistically significant (p > 0.01).

Before drawing conclusions about Elizabeth's progressiveness in the change, it is important to examine the personalisation of *wh-* relatives from another perspective. Although it is convenient to treat *who* and *which* as a bipartite variable, and my analysis frequently follows the macro-level studies in adopting this approach, the dehumanisation of *which* and the emergence of *who* are in fact distinct, albeit connected, changes in the EModE relative system. This can be clearly shown if the percentage of animate antecedents is calculated separately for each marker from the total occurrences with animate and non-animate antecedents (Table 27).[22]

In QEIC correspondence the dehumanisation process of *which* has almost completed, with less than 10% of *which* tokens taking animates. These figures reaffirm Elizabeth's leading position in the personalisation of the relative system. Macro-level studies show that *which* took animate antecedents about 30% of the time in the sixteenth century as a whole

Table 27. Animate *who* and *which* (%) out of all tokens (animate and non-animate antecedents) (QEIC correspondence)

	Total *who*	% *who* (animate)	Total *which*	% *which* (animate)
Pre-accession correspondence	4	100%	10	0%
Post-accession correspondence	49	95.9%	51	7.8%

[22] The difference between the animate/non-animate status of the antecedent with each marker is highly significant (p > 0.001) in the post-accession period. The token count is too low to assess the pre-accession period statistically.

(Rissanen 1999: 294). Indeed, Dekeyser's (1984: 71) corpus-based analysis of the seventeenth century finds that the average frequency for *which* is still around 10%. The role of *who* as a marker of person is also clearly established in Elizabeth's idiolect, with over 90% of tokens occurring with animate antecedents. On this basis, the evidence for Elizabeth's progressiveness in animacy and *wh*-relatives is persuasive.

9.2 *Systemic Factors*

Before considering the social factors for this linguistic feature, it is necessary to test the interpretation of Elizabeth's leadership in this change. Currently, the breadth of the animate category may create a misleading picture of her usage. As noted above, the relative marker *who* originated in the closing formulae of correspondence to mark reference to the deity, a function that was well established in English before Elizabeth's birth. The generalisation of *who* to non-divine antecedents took longer, and macro-level studies trace the process throughout the sixteenth and into the seventeenth century. Because the data in Table 27 is drawn from the QEIC correspondence, the high frequency of animate *who* may be a consequence of closing formulae rather than a more general distribution.

To assess this possibility, the animate antecedents of each relative marker are split into different types: God, spirit, king, human (singular) and human (plural), and the percentage of *who* calculated for each (Table 28). The data collates both pre- and post-accession correspondence.

Overall, Elizabeth uses *who* exclusively to refer to the deity, spiritual beings and monarchs. In the singular human category, *who* is also the dominant variant, although it is not exclusive (96%). In the final category *who* is the least dominant, accounting for 57% of tokens with plural human antecedents. The four tokens in the pre-accession correspondence are too few to be used for diachronic quantitative comparison, although they can offer qualitative insight into Elizabeth's early usage. Three occur with God as an antecedent, and the fourth has a human (singular) antecedent, examples (90)–(93), which suggests that *who* was established as a

Table 28. Animate *who* (%) out of *who*/*which* by antecedent category (QEIC correspondence)

	Total (*who*/*which*)	% *who*
God	18	100
Spirit	1	100
King	4	100
Human (sing.)	25	96
Human (pl.)	7	57

non-formulaic marker in her adolescent idiolect. There is no clear evidence that *who* expanded into different categories over time.

(90) in God's hand **who** keep you from all evil (June 1548, to Thomas Seymour, QEIC correspondence).

(91) God (**who** shall judge my truth) (17th March 1554, to Mary I, QEIC correspondence).

(92) As knoweth God **who** judgeth all (29th October 1555, to William Paulet, QEIC correspondence).

(93) desiring you to give him thanks for me, **who** can ascertain you of mine estate of health (1549, to Edward Seymour, QEIC correspondence).

Macro-level studies indicate that the syntactic category of an antecedent is also relevant to the progression of the change. The spread of *who* began with divine and non-divine explicit referents of person such as proper names before diffusing to less explicit forms, encompassing collective nouns and pronominal forms such as demonstratives (e.g. *those*) on a similar scale to the semantic development from deity > human (Hope 1994: 39; N&R-B 2002: 118). To calculate the significance of this systemic factor in Elizabeth's idiolect, the animate antecedents of *which* and *who* are categorised into three syntactic groups: proper name/title, common noun and pronoun. When the percentage of *who* is calculated for the combined tokens (*who/which*) in each group, it appears that Elizabeth's selection is sensitive to the syntactic explicitness of the antecedent (see Appendix, Table 71). In the most explicit category, proper name/title, Elizabeth only uses *who*. This includes 18 references to God (God, Lord, the Almighty), as well as spiritual (Fame) and human antecedents (Lord Chamberlain, Monsieur). *Who* is also the preferred marker with common nouns (93%), with only one antecedent of this type occurring with *which* in Elizabeth's correspondence:

(94) to request this just desire, that you never doubt my entire good will in your behalf and do protest that if you knew even since the arrival of your Commissioners (**which** if they list they may tell you) the extreme danger my life was in (January 1587, to James VI, QEIC correspondence).

In the least explicit category (pronouns) there is greater variation. *Who* accounts for 82% of the tokens, with *which* occurring three times: twice with a demonstrative and once with a reflexive pronoun.

The four tokens for the pre-accession correspondence again prohibit an accurate assessment of diachronic development. Three tokens occur with proper names, and one with a common noun, and these are subsumed into the overall figures. The level of generalisation for *who* in the post-accession period, however, suggests that the change was probably at an advanced stage in Elizabeth's adolescent idiolect. There is no evidence to indicate that this was a rapid development, and nothing to indicate that her accession had a direct influence on the variable.

The macro-level data supports this interpretation. CEEC shows only 60% *who* in the least explicit category (pronouns) for 1560–1599, compared with 82% for the whole QEIC correspondence (figures adapted from N&R-B 2002: 118). N&R-B (2002: 119) also found that *who* accounted for a greater proportion of markers in non-restrictive clauses than restrictive clauses. However, the restrictiveness of the clause appears to have only a minor influence upon Elizabeth's selection of marker, although the low token counts require caution. 90% non-restrictive clauses occur with *who* and 86% restrictive clauses occur with *who*. Animate *which* occurs twice in each context.

The systemic factors thus confirm the initial interpretation of Elizabeth's progressiveness in the generalisation of *who*, making her a leader in this linguistic change. The dehumanisation of *which* is similarly well established, and the marker is limited to the least explicit animate categories.

9.3 *Social Factors*

It is widely held that *who* first developed in formulaic contexts as a result of Latin letter-writing manuals influencing English epistolary practice. The subsequent diffusion of *who* into other contexts was therefore a change 'from above', as the form permeated down via the educated elite who were familiar with Latin and Classical standards (Rissanen 1999: 294; D'Arcy & Tagliamonte 2010: 385). Some of the earliest users of non-formulaic *who* in the early sixteenth century include Lord Berners and Thomas Elyot, both of whom were upper-class, highly educated individuals (Hope 1994: 39).

The CEEC data (N&R-B 2002: 112) suggests that *who* rapidly acquired prestigious connotations following its initial emergence in English. In the early sixteenth century, informants from the middle ranks and social climbers use *who* with animate antecedents over 70% of the time. By comparison, the upper-ranks use *who* only 49% of the time. The figures provide a different perspective on Elizabeth's early adoption of *who*, and suggest that her leading uptake may be driven by her awareness of the prestigious associations of the marker. If this assessment is accurate, then it represents a comparable context to the uptake of single negation, which was also a change from above.

The domicile data indicates that Elizabeth is a leader in the change throughout her life. N&R-B (2002: 118) provide figures for the CEEC domiciles for 1560–1599 (Table 29). Elizabeth's near-exclusive use of *who* in the post-accession period is ahead of the usage of others at the Court. Here, *who* has reached the upper-end of the 'near-completion' stage at 81%, significantly lower than Elizabeth's completed usage ($p > 0.001$). The

Table 29. Animate *who* (%) by domicile
(CEEC 1560–1599) adapted from N&R-B
(2002: 112)

	Total *who/which*	% *who*
Court	204	81
London	42	83
North	4	100
East Anglia	237	69

difference between Elizabeth and her domicile is surprising if we consider that many courtiers were also educated to a high level, familiar with Classical languages, and thus potentially receptive to any prestigious connotations.

Although I am not aware of any macro-level investigations that consider the role of gender as a social factor, the provenance of the change suggests that men would lead the generalisation of *who* based on the trends for other changes from above during this period (e.g. the decline of multiple negation; see Nevalainen 2006c). PCEEC letters by sixteenth-century female informants provide some information for this social factor. The writers largely represent the upper echelons of Tudor society (N&R-B 2003: 45), including royalty (for example, Margaret Tudor, Queen of Scotland) and the nobility (such as Arabella Stuart and Jane Grey), and many received a high level of education. The data is not substantial enough to provide a quantitative overview of the change (which may explain the lack of a macro-level gender analysis), but from a qualitative perspective the replacement of *which* with *who* for animate antecedents appears more likely in letters written by highly educated women towards the end of the sixteenth century. For example, Margaret Tudor, writing in 1504, uses *which*:

(95) Thomas, **whych** was footman to the Quene my moder (Margaret Stuart [n. Tudor], 1504; Origin1, 42).

Who is the dominant form in the mid-century letters written by Elizabeth's sister, Mary I, and her contemporary and childhood acquaintance Jane Grey—women of a comparable educational background and, in the case of Jane Grey (b. 1537), close in age. In the latter half of the century, *who* appears to be the preferred form for animate antecedents amongst the upper-ranking women, including Elizabeth D'Oyly and Arabella Stuart.[23]

---

[23] CEEC does not document the level of Elizabeth D'Oyly's education, but as the daughter of Sir Nicholas Bacon, who professed an interest in educational matters and ensured his sons received a high level of education (ODNB), we can speculate that she received a higher-than-average education for her gender.

(96) Mr Smythe, **who** telleth me (Elizabeth D'Oyly/Neville, 1583; Bacon, II, 236).

Whilst necessarily impressionistic, the PCEEC data appears to support the interpretation that the education of an informant was an important factor of the generalisation of *who* and dehumanisation of *which* in the sixteenth century. A more nuanced view of gender is not possible from the present data.

9.4 *Interactive Factors*

The origin of *who* in epistolary formulae, and its subsequent diffusion across the upper ranks, means that the form is part of conventional epistolary practice in the Early Modern period. The analysis of interactive factors for *who* and *which* thus considers how Elizabeth's usage compares with these norms, and how they may explain her leading position in the change. The first important feature of the QEIC correspondence data is the presence of formulaic *who*. Formulaic *who* formed part of the *conclusio*: 'the formal ending, often involving a blessing and the place and date of the letter' (Richardson 2007: 56). The earliest example of *who* in QEIC occurs in a letter dating from 1548, addressed to Thomas Seymour.[24] The dating reveals that Elizabeth was familiar with the epistolary formulae from an early age. Perhaps the tuition of Kat Ashley or Dr Richard Cox, also tutor to the young King Edward VI, introduced her to the epistolary convention, as part of her early Latin schooling. Certainly, from this date onwards, formulaic *who* is an established component of Elizabeth's letters: 17 of the 18 references to God with *who* in the correspondence occur in the closing formulae of a letter.

(97) In God's hand **who** keep you from all evil (June 1548, to Thomas Seymour, QEIC correspondence).
(98) As knoweth God **who** ever bless you and guide you (September 1589, to James VI, QEIC correspondence).

The evidence of Latin-influenced formulaic *who* supports the hypothesis that Elizabeth's education is significant for this change. However, this does not necessarily entail that she would also use *who* for non-formulaic, non-deity contexts, or that she would be a leader in the change. To explain *who* in those contexts, the socio-historical background offers a persuasive

---

[24] Marcus (2008: 214) reports that the manuscript of this letter is unusual, because Elizabeth has decorated the border of her text using red ink. The letter is addressed to Thomas Seymour, on whom Elizabeth is assumed to have had an adolescent crush 'at the very least'. The presence of the closing formula, therefore, could be interpreted as another 'adornment', differentiating the letter from those previously written by Elizabeth (i.e. those to Catherine Parr).

scenario. Rissanen suggests that the spread of *who* in the sixteenth century was driven by social pressures arising from

> the polite and formal expression of Tudor and Stuart society, which probably emphasise[d] the observation of the 'personality' of the reference (Rissanen 1999: 294).

Elizabeth's social status and experiences, as both princess and queen, position her within those circles that would be interested in 'polite and formal expression'. As Borman (2009: 77; see also Perry 1990: 29) observes, Elizabeth's early education under Kat Ashley covered titles of address, which may have highlighted *who* as a marker representative of deferential, formal and polite language appropriate to her station. The sibling address terms used in the post-accession letters between Elizabeth and James VI of Scotland are perhaps a legacy of this early instruction. Elizabeth's sister, Mary I, who had a comparable social status, also uses non-formulaic *who* in letters from the mid-sixteenth century:

> (99) I am nothyng able to perswade her to forget the losse of hyme [Henry VIII], **who** is as yet very rype in myn owne remembrance (1547, Mary Tudor I; Origin2, 151).

The social pressures at the interactive level would not have changed at the point of Elizabeth's accession, offering an explanation for why the results show little evidence of a change anchored around this event.

9.5 *Stylistic Factors*

The final stage of my analysis considers the influence of stylistic factors. The prestigious and learned origins of *who* in English are reflected in its macro-level distribution in different genres. Catherine Ball's (1996: 246–247) diachronic corpus study found that *who* generalised rapidly in written mode genres, whereas spoken genres used *which* for both animate and non-animate antecedents through the sixteenth and seventeenth centuries. Raumolin-Brunberg's analysis of the language of Sir Thomas More corroborates the stylistic patterning; the two instances of *who* in her corpus occur in 'one of the most complex and formal registers, official letters' (Raumolin-Brunberg 1991: 232). Of the three genres representing Elizabeth's idiolect in QEIC, her correspondence has the closest affinity to spoken, informal language. The advanced stage of the change in her letters therefore suggests that there should be minimal stylistic variation in the more formal and literary speeches and translations. Ball's macro-level data leads me to expect that *who* and *which* in these genres will show a comparable distribution with the correspondence.

Table 30. *who* (%) with animate antecedents out of *who/which* (QEIC)

	Total (*who/which*)	% *who*
Pre-accession correspondence	4	100
Post-accession correspondence	49	91.8
Speeches	6	50
Pre-accession translations	83	16
Post-accession translations	16	94

Table 31. Animate *who* (%) out of *who/which* by antecedent category (QEIC pre-accession translations)

	Total (*who/which*)	% *who*
God	18	44%
Spirit	1	0%
King	–	–
Human (sing.)	32	9%
Human (pl.)	31	6%
Other	1	0%

The findings for Elizabeth's translations and speeches do not support this hypothesis (Table 30). The most striking result is for the pre-accession translations, which contain only 16% *who* with animate antecedents. Calculating the results according to antecedent category reveals that the distribution of *who* and *which* replicates the macro-level pattern of diffusion discussed above, with *who* occurring most frequently with God (44%) and least frequently with human antecedents.

The occurrences of *which* with deity antecedents are especially interesting given the purported Latinate provenance of *who* via epistolary formula, which granted the marker a prestigious status from the beginning of the Early Modern period. The presence of *which* in the pre-accession translations is unexpected, particularly given the pious topic of both works.[25]

(100) Bountiful God, brother, and true Moses, **which** doth all things with goodness, and justice (1544, Navarre, QEIC translations).

---

[25] Elizabeth's preferences in her translations contrast with the attitudes of later centuries. Beal (2004: 76) notes that animacy and marker became a prescriptive concern in the eighteenth century. The grammarian Lowth, for example, 'explicitly condemns the use of *Our Father, which* [...] in the King James Bible (1611)'. Presumably, he would have found Elizabeth's translations similarly offensive.

(101) God, **who** doth inspire the hearts of the faithful (1545, Calvin, QEIC translations).

The syntactic category of the antecedent appears to have more influence on Elizabeth's marker selection than the antecedent category. For deity antecedents the frequency of *who* decreases as the syntactic explicitness of the deity antecedent also declines. In the proper name category (e.g. God, Lord), *who* accounts for over half the tokens at 66.7%, whereas there are no examples with nominal or pronominal antecedents. *Which* occurs in the more complex cases in the proper name category, either referring to multiple antecedents and/or containing intervening material between the antecedent and relative marker, as can be seen in example (100). Rissanen (1999: 295) has suggested that ambiguity between antecedent and the relative clause was a common trigger for *which* in EModE, and this would certainly explain the distribution seen here. The same pattern is evident across the syntactic categories for all types of animate antecedents.

This trend problematises the interpretation of *which* as stylistically motivated, as we would expect the relative marker to occur more evenly across the different antecedent and syntactic categories, rather than diffusing in a pattern that corresponds to the progression of the change at the macro-level. The distribution of *who* and *which* in the pre-accession translations in fact makes a more persuasive case for systemic variation. The pre-accession translations are the only source of data for animate *who/which* in the mid-1540s as, unfortunately, the first token in the QEIC correspondence occurs in a letter written in 1548 ((97)). The three-year gap between these works and the first letter spans Elizabeth's adolescent years (ages 12–14), suggesting that the interpretation of Elizabeth's progressiveness in the personalisation of the relative system, based on her pre-accession correspondence, may have been premature. Although the presence of *who* in the translations confirms that this marker was active in Elizabeth's idiolect throughout her youth, it is possible that the dehumanisation of *which*, as a related but distinct change, developed more slowly over the course of the pre-accession period. The biographical evidence provides a possible motive: Elizabeth received tuition from Classicists Sir John Cheke and Roger Ascham in the 1540s, who replaced her earlier (female) tutors.

If this is the case, then the evidence still supports the hypothesis relating to the social and interactive factors. *Who* becomes the more frequent form over the course of the pre-accession period, whilst the dehumanisation of *which* sees the marker restricted to the least explicit antecedent categories. Both developments parallel Elizabeth's advancing age and education, and her increasing participation with the social events at the Court. These experiences would foreground the social and interactive associations of *which* and *who* noted above, and potentially accelerate the change to the completed stage in her later adolescent idiolect.

The pre-accession data does not change Elizabeth's leading position in the post-accession period. The post-accession translations show a near-exclusive use of *who* with animate antecedents; the only exception is a single token of animate *which* in the Boethius translation ((102)). Interestingly, animate *which* occurs alongside a multiple negation construction and the combination of archaic features suggests Elizabeth may have deliberately selected *which* for stylistic purposes. This may explain why she uses the interrogative pronoun *who* in the same quote, but not relative *who*:

(102) '**Who** suffered' quoth she 'these stage's harlots approach this sick man? **Which** not only would not ease his sorrow with no remedies but with swift venom nourish them?' (1593, Boethius, QEIC translations).

Overall, the results for the post-accession translations conform to the existing trend in Elizabeth's correspondence, and support the hypothesis based on Ball's (1996) macro-level data.

The parliamentary speeches, on the other hand, offer a contradictory picture of Elizabeth's position in the change. *Who* accounts for only 50% of animate antecedents, a frequency much lower than the post-accession correspondence or translations. The macro-level data offers a possible precedent: Ball (1996: 246) found the dehumanisation of *which* to be much slower in trial records and other genres representing formal spoken language, a feasible comparison with Elizabeth's parliamentary speeches.

However, the distribution of animate *which* warrants attention. Significantly, the three tokens all occur in the 1576 speech and the syntactic categories show that *who* is used only to refer to the deity, with all human antecedents marked by *which*:

(103) the Almighty **who** will preserve you safe (1576, QEIC speeches).
(104) Can a prince, **which** of necessity must discontent a number to delight (1576, QEIC speeches).
(105) one **which** yieldeth you more thanks (1576, QEIC speeches).

In the other speeches, as with the other post-accession genres, Elizabeth uses *who* with human antecedents in both more and less explicit syntactic categories. It seems unlikely that she would deviate from her general preferences for one speech. Instead, the frequency of animate *which* may reflect third-party interference in the text. The transcription of the speech is based on an apograph that itself was based upon a contemporary copy. The concentration of animate *which* in this speech may replicate the scribe's preferences, whose own use of *who* and *which* was not at quite so advanced a stage as Elizabeth's practice (e.g. *who* with deity but not human antecedents).

This is the first evidence that suggests the 1576 speech may not be an accurate representation of Elizabeth's idiolect, although I was concerned that this might be the case when selecting the text for the corpus (see Appendix). On the premise that this interpretation is accurate, it would be interesting to know at what point the 1576 text deviated from Elizabeth's original. Did the Queen see the copy before it was sent to her godson, complete with changes, or did she approve the text without seeing the transcribed version? This particular case emphasises the need for an investigation into the relationship between Elizabeth and her scribes in manuscript production.

Overall, stylistic variation has only a small influence on Elizabeth's usage of *who* and *which*. Comparison of the genres has instead revealed the possible diachronic development of the change in the pre-accession period, and the scribal interference in the post-accession 1576 speech. These are perhaps not the expected findings, but nevertheless highlight the value of cross-genre comparison in a sociolinguistic idiolectal study.

9.6 Objective Case: whom/which

The situation for the objective case, *whom* and *which*, is very different. The figures for *whom* in QEIC indicate that it was the dominant form for animate antecedents in Elizabeth's idiolect (Table 32).

Only in the pre-accession translations is there evidence of variation, a pattern that correlates with the lower level of *who* also seen in these texts. *Which* occurs with deity and human antecedents in proper name, noun and pronominal categories. The greater frequency of *whom* (87%, compared to only 16% *who*), however, offers support for my hypothesis that the personalisation of the relative system stabilised in Elizabeth's idiolect during her adolescence. If she were selecting animate *which* for stylistic purposes, then we might expect this to occur as extensively in object position as in subject position.

(106) he is the God **whom** they must honour (1545, Calvin, QEIC translations).

Table 32. *whom* out of *whom/which* (%) in object/ prepositional position (QEIC)

	Total (*whom/which*)	% *whom*
Pre-accession correspondence	4	100
Post-accession correspondence	43	100
Speeches	3	100
Pre-accession translations	31	87
Post-accession translations	9	100

(107) he is God alone, **the which** we all must worship (1545, Calvin, QEIC translations).

Overall, animate *whom* is well established in Elizabeth's idiolect. It is possible that the trends for *whom* and the infrequency of animate *which* in object position contributed to her uptake of *who* through analogy.

9.7 *Summary*

The analysis of *who* and *which* with animate antecedents shows that Elizabeth was a leader of the change during the sixteenth century. The social correlates indicate that her age, rank and level of education are important factors in explaining the advanced stage of the change. There is no evidence that Elizabeth modified her usage in response to her accession. Developments in her education and social interaction during the pre-accession period, however, may have hastened the personalisation process in her adolescence. The results indicate that a series of biographical elements and events, rather than the most obvious social change (her accession), shape and influence the development of this variable.

Who and *which* is another change characterised by its progression 'from above' and Elizabeth's leadership testifies to her responsiveness to language change from across the social spectrum, in contrast to the behaviour of many of her contemporaries (see Nevalainen et al. 2011: 32). As the evidence from the 1576 speech suggests, the dehumanisation of *which* and animate *who* may offer productive evidence for authorship analysis.

10. WHICH AND THE WHICH

The analyses presented so far offer a consistent picture of Elizabeth's progressiveness in sixteenth-century morphosyntactic change. The replacement of relative marker *the which* with *which* reveals a somewhat different picture, and illustrates the complex relationship between linguistic variation, language change and social experience at the site of the individual speaker.

The life span of *the which* in English was relatively brief. First attested in northern dialects in Late Middle English, *the which* diffused into southern varieties and temporarily became a competing variant with relative marker *which* at the beginning of the Early Modern period (Rissanen 1999: 296–297). By Elizabeth's lifetime, however, the northern variant was already on the wane with its replacement, *which*, reaching the near-completion stage of the change in the mid-sixteenth-century (N&R-B 2003: 74). By the 1600s, *which* had become the dominant variant.

10.1 *Results*

The results for the QEIC correspondence are shown in Table 33, with no discrimination between different types of relative clause, i.e. adnominal or sentential types. The results show that the generalisation of *which* was at the upper-edge of the near-completion stage in Elizabeth's youth, accounting for 83.1% of tokens. In the post-accession period, the change has reached completion with *which* the dominant variant at 98.2% ($p > 0.001$).

The overall percentage of *which* in the QEIC correspondence (94.2%) is very similar to the macro-level norm for the sixteenth century, with CEEC informants using *which* 96.6 % for the period 1520–1619 (N&R-B 2003: 222). However, it appears that the development of the change in Elizabeth's idiolect progressed at a different rate than at the macro-level, despite the similarity for the overall percentages. The pre-accession frequency is lower than the macro-level average of 90.8% (for the sub-period 1540–1579) (see Table 34).

The difference marks the division (< 85%) between near-completion and completion stages, although it is not statistically significant. However, within the context of Elizabeth's idiolect, any suggestion of lag is striking and contrary to the norm. This finding is not wholly unexpected. Nevalainen et al. (2011) found Elizabeth to be a mid-range user for this variable, the only such case out of the six variables studied in their investigation. However, the scope of QEIC suggests that there is a more

Table 33. *which* (%) out of *which/the which* tokens (QEIC correspondence)

	Total (*which/the which*).	% *which*
PreA	59	83.1
PostA	166	98.2
Overall	225	94.2

Table 34. *Which* (%) out of *which/the which* in CEEC, adapted from N&R-B (2003: 222, Table 12)

	Total *which/the which*	% *which*
1500–1539	1423	89.6
1540–1579	2552	90.8
1580–1619	3975	97.6

striking diachronic dimension to Elizabeth's preferences than the CEEC findings are able to reveal. Closer analysis indicates that all *the which* tokens for the pre-accession correspondence occur in letters dating from the 1540s, after which the variant does not occur again until a letter to James VI written in 1588. The difference between the two decades of the pre-accession period, the 1540s and 1550s, is statistically significant (p > 0.5) and the diachronic distribution suggests that Elizabeth modified her preferences in the early 1550s. The change cannot, therefore, be explained by the social changes connected to her accession, although other biographical experiences may be relevant.[26]

10.2 *Social Factors*

Macro-level trends indicate that gender and domicile are the most significant social factors for this linguistic change. In CEEC, male informants lead the change. Between 1500–1539, men use *which* around 90% of the time, with women's usage hovering around 75% (N&R-B 2003: 128). By the period of Elizabeth's adolescence and early reign (1540–1579) the difference narrows and both groups use the variant about 90% of the time. When Elizabeth's pre-accession usage is compared with the CEEC sub-period, the frequency of 83.1% suggests that she in fact lagged behind both genders.

However, it may be significant that Elizabeth's earliest years fall within the final decade of the 1500–1539 sub-period, when the difference between genders is more pronounced. Scholars (McIntosh 2008: para.29; Borman 2009, esp. 44–126) have commented on the influence of Elizabeth's caregivers during her childhood, and the presence of *the which* in Elizabeth's 1540s correspondence may show the linguistic effect of this influence, with the female caregivers exposing Elizabeth to the form from earliest childhood.

To test this hypothesis, the frequency of *the which* and *which* in the letters of female informants involved in Elizabeth's early upbringing can provide some indication of her childhood linguistic environment, although PCEEC offers only a few relevant examples. The letter by Catherine Parr contains only *which*. In the two letters representing Mary I, the dominant form is *which*, but there is one example of *the which*. The overall scarcity of the outgoing variant at this time means that the macro-level corpus cannot offer much evidence to support the correlation with female informants specifically connected to Elizabeth's early life. However, Nevalainen (1996a: 81) suggests that unfamiliarity with the literary trends of the period

---

[26] Elizabeth's usage is not as striking as that of Sabine Johnson, where *the which* accounts for over 90% of occurrences in Sabine's letters in CEEC (1520–1550). Nevalainen (1996a: 82) suggests that Sabine's 'relative lack of exposure to the changing literary usage of the time' could explain her unusual preference.

could affect the rate of an individual's replacement of *the which* by *which*. The women of Elizabeth's household, whilst educated, would potentially be less familiar with current literary trends than their male contemporaries.

Gender thus provides the strongest, if chiefly theoretical, correlate for this period. The macro-level figures for domicile, whilst significant in the fifteenth century, show that the Court, London and North use *which* around 90% of the time in the 1520–1559 sub-period (N&R-B 2003: 176). The similarity across the social spectrum is also shown by social rank; in 1520–1550 the nobility use *which* 94%, social climbers 89% and non-gentry 87% (Nevalainen 1996b: 68).[27]

In the post-accession period, Elizabeth's usage is comparable to the macro-level trends across the social categories. The point of interest for this variable therefore lies in her earliest usage, and the following analysis will focus on the pre-accession period. Currently, the social factors offer one reason for the lag in the generalisation of *which*. They cannot explain the rather abrupt and rapid completion of the change in the 1550s.

10.3 *Systemic Factors*

In ME *the which* occurs 'particularly in contexts in which an unambiguous link between the relative clause and the antecedent is needed' (Rissanen 1999: 297), such as relatives with sentential antecedents. Rissanen (1999: 297) states that ambiguous contexts remain the favoured location for *the which* until the end of the sixteenth century. In order to establish if this specialist usage relates to, and may explain, the frequency of *the which* in Elizabeth's idiolect, I have examined five contexts that may require an unambiguous link:

- Non-restrictive clauses, which do not limit the reference of the antecedent and thus have a greater scope for ambiguity.[28]
- Continuative clauses, which are clauses in coordination rather than with a subordinate structure. They are a particular type of a non-restrictive clause, with a weak tie between the relative marker and the antecedent; e.g.: 'we can send you more **which** with all speed we mean to do' (December 1601, to James VI, QEIC correspondence).
- Clauses with sentential antecedents, which are less explicit than nominal antecedents.

---

[27] These figures use the 1994 version of CEEC. Unfortunately, N&R-B (2003) do not provide specific figures in their discussion, which uses CEEC 1998.

[28] Over the years, scholars have debated the validity of the restrictive/non-restrictive distinction, particularly in EModE (e.g. Romaine 1982; Dekeyser 1984; Hope 1994). However, the apparent significance of non-restrictive clauses in macro-level accounts made the categorisation a necessary one for the present analysis. I omit five tokens from the analysis of this context in the post-accession correspondence where the semantic distinction was ambiguous. One ambiguous token is excluded from the pre-accession translations.

- Clauses with the marker used as a determiner, which always occurs in non-restrictive clauses, and are thought to be the product of foreign linguistic influence and 'the demand for structural clarity' (Rissanen 1999: 296); e.g.: 'And therefore have I (as for assay, or beginning, following the right notable saying of the proverb aforesaid) translated this little book out of French rhyme [...] **The which** book is entitled, or named the mirror or glass, of the sinful soul' (31st December 1544, to Catherine Parr, QEIC correspondence).
- Prepositional clauses, which have a greater level of complexity than other relative marker syntactic positions.

Calculating the percentage of *which* and *the which* in each context, from all the tokens for each marker in QEIC correspondence, provides a more accurate picture of the function of each relative marker in Elizabeth's idiolect than calculating only the percentage of *the which* in each context (see Appendix, Table 72). For example, *the which* accounts for 25% of non-restrictive tokens for both markers in the pre-accession period, which simply illustrates the low frequency of *the which*. Working out the figures for each marker individually shows that all instances of *the which* in the pre-accession corpus occur in non-restrictive contexts, whereas only 63.3% *which* tokens occur in non-restrictive clauses in the data. This suggests that *the which* had a narrower systemic function than *which* in Elizabeth's idiolect. The results for the five contexts for *the which* and *which* are shown in Figure 8.

In the QEIC pre-accession correspondence there is a clear connection between *the which* and four of the five contexts. The outgoing relative marker occurs only in non-restrictive clauses, and half of the tokens are located in continuative clauses. Over one third of the tokens use the marker as a determiner.[29] The prepositional context is also a significant factor in promoting Elizabeth's use of *the which*, with 60% of *the which* markers found in this context (p > 0.001). This fits the macro-level data. In the HC prepositional relative clauses account for the majority of *the which* in the sixteenth century (Raumolin-Brunberg 2000).

By contrast, the scope and function of *which* in the pre-accession period is broader, and a lower proportion of tokens occur in the five contexts. The low percentage (6.1%) for *which* in prepositional clauses, in particular, suggests that Elizabeth preferred to use *the which* for this context in the pre-accession period. Overall, it appears that *the which* had a specialist role in her idiolect, relating to semantically complex clauses; a distribution that can be described as grammatical specialisation, a postulated symptom of a variant's outgoing status in a language (Raumolin-Brunberg 2000).

---

[29] The figures for restrictiveness of the clause and continuative clauses are statistically significant (p > 0.5); the figures for determiner type and sentential clauses are not.

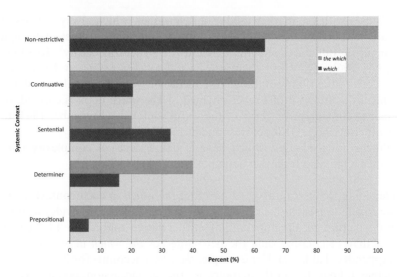

Figure 8: *which* and *the which* in five systemic contexts (%), pre-accession QEIC correspondence

10.4 *Stylistic Factors*

The stylistic distribution of *which* and *the which* during the Late Middle and Early Modern periods has been characterised as 'disordered heterogeneity' (Raumolin-Brunberg 2000: 221). Perhaps as a result, few studies have attended to the relationship between genre and variant; Romaine (1982), for example, does not distinguish between *which* and *the which* in her analysis. Raumolin-Brunberg's (2000) study, which explores the variable in the fifteenth-century samples in the HC, finds little consistency. *The which* is the more frequent form in some formal genres (fifteenth-century depositions), whereas *which* is the dominant marker in others (statutes and non-private letters) (Raumolin-Brunberg 2000: 216). In the sixteenth century (1500–1570), the distribution remains haphazard. In the breakdown by individual samples for the sub-period, texts with a frequency > 20% include private letters, travelogues, diaries, handbooks and treatises. Yet other samples of the latter three genres occur with < 10% *the which* (Raumolin-Brunberg 2000: 217). It is thus difficult to summarise the stylistic significance of *the which* at the macro-level during Elizabeth's lifetime, with 'individual and textual variation' occurring with no discernible connection to broader conventions of genre or style (Raumolin-Brunberg 2000: 221). On this basis, a feasible hypothesis is that *the which* had different stylistic properties in different idiolects, a suggestion that may explain the concentrated use of *the which* in Elizabeth's 1540s correspon-

Table 35. *which* (%) out of *which/the which*
(QEIC translations and speeches)

	Total *which/* *the which*	*% which*
PreA translations	268	73.5
PostA translations	35	100
Speeches	30	100

dence. If so, we would expect to find supportive evidence in the other, more literary examples of her writing.

Table 35 shows the percentage of *the which* in Elizabeth's translations and speeches. The first observation is that the diachronic distribution seen in her correspondence represents an idiolect-wide change in preference. There are no instances of *the which* in her parliamentary speeches (1563–1586), nor in her post-accession translations (1592 and 1593). In the pre-accession translations, *which* is at 73.5%, equating to the 'near-completion' stage—the same stage as her pre-accession correspondence.[30] The date of composition for the translations overlaps with the dating of *the which* in Elizabeth's letters. If stylistic associations contribute to the lag in the replacement of *the which* in her idiolect, then it appears to be confined to a five-year window: 1544–1549. After that, any stylistic attributes that promote the variant appear to have been lost.

To gain a better impression of the cross-genre distribution of the variable, and to focus on the years of lag in Elizabeth's idiolect, Table 36 shows recalculated frequencies using the 1540s correspondence only. The proportion of *which* in the 1540s correspondence is 76.2%, comparable with the translation frequency of 73.5%. Also comparable is the trend for specialist systemic functions, with *the which* showing a narrower range of contexts than *which* in the pre-accession translations (see Appendix, Table 73).

The results may suggest that *the which* was an idiosyncratic feature of Elizabeth's idiolect during the 1540s, before her preferences changed and *the which* fell out of use. The macro-level studies give this explanation clear

Table 36. *the which* (%) out of *the which/which*, 1544–1549 (QEIC correspondence and translations)

	Total (*which/* *the which*)	*% which*
Correspondence: 1540s	42	76.2
Translations: 1540s	268	73.5

[30] The difference between the pre- and post-accession translations has a p value > 0.001.

precedent. The HC trends show no discernable genre-based pattern, but there is evidence of idiolectal and text-specific variation. Raumolin-Brunberg (2000: 215–216) notes that texts in different genres written by the same author show comparability in the frequency of *the which*. Rissanen also acknowledges that the form is 'favoured by certain authors' (1999: 297). One could simply use the concept of idiolectal variation to explain the findings for Elizabeth's 1540s correspondence and translations.

However, the biographical and socio-historical context allows a more precise explanation to be explored. In the ME and EModE periods, the progression of *wh-* relatives in English was largely a change from above, with upper-ranking, educated authors promoting the forms in formal and literary genres (Rissanen 1999: 295). The ambiguous 'loosely appended relative clauses', analysed under systemic factors, are associated with the 'influence of Latin and Latinate prose', and the Latin relative marker system (ibid.). Thus, *which* and *the which* are the tools with which to achieve the literary and stylistic ideals of sixteenth-century prose. Determiner *(the)which*, for example, is explicitly identified with 'the literate mode' in Rissanen's account (1999: 296). In the 1540s, an intense decade for Elizabeth's education, she may have noted the prestigious and specialised role of *the which* in learned and literary texts, and made an association between particular systemic contexts and the marker in her own writing. The rather earnest use of the determiner context illustrates the connection between style and form ((108) and (109)), particularly when compared with the more organic examples found in her later writing ((110)).[31]

(108) wherefore I trust you shall never find that fault in me, to **the which thing** I do not see that your grace has made any direct answer at this time (21st February 1549, to Edward Seymour, QEIC correspondence).

(109) it should please God to mitigate his judgement: **The which thing** thou couldst not obtain (1545, Calvin, QEIC translations).

(110) the good justice that with your own person you have been pleased to Execute together with the large assurance that your words have given to some of my ministers **which all** doth make me ready to drink most Willingly (15th May 1588, to James VI, QEIC correspondence).

The analysis of other linguistic variables frequently reveals that the patterns for Elizabeth's pre-accession translations are often a heightened or contrasting version of the distribution seen in her correspondence; for example, the frequency of affirmative *do* or the use of the ME pronoun

---

[31] Elizabeth's stepmother, Catherine Parr, also uses this determiner type, although with *which*: 'suche as ye schall thynke convenyent, **wyche thynge** obtayned *shall*be{TEXT:schalbe} no small schame to yowr brother' (Catherine Parr, 1547; ORIGIN2, 152).

system. In the case of *(the)which*, it appears that the stylistic significance of the relative marker was equally relevant to both genres in her pre-accession writing.

10.5 *Interactive Factors*

QEIC letters for the 1540s include only three recipients: Catherine Parr, Edward Seymour and Thomas Seymour. Only Parr and Edward Seymour receive letters containing *the which* or *which*, although the omission of Thomas Seymour is most likely a reflection of the limited corpus data for this individual (one short letter), rather than evidence of interactive variation. The letters to Parr and Edward Seymour contain both *the which* and *which*. *The which* occurs in only one of three letters to Parr: the 1544 preface to Elizabeth's translation of Navarre:

> (111) the words (or rather the order of my writing) **the which** I know in many places to be rude (June 1544, to Catherine Parr, QEIC correspondence).

All five letters to Edward Seymour written during the Seymour affair contain examples of *the which* ((112)). An earlier letter to him, written in 1548, contains no tokens of either relative marker.

> (112) these are shameful slanders, for **the which** besides the great desire I have to see the King's Majesty I shall most Heartily desire your Lordship (28th January 1549, to Edward Seymour, QEIC correspondence).

The letters to Parr and Seymour differ in their compositional context and function. Analysis of other linguistic features in the letters to Seymour, for instance, has highlighted aspects connected to more spoken and discursive linguistic modes such as affirmative *do*. The preface to Elizabeth's translation, addressed to Parr, is carefully constructed and shares the literary tone of the text that follows it. Thus, the interactive context appears to have little influence upon Elizabeth's selection of the variant. Systemic, social and stylistic factors have a more significant role in her status as lagger in the 1540s.

10.6. *Summary*

Overall, the marginal status of *the which* in Elizabeth's idiolect conforms closely to macro-level norms for the sixteenth century. The diachronic developments show no evidence that Elizabeth modified her usage in response to her accession, reinforcing the suspicion that her accession, whilst a historically significant event, may not be the most significant episode for her idiolect. However, more unexpectedly, Elizabeth was found to lag behind the macro-level norm in her earliest writing (1544–1549): a trend possibly explained by the contact with her female caregivers in her early childhood, as well as the development of a specialised systemic function connected to prose ideals of the sixteenth century.

It is also curious that *the which* disappears so abruptly after 1549. The literary and rhetorically influenced correspondence to Edward VI, written only a few years later (1551–1553), contains plenty of prepositional and non-restrictive clauses that promote *the which* in her earlier correspondence. How might this be explained? Elizabeth's biographical experiences in the 1550s offer one possible and quite persuasive scenario. Elizabeth's activities and social experiences in the 1550s marked a significant change from the preceding years, when Elizabeth was still under the protection of her stepmother, Catherine Parr. It is plausible that the change in Elizabeth's social context, as she strengthened her relationship with her brother Edward VI and attended the Court more frequently, provided an extralinguistic impetus that accelerated the loss of *the which*. Notably, the HC sample of King Edward's diary from this time shows no examples of outgoing variant *the which* (Raumolin-Brunberg 2000: 217). The adolescent Elizabeth could be seen as adjusting her linguistic preferences to accommodate towards those around her, and thus position herself linguistically within the new social group.

Throughout the analysis, I have characterised Elizabeth's position in this change (in the 1540s, at least) as a lagger. However, this description needs to be refined. Smith (1996: 114) makes a useful distinction between types of language change. His terms 'innovative failure' and 'innovative success' distinguish new forms in the language according to their period of functionality. The decline of *the which* is one of innovative failure, the Northern form losing out to a variant, *which*, that was already established—indeed, too firmly established—in the language. Elizabeth's status as lagger in this change refers to her slower-than-average loss of the failed form. This, I believe, is significantly different to cases where the lagger status is defined by the slow acquisition of an innovative success, an incoming form that goes on to become the generalised norm in the language (e.g. negative *do*) and can be considered conservative in type.

It is possible to speculate that, from a synchronic perspective, Elizabeth may have perceived *the which* as the new, incoming form, with qualities distinguishing it as a prestigious and learned variant. Had *the which* made a more definitive impression on the English language, Elizabeth's early preferences may again have placed her in the leader category. Instead, the events of the 1550s caused her to re-evaluate the form and replace it with *which*. Conceptualising the change in this way emphasises the importance of Elizabeth's stylistic sensitivity in her participation in language change. She may well be a lagger in a quantitative, diachronic sense, but this is because her valuation of the variant at a stylistic level, which held a distinctive systemic role in her idiolect, differed from the macro-level norm. The results do not suggest her lagger status reflects a conservative attitude towards language change, but rather a keen synchronic concern for stylistic appropriateness and the social connotations of linguistic forms.

It is not clear how useful this variant will prove for authorship attribution, unless the text in question can be confidently dated to the 1540s, when her usage is most deviant.

11. Superlative adjectives

One of the central questions underpinning the analysis of Elizabeth's idiolect concerns the potential relationship between her language use and the impact of her accession. Highlighted as a key event by historians and biographers, the ascent to the throne has thus far shown little significance in the diachronic patterns and trends identified in her idiolect. Broader social factors (i.e. education), social networks (i.e. female caregivers) and other biographical experiences (i.e. contact with the Court of Edward VI) have been identified as strong correlates and provided a persuasive basis for interpretation and explanation. However, in the two analyses that follow, it becomes clear that Elizabeth's accession does have an impact on her idiolect; notably, the correlation emerges for features that are most explicitly concerned with the interpersonal or interactive dimension of communication, and thus most sensitive to the change in her social status. The first of these is the formation method for adjectival superlatives; the second, which I discuss in the subsequent chapter, is the first-person pronoun *royal we*.

In the Early Modern period, there were three methods for creating a superlative: the synthetic variant using terminal inflection, *-est* ((113)); the analytic variant with periphrastic *most* ((114)); and the double form, which combines both methods ((115)).[32]

(113) Your **dearest** chamber (16th March 1589, to James VI, QEIC correspondence).

(114) My **most** dear brother (September 1589, to James VI, QEIC correspondence).

(115) Your **most necessariest** weapons (3rd December 1600, to Charles Blount, QEIC correspondence).

The inflection method dates back to Old English, and periphrasis—whilst previously held to have emerged in Middle English (e.g. Pound 1901: 3)—has recently been back-dated to the Old English period as well

---

[32] Many of the macro-level studies consulted assess both comparative and superlative forms in their analysis. Comparisons are made with the superlative data only, unless otherwise stated.

(González-Díaz 2006). The third method, the double form, is far less common, accounting for only 2% of superlatives in the EModE section of the Helsinki Corpus (Kytö & Romaine 1997). As Kytö puts it, the double form is 'of sporadic use only; the real rivalry is between the inflectional and the periphrastic form proper' (Kytö 1996: 128). Thus, periphrastic and inflected superlatives are treated as a bi-partite system, with a separate discussion of the double superlative.

The superlative variable is not a linguistic change of the kind investigated in the preceding chapters—neither periphrasis nor inflection has generalised to the detriment of the other. Instead, the Early Modern period saw a movement away from free variation towards systematic variation, whereby the choice of method is largely predictable based on systemic and stylistic factors. It may be for this reason that historical sociolinguists have yet to conduct a macro-level investigation of the social distribution of superlative formation, but have instead focused upon the systemic and stylistic development of the system now found in PDE. As a result, the discussion has a slightly different comparative focus than other morpho-syntactic features analysed in QEIC.

Whilst some linguists (e.g. Lass 1999) discuss adjective and adverb superlatives collectively, the QEIC analysis is restricted to adjectives, following the methodologies of previous studies (Kytö 1996; González-Díaz 2003, 2008). I disregard adjectives that change lexical form (i.e. *bad*, *worst*) and focus on those that are modified only by inflection or periphrasis, e.g. *happy*, *happiest*; *beautiful*, *most beautiful*. Tokens (*-est* and *most*) were located in QEIC using the AntConc concordance program, before being manually checked and sorted.

11.1 *Results*

In the QEIC correspondence, periphrasis is Elizabeth's preferred strategy and accounts for 61.1% of all superlative forms. The diachronic distribution shows that her preference for periphrasis is most pronounced in the pre-accession period, with a frequency of 84%. In the post-accession period this figure drops to just over half, at 57.3%. The difference between periods is statistically significant ($p > 0.5$). The decrease in periphrasis over time fits with the macro-level trends. Results from the HC (all genres) show that inflection was the rising variant, increasing from 47% in the Late Middle English period to over 50% in the Early Modern period (1500–1710) (Kytö 1996: 129; Kytö & Romaine 1997). In the correspondence sub-section of the HC, Kytö (1996: 131) reports an overall percentage of 66% inflection for the Early Modern period (1500–1710), similar to the figure for the QEIC correspondence.

11.2 *Systemic Factors*

There are a number of systemic factors that have regularised and can be used to predict the choice of inflection or periphrasis in PDE. During the Early Modern period, the influence of these factors was more variable and still developing (González-Díaz 2008: 77). The first factor to consider is word length (syllable count). Although Louise Pound (1901: 10) assigns tentative significance to word length, suggesting the associations were 'well on the way, but not fully established' in Elizabeth's lifetime, more recent analysis of the HC has led Kytö and Romaine (1997) to describe it as 'a powerful factor' in the Early Modern period. Over 70% of monosyllables take inflection at the start of the Early Modern period, rising to 90% by 1700. Trisyllabic words (and longer) take periphrasis more than 95% of the time. Only disyllabic words show a more variable distribution between the two methods, although Kytö's (1996: 133) analysis of the HC found that periphrasis accounted for more than 60% of disyllables in the Early Modern period.

In the QEIC correspondence, the rate of inflection with monosyllables is 81.8% (Table 37), which shows a convincing correlation with the HC trends. The frequency of inflection in this word-length is largely attributable to recurrent and consistently modified adjectives. For instance, *greatest* occurs 19 times in the superlatives data, and other recurrent monosyllabic adjectives, such as *sure* (n = 5), *high* (n = 5), *meet* (n = 4) and *safe* (n = 2) also occur only with the inflected form. Some monosyllables do show variation in comparison strategy: *dear* occurs three times with inflection and three times with periphrasis; *true* occurs only once with inflection and twice with periphrasis. Unfortunately diachronic analysis of the monosyllabic items is not possible, as the token count (n = 5) for the pre-accession period is too low. In her survey of adjective comparatives, González-Díaz (2008: 77) suggests that 'the higher the frequency of the adjective, the greater the likelihood of inflectional forms being selected'. Whilst comparatives and superlatives show different properties in the history of English (e.g. Kytö & Romaine 1997), González-Díaz's hypothesis provides an accurate prediction of the properties of monosyllabic superlatives in the QEIC correspondence.

Table 37. Inflection/periphrastic superlatives (%) by word length (QEIC correspondence)

Word length	Inflection	Periphrasis
Monosyllables	54 (81.8%)	12 (18.2%)
Disyllables	14 (19.2%)	59 (80.8%)
Trisyllables (+)	0 (0%)	36 (100%)

High frequency items also occur in the trisyllabic (+) data, suggesting that they may contribute to the exclusive use of periphrasis for this word length. *Most affectionate* occurs 16 times in the correspondence, for example. The correlation between polysyllables and periphrasis fits with the macro-level trends identified in historical corpora (Kytö & Romaine 1997). Again, the pre-accession correspondence data for trisyllabic forms (n = 3) is insufficient for diachronic analysis.

Finally, the relationship between disyllabic adjectives and formation method also fits with the macro-level patterns, with Elizabeth's clear preference for periphrasis (80.8%) at the upper-end of the figures identified at the macro-level. Kytö's (1996) study of the E1 and E2 periods in the HC (1500–1640) finds an average frequency of 79% periphrasis, with a slight decline between the two periods (see Table 38).

In the QEIC correspondence, the token count for disyllabic adjectives is higher than the other word lengths, and can be examined diachronically. The findings show that disyllabic adjectives promote periphrasis in the pre-accession period, with 16 of the 17 tokens formed with this method (94.1%). In the post-accession data, the rate of periphrasis drops to 75% (42 of 56 tokens), showing a parallel decline with the overall (cross-genre) figures from the HC. Recurring adjectives may explain the dominance of periphrasis in Elizabeth's pre-accession correspondence: 12 of the 16 periphrastic superlatives constitute only three adjective forms, *humble*, *noble* and *hearty*, and Elizabeth uses periphrasis consistently for each.

Previous macro-level analyses have focused on the disyllabic group when analysing systemic factors. This is because disyllables show the greatest variation in the selection of inflection or periphrasis, indicating that they are susceptible to systemic properties other than word length (e.g. González-Díaz 2008: 75–88). One such property is the ending of the adjective. Whilst a range of endings has been identified as promoting one method over the other (see Elzinga 2006: 759; Kytö & Romaine 2000: 181; Lass 1999: 156; Kytö 1996: 136), the QEIC analysis is restricted to the available forms in the data. Table 39 shows the six most frequent endings for the disyllabic superlative adjectives, listing the expected formation method where

Table 38. Inflection/periphrasis (%) in disyllabic adjectives (Helsinki Corpus (all genres)), adapted from Kytö (1996: 133)

Period	Disyllables: inflection	Disyllables: periphrasis
E1 (1500–1570)	12 (14%)	72 (86%)
E2 (1570–1640)	16 (33%)	33 (67%)
Overall	28 (21%)	105 (79%)

Table 39. Word ending and formation method (number per period), disyllables only (QEIC correspondence)

Word ending	Expected	PreA inflection	PreA periphrasis	PostA inflection	PostA periphrasis
ed	–	–	–	0	22
en	periphrasis	–	–	1	0
ful	periphrasis	1	2	5	5
ing	inflection	–	–	0	7
le	inflection	0	10	1	0
y	inflection	0	3	5	4

applicable (based on Lass 1999: 156) and the number of tokens for each method in Elizabeth's correspondence.

The influence of this systemic factor appears to be limited. In general, Elizabeth's usage is fairly erratic, with the exception of –ed and –ing both taking only periphrasis. The endings –le and –y show no clear correlation with the macro-level norm: less than half of the tokens ending in –y take inflection, and only 1 of the 11 tokens ending in –le occur with the synthetic variant. Interestingly, Kytö (1996: 136) notes that periphrasis also 'hangs on' with these word endings in the EModE HC data, contrary to the accepted literature. The word ending –ful, which in LModE is most likely to take periphrasis (Kytö & Romaine 2000: 181), occurs six times with inflection and seven times with periphrasis in Elizabeth's correspondence. Some adjectives even occur with both methods (*most careful, carefulest*). Elizabeth's preferences correlate and deviate with the macro-level trends, suggesting she does not lead the change in regards to this systemic factor. Other factors must instead contribute to the high frequency of periphrasis in her pre-accession correspondence, and the subsequent decrease in periphrasis in the post-accession period.

The sequential superlative may be one such factor ((116)). In Elizabeth's correspondence, sequential forms account for 14.8% (26 of 175) of all tokens, and these occur in both the pre- and post-accession periods. All but one occurs with periphrasis. Proportionally, this equates to almost a quarter of the periphrastic superlative tokens in the correspondence data (statistically significant $p > 0.001$):

(116) our **most** noble and virtuous queen Catherine (June 1544, to Catherine Parr, QEIC correspondence).

Interestingly, the exception does not use inflection, but instead contains both periphrasis and inflection to modify the adjectives separately:

(117) Your **most** assured and **faithfullest** sister and cousin (1st August 1583, to James VI, QEIC correspondence).

Finally, there is a striking distribution pattern in the data when the superlatives are sorted according to type. As a true superlative expression, the adjective should have a reference point (i.e. the item with which it is being compared). However in the QEIC correspondence there is only one token that occurs in an expression of explicit comparison:

(118) I may die the **shamefullest** death that ever any died afore I may mean any such thing (17th March 1554, to Mary I, QEIC correspondence).

The majority of superlatives from Elizabeth's correspondence are 'elative (absolute) superlative[s]' (Pound 1901: 57), also known as 'laudatory superlatives' (Kytö 1996: 136), which have no point of comparison. Pound's analysis of EModE literary texts shows that elatives were frequent in the late fifteenth century, and continue to be prevalent throughout the sixteenth century, including the writings of Thomas Elyot and Roger Ascham (Pound 1901: 58); Kytö (1996: 136) makes a similar observation in regards to the frequency of elative superlatives in the EModE HC data. Pound (1901: 58) observes that elatives are used 'before titles, in phrases of compliment, in direct address, in exclamations'. The implied interactive properties suggest that closer analysis of this factor may reveal a connection to the trends in Elizabeth's correspondence.

11.3 *Interactive Factors*

Whilst elative superlatives account for all except one of the examples in Elizabeth's correspondence, it is possible to further refine the category into the different contexts (i.e. function) in which the elatives occur. A third of all elative tokens in the QEIC correspondence occur in the opening and closing sections of Elizabeth's letters, thus showing semi-formulaic qualities. I term these ADDRESS-FORM SUPERLATIVES ((119)):

(119) Your **most** loving cousin and sovereign (1575, to Walter Devereux, QEIC correspondence).

The connection between address-form superlatives and periphrasis is striking, with 96.6% tokens taking periphrasis. By comparison, elative superlatives that do not occur in address-form contexts take periphrasis only 43.6% of the time ($p > 0.001$). Without the address-form superlatives, Elizabeth's preferred formation method would be inflection.

In their analysis of the HC, Kytö and Romaine include correspondence in the periphrasis category, a group that otherwise contains genres 'less likely to reflect spoken language' (Kytö & Romaine 1997). In her earlier study, Kytö (1996: 138) explains this apparent abnormality. She observes that the high percentage of periphrasis documented in private correspondence

Table 40. Periphrasis (%) in address-form and non-address-form adjectival superlatives (QEIC correspondence)

	Total periphrasis and inflection	% periphrasis
Address-form	58	96.6
Non-address-form	117	43.6

across the Early Modern period is attributable to the 'highly rhetorical use of adjectival comparison' in epistolary formula, i.e. address-form superlatives.

In Elizabeth's correspondence, the address-form superlatives overlap with the systemic factors discussed above. The address-form superlatives are mainly disyllabic (*noble, humble, faithful*) or trisyllabic (+) forms (*excellent, affectionate*) with a high percentage of periphrasis. They are also high frequency adjectives; for instance, 15 of the 16 occurrences of trisyllabic periphrastic *affectionate* occur in closing subscriptions. Disyllabic *assured* (21 tokens) and *loving* (7 tokens) are also predominantly address-form superlatives, and Elizabeth consistently modifies these adjectives with periphrasis. Address-form superlatives also overlap with the word-ending data. The most consistent context, the 22 examples of past participle *–ed* modified by periphrasis, all occur in adjectives used in Elizabeth's subscriptions.

The type of superlative, as an address-form or non-address form, can also help explain variation in Elizabeth's choice of method for particular adjectives. The adjective *dear* occurs six times in QEIC correspondence: three periphrastic and three inflected forms. The periphrastic examples are all address-form (e.g. (120)). Conversely, two of the inflected forms are non-address-form elative superlatives positioned in the main body of the letter ((121)). The third inflected form is an address-form ((122)). However, the context is somewhat different from the other examples, as it occurs in that letter's exterior address label rather than as part of the letter itself.

(120) My **most** dear brother (1593, to James VI, QEIC correspondence).

(121) soon after to be extolled to your **dearest** chamber (1589, to James VI, QEIC correspondence).

(122) To my **dearest** brother and Cousin the King of Scots (1586, to James VI, QEIC correspondence).

From one perspective, the dominance of the address-form superlatives skews the data, and prohibits accurate analysis of the general patterns of inflection and periphrasis in Elizabeth's idiolect. On the other hand, the data offers a valuable insight into language use specific to the correspondence. The address-form superlatives characterise her use of the linguistic feature in this particular interactive and generic context and hence provide important evidence of the role of style in her idiolect.

Indeed, the insight offered by these forms permits the suggestion that the address-form superlatives explain the decrease in periphrasis between the pre- and post-accession periods. Significantly, the diachronic change is connected to the function of the address-form superlatives, and their sensitivity to social relationships between Elizabeth and the recipient. Elizabeth's social status, before and after her accession, affects her use of this particular type of superlative.

The correlation between address forms and social status has been identified elsewhere in sixteenth-century correspondence. Nevala (2004) examines the diachronic development of address forms in CEEC using a socio-pragmatic framework, and finds them to be a powerful tool in creating and maintaining social relationships in epistolary communication. Some of her most relevant findings concern the address forms used by social climbers. In letters to individuals who ascend the social ranks, Nevala found that writers would address the recipient in different ways, before and after their promotion. For example, letters addressed to Thomas Cromwell before his ascent are less deferential than after he assumed the title Earl of Essex (2004: 123–124). Nevala (2004: 87) also suggests that the selection of periphrasis for address-form superlatives is a highly formalised feature of Early Modern correspondence, observing that 'intensifiers such as *very*, *entirely* and *most* often appear in the material'. This applies particularly to address-forms in the honorific category (e.g. 2004: 91). She further notes (2004: 124) that opening address forms are 'more bound to address rules'—such as the formulaic use of intensified expressions—than the closing formulae, which 'can be more freely constructed'.

Nevala's observations are echoed in the data from Elizabeth's correspondence. In the pre-accession period, the most frequent address-form superlatives are deferential and flattering terms: *noble*, *humble* and *excellent*. They are typical adjectives of the period in this context, and Kytö (1996: 136) remarks upon the prominence of the first two forms in her study of address-form superlatives in private correspondence in the HC.

Contrastingly, the address-form superlatives in the post-accession correspondence communicate Elizabeth's equal and indeed superior relationship with the recipient, including adjectives such as *affectionate*, *assured* and *loving*. These forms are not listed as elative in Kytö's (1996) analysis of the HC correspondence. Significantly, address-form superlatives are less common in the opening lines of her post-accession letters. The formulaic superlative adjectives have been replaced with less intensified address-forms, 'my lord' (11th April 1572, to William Cecil, QEIC correspondence) or 'my dear brother and cousin' (7th August

1583, to James VI, QEIC correspondence). Likewise, Elizabeth does not always use address-form superlatives in the closing sections of her correspondence. Un-intensified expressions such as 'your loving kinswoman' (26th February 1570, to Henry Carey, QEIC correspondence) are also found.

To summarise: in the pre-accession period, address-form superlatives constitute the majority of superlative tokens. These occur primarily in the opening lines of the letters and use highly formulaic expressions of deference (*most noble, most humble*) appropriate to Elizabeth's social status, thus providing a significant contribution to the percentage of periphrastic superlatives in this period. In the post-accession correspondence, the change in Elizabeth's social status allows for a greater degree of flexibility in the opening and closing formulae. As a result, the addressform superlatives are less frequent, and make up a lower proportion of superlative tokens. Overall, the diachronic differences in the correspondence superlatives are connected to the changes in Elizabeth's social status specifically associated with her accession. Her correspondence suggests that social climbers (if that category can be used to describe her change in status) change the address-forms that they use to others, as well as the changes in address-forms used to address social climbers documented by Nevala (2004).

11.4 *Stylistic Factors*

The relationship between the superlative patterns and interactive factors in Elizabeth's correspondence raises questions about the potential for diachronic change in other genres, which have different interpersonal requirements. The macro-level data shows that cross-genre variation does occur. In the HC 'matter-of-fact text types' encompassing handbooks and spoken mode genres show a preference for inflection. More literary genres, including philosophical and religious treatises, are more likely to use periphrasis (Kytö 1996: 130; Kytö & Romaine 2000: 185). It has been suggested that the distribution may reflect the written origin of the periphrastic form and the association with Latinate lexis. The patterns may also relate to the greater markedness of the periphrastic form, which allows the element of degree and the adjective to be individually foregrounded, and would be more appropriate in literary, rhetorical texts (Kytö 1996: 123; Kytö & Romaine 2000: 185; González-Díaz 2008: 89).

The results for the three genres in QEIC are presented in Table 41. The frequency of periphrasis in the parliamentary speeches is 15%, much lower than the post-accession correspondence (57.3%), and the difference is further illustrated when re-calculated according to word length: 0% monosyllable, 50% disyllabic, 0% trisyllabic. Most striking is Elizabeth's

Table 41. Periphrastic (%) superlatives (QEIC speeches and translations)

	Total inflection/ periphrasis	Periphrasis (%)
Pre-accession correspondence	25	84%
Post-accession correspondence	150	57.3%
Speeches	20	15%
Pre-accession translations	13	84.6%
Post-accession translations	61	3.3%

use of inflection, not periphrasis, for the trisyllabic and quadsyllabic adjectives:

(123) If I should say the **sweetest** tongue or **eloquentest** speech that ever was in man were able to express that restless care (1576, QEIC speeches).

(124) I might be thought **indifferentist** judge in this respect (1576, QEIC speeches).

Although the numbers are not large enough to be statistically significant, I suggest the trisyllabic (+) adjectives are persuasive evidence for a stylistic difference between Elizabeth's speeches and correspondence. Periphrasis accounts for all trisyllabic (+) words in her letters.

Another difference between the speeches and post-accession correspondence is the superlative type. Elative superlatives comprise the majority of tokens (65%) in the speeches, but to a lesser degree than in the correspondence. The resultant effect on the rate of periphrasis is clear in the non-elative examples: six of the seven true comparison superlatives (out of 20 superlatives overall) take inflection. More significantly, there are no address-form superlatives in the speeches data, and this is the type of superlative with which Elizabeth most consistently uses periphrasis. Thus adjectives also found in Elizabeth's correspondence, such as *humble* and *noble*, take inflection in the speeches, presumably because of the difference in function:

(125) to give Him my **humblest** thanks (12th November 1586, QEIC speeches).

Overall, the greater frequency of inflected forms in this genre correlates with the macro-level trends, which show that spoken genres (excluding correspondence) contain a larger proportion of inflected forms.

In the pre-accession translations, periphrasis is the dominant method. Whilst the token counts are fairly low, the 84.6% periphrasis is nearly identical to the contemporary correspondence (84%). The disyllabic and trisyllabic forms, which account for just over half of the tokens, take 100% periphrasis and this may skew the data slightly. Yet three of the five monosyllabic forms also use the periphrastic strategy, which suggests periphrasis has a prominent role in these texts, despite the low token counts. The superlatives are primarily comprised of elative adjectives, but there are no address-form contexts. Instead, the non-address-form superlatives contribute to the intensified and emphatic expressions in the religious prose:

(126) When I was going in the **most** deep place of hell (1544, Navarre, QEIC translations).

(127) Therefore the **most** wicked men are an example unto us (1545, Calvin, QEIC translations).

When compared with the macro-level data, there is a strong case for stating that Elizabeth's preferences in the pre-accession period as a whole epitomise Kytö & Romaine's (2000: 185) assertion that literary texts and correspondence show a preference for periphrasis during the Early Modern period. However, it is important to emphasise that whilst the figures are nearly identical (c. 84%), Elizabeth's choice of method is sensitive to very different functions in each genre: the literary, more formal style in her translations and the formulaic address-form superlatives in her correspondence.

In the post-accession translations, periphrasis accounts for only 3.3% of superlatives, a clear downward trend that mirrors the decline of periphrasis in Elizabeth's correspondence, as well as fitting the macro-level development. However, the actual percentage of periphrasis is much lower than the comparative material would predict. In Kytö's (1996: 131) investigation of the HC, for instance, handbooks contained the lowest level of periphrasis at 27%. The low frequency of periphrasis in Elizabeth's post-accession translations can partly be attributed to systemic factors. The majority of tokens are monosyllabic adjectives, which are known to promote inflection in her idiolect. Two disyllabic adjectives take periphrasis. Yet there is also an inflected trisyllabic form and, like the examples in Elizabeth's parliamentary speeches, this is a marked occurrence when compared to the patterns in her correspondence:

(128) among all your deeds this day hath won you the **generalest** praise (1592, Cicero, QEIC translation).

Boethius contains only inflected superlatives, largely occurring with monosyllabic adjectives. The lack of periphrastic forms is interesting, as we might have expected the different syllable lengths of each method to be implemented in the sections of verse.

One explanation for the low frequency of periphrasis in the post-accession translations is that it is a stylistic decision prompted by the source language of the original texts. Elizabeth composed both translations from Latin, and it is possible that her preference for inflection in the later period (evident in the speeches and non-address-form superlatives in her correspondence) is further enhanced by a desire to mark her English version from the source language.

Overall, the results for the three genres reflect the relationship between the variable and the interactive and stylistic dimensions of the texts. In the translations, there is a decisive shift from periphrasis to inflection across the two periods, but this cannot be explained by a decrease in address-form superlatives. The figures suggest that Elizabeth attached stylistic significance to the periphrastic method in her pre-accession writing, and re-evaluated this over time. If she had attached prestige to the periphrastic method in the post-accession period, then I would expect it to occur at least in the most salient contexts, such as trisyllabic (+) adjectives. Instead, inflection is the dominant and preferred method. The parliamentary speeches corroborate her post-accession preferences for inflection. If the hypothesis is accurate, then Elizabeth's usage corresponds to the macro-level trend that saw inflection increase over time, but to an exaggerated degree. The role of Elizabeth's accession in the diachronic trends is less clear in the more literary material, most likely because they lack the social interactive properties that explain the change in address-form superlatives in the correspondence.

11.5 *Double Forms*

In addition to periphrasis and inflection, there was a third option available to speakers during the sixteenth century: the double superlative. The status of the third comparison strategy in Early Modern English has been described as 'marginal' and limited to 'literary language' (Kytö & Romaine 2000: 173). Whilst some vital work has been conducted on the social dimension of double comparatives (e.g. Kytö 1996; González-Díaz 2003), Early Modern double superlatives remain largely overlooked. To investigate Elizabeth's idiolectal preference, it has been necessary to compile a macro-level baseline using the sixteenth-century files in PCEEC, and to explore the distribution of double superlatives at both macro- and micro-levels.

11.6. *Results*

In their study of superlative forms, Kytö and Romaine (1997; also Kytö 1996: 129) note that double superlatives comprise an average of 2% of all superlative forms in the Early Modern section of the HC, with a downward trend across the period. PCEEC data suggests that the doubled form is marginal in the letter corpus, although I have not been able to calculate the percentage. The normalised frequencies (0.08 per 10,000 words, falling to 0.01 per 10,000 words) offer a persuasive alternative perspective on the peripheral status of the double superlative in the corpus, and, importantly, also show a downward trend.

Double superlatives are similarly marginal in the QEIC correspondence, comprising 2.2% of all superlative forms. The normalised frequencies suggest that they may, nevertheless, occur more frequently than the macro-level norm. Whilst there are no examples in the pre-accession correspondence, the post-accession data shows a normalised frequency of 0.12 times per 10,000 words—rare, but not as rare as the PCEEC figure of 0.01 times per 10,000 words.

Although little sociolinguistic work has been conducted on EModE double superlatives, González-Díaz (2003, 2007) has conducted extensive analysis of double comparatives. Her findings suggest the form had social significance during the Early Modern period. Shakespeare, who contributes 66% of the examples in her study of dramatic dialogue, aligns the form with 'the speech of important members of society', such as kings (e.g. Lear) or noble Romans, and also the dialogue of social climbers (González-Díaz 2007: 646). The relationship between frequency of adjective and superlative formation method was compatible with a hypothesis González-Díaz proposed for comparative forms (2008: 77). The social properties of the double comparative may therefore also apply to double superlatives in the same period. To this end, I have analysed the distribution of the forms in PCEEC according to the social rank of the informant (Figure 9).

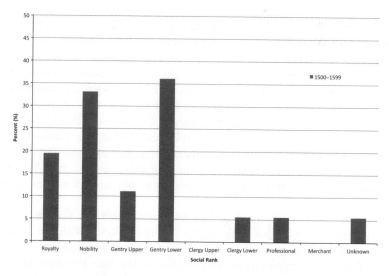

Figure 9: Distribution (%) of double superlatives by social rank, 1500–1599 (PCEEC)

The results suggest that double superlatives were socially stratified, with a clear weighting towards the upper-ranks, including informants of royal and noble status. This includes the sisters of Henry VIII, Mary and Margaret Tudor, and Elizabeth's own courtiers Robert Dudley and William Cecil. The trend initially suggests that Elizabeth conforms to the linguistic preferences of her peers in her (marginal) usage of double superlatives.

However, the correlation is less convincing when the data is examined qualitatively. Mary Tudor, Queen of France, and Margaret Tudor, Queen of Scotland (both writing to their brother, King Henry VIII), use the double superlative in an elative address-form context:

(129) My **most derest** and ryt entierly belowyde Lord (1515, Mary Tudor; Origin1, 124).

(130) And the Holy Trenyte have you my **most derest** broder in tuycion and Governance (1515, Margaret Stuart [n. Tudor]; Origin1, 129).

In (129) the double superlative sits in a cluster of emphatic statements designed to flatter and show respect towards the sovereign in the opening superscription to the letter. Example (130) is extracted from the subscription, and has similar qualities. Other users of the double superlative in an address-form context include Anne Boleyn writing to Cardinal Wolsey in 1528. Her use of the double superlative forms part of an opening expression of humility:

(131) My Lord, in my **most humblyst** wyse that {in} my powuer hart can thynke I do thanke your Grace for your kynd Letter (1528, Anne Boleyn; Origin1, 306).

Kytö (1996: 138–139) also notes that double superlatives typically occur in address-forms in the HC correspondence. Interestingly, her cited examples are all taken from the E1 (1500–1570) period, suggesting that there may be a diachronic weighting in the use of address-form double superlatives. When the PCEEC data is divided into sub-periods, more than 80% of the address-form tokens occur in the E1 (1500–1569) period (22 of 25 tokens). This figure declines significantly to 18.2% in the E2 (1570–1639) period (2 of the 11 tokens). This could show that the address-form superlative was re-evaluated as a feature of formulaic opening and closing expressions. In the latter period, upper-ranking individuals such as William Cecil and Robert Dudley use the double form but not as address-form superlatives.

In fact, the downward trend in PCEEC may reflect the first stages of stigmatisation of the double form, as the timing co-occurs with the decline of the double comparatives in dramatic dialogue. In González-Díaz's survey of double comparatives, playwrights of the late Elizabethan and early Jacobean period use the form very rarely. Works by Jonson,

Middleton, Heywood and Fletcher contain only one or two occurrences for each author, from a corpus of 3.3 million words, occurring in the dialogue of upper and lower class characters. González-Díaz explains the difference by referring to the age of the playwrights, all being of a generation younger than Shakespeare. The shift, she suggests (2003: 94), indicates the 'very beginnings of the loss of prestige of double forms'.

In the PCEEC correspondence, the decreasing frequency of the address-form double superlative feasibly shows the same phenomenon. The important social role of address forms in opening or closing epistolary formula make this context a logical starting point for the stylistic re-evaluation of the double superlatives. The rhetorical style shown in examples (129) and (131) offers depth to this interpretation. The clustering of intensifying deferential and flattering forms, including the double super-lative, compares to the rhetorical figure of HYPERBOLE. George Puttenham's cautionary definition of hyperbole (the over reacher) states that:

> This maner of speech is used, when either we would greatly advaunce or greatly abase the reputation of any thing or person, and must be used very discreetly, or els it will seeme odious, for although a prayse or other report may be allowed beyond credit, it may not be beyond all measure (1589/2007: 108).

In her astute discussion of the figure, Katrin Ettenhuber (2007: 200) remarks that Puttenham's account is 'genre-specific: the main province of hyperbole is now epideictic, the rhetorical form in which reputations can be made or destroyed'. She suggests that Puttenham was thinking of the environment of the Elizabethan Court, and the principles of 'how to make friends and influence people', when composing his definition. In such a context, hyperbole is an inappropriate tool for social negotiation 'incompatible with prudence and discretion' (2007: 200).

The address-form double superlative fits neatly into the epideictic category. The construction enhances and intensifies the conventional expressions of address, which construct the relationship between author and recipient, and is used most frequently by the upper ranks; those for whom social decorum and social advancement were most (if not necessarily equally) important. Puttenham's contemporary, Henry Peacham, consid-ered hyperbole as an important

> sentence or saying surmounting the truth onely for the cause of increasing or diminishing, not with purpose to deceive by speaking untruly, but with desire to amplifie the greatnesse or smalness of things by the exceeding similitude (1593: 31).

Hyperbole, as a means of amplification, is a useful device, although Peacham, too, cautions that 'there be not too great an excesse in the comparison: but that is may be discreetly moderated' (1593: 33). The line between genuine superlative expression and calculated aggrandising flattery is a fine one, particularly if one is addressing a King or noble in the pursuit of self-advancement.

Puttenham's *Art of English Poesie* was published in 1589, and it is striking that his Court-specific advice for the use of hyperbole coincides with the decline of the double superlative in PCEEC. As a device, it is possible that the hyperbolic role of the double superlative was considered unfit for the epistles of Elizabethan nobles and gentry in the latter-half of the sixteenth century.

Address-form (periphrastic) superlatives comprise a large proportion of the QEIC correspondence data. This suggests the double forms should also occur in this context, especially since Elizabeth is a member of the social groups (upper-ranks, the Court) found to use the construction most frequently in PCEEC. Yet the QEIC correspondence does not conform to expectations, with only one double superlative used as an address-form ((132)):

(132) Your **most Assuredest** Sister and Cousin/Elizabeth R (1st July 1588, to James VI, QEIC correspondence).

(133) I must not omit for conscience sake to speak a few words of the master of gray with whom I have had long discourse in which I find him the **most greediest** to do you acceptable service that I have ever heard any (October 1594, to James VI, QEIC correspondence).

(134) I rejoice with who is **most gladdest** that at length (though I confess almost too late) it pleaseth you so kingly and valiantly to resist with your person their outrecuidant malignant attempt (October 1594, to James VI, QEIC correspondence).

(135) And learn this of me, that you must make difference betwixt admonitions and charges, and like of faithful advices as your **most necessariest** weapons to save you from blows of princes mislike (3rd December 1600, to Charles Blount, QEIC correspondence).

Most interesting, however, is the absence of address-form double superlatives in Elizabeth's pre-accession correspondence. The PCEEC data shows that the form occurred in expressions of humility and deference, a function that corresponds to the address-form periphrastic superlatives identified in Elizabeth's early correspondence. The PCEEC evidence also shows that double superlatives were common in letters by Elizabeth's counterparts of social rank and domicile at this time. The lack of address-form double superlatives is therefore surprising, showing a deviation from the interactive style choice of her contemporaries. One hypothesis is that Elizabeth did not approve of the address-form double superlative during her youth; perhaps anticipating the 'odious' connotations decried by Puttenham (1589). However, this interpretation is weakened by the example in the post-accession period. Further research is needed to confidently attribute the absence of address-form double superlatives to Elizabeth's preferences, rather than to the limited correspondence data available for the pre-accession period.

11.7 *Stylistic Factors*

In Shakespearian dialogue, González-Díaz (2003: 91) finds that the double comparative construction typically co-occurs with other markers of more formal or high register speech, such as periphrastic *do* and the *–th* variant for third-person singular verbs, providing support for a reading of the doubled form as a marker of learned, upper-class speech. In other genres, the double comparatives occur in blank verse or poetic prose, and are also associated with the high style.

Previous results for the literary genres indicate that Elizabeth is highly sensitive to the stylistic significance of linguistic forms. It is therefore surprising that there is no evidence of an associated prestige with the double superlative in either the pre- or post-accession period. There are no examples in the QEIC speeches or translations, despite many occurrences of inflected and periphrastic superlatives. On this basis, we might ascribe double superlatives more informal or less literary associations in Elizabeth's idiolect, an interpretation that suggests that the stylistic significance of double superlatives perhaps differed from that of comparatives in EModE. Further analysis is needed to ascertain the prevalence of the construction across different genres of the Early Modern period to establish if Elizabeth's usage corresponds with macro-level trends.

11.8 *Summary*

The most significant finding for the superlative variable in QEIC is the connection with Elizabeth's accession, with the change in her social status affecting her selection of epistolary address-forms and in turn shaping the proportion of periphrastic address-form superlatives in the correspondence. This is the first linguistic feature to show any correlation to the accession, and the connection to the interactive dimension of communication is thus highly significant.

The analysis highlights the importance of accounting for the interactive and stylistic dimensions when interpreting trends in linguistic data. Whilst the macro-level results hint at the role of address-form superlatives, discriminating between superlative type is essential for interpreting the patterns in Elizabeth's idiolect, and this may also be the case for other writers discussed in macro-level studies. The superlative data may have a high value for authorship analysis, particularly when considering high-frequency adjectives and address-form contexts. However, more macro-level social data may be required before the value of the feature can be properly exploited.

The analysis of double superlatives offers new information about the sociolinguistic properties of the variable at both the macro- and micro-level. The diachronic trends in PCEEC suggest that the double superlative possessed particular social and stylistic associations, comparable with the socio-stylistic evidence identified for double comparatives in the same period (González-Díaz 2003). The results also highlight the importance of address-forms, both in the macro-level data and in Elizabeth's own correspondence. The lack of double address-form superlatives in her pre-accession correspondence, when compared with the consistent use of the form by others of her social rank, is both interesting and unexpected. Indeed, the role of social and stylistic factors in the PCEEC and QEIC data suggests that further research into the double superlative would be a fruitful pursuit, in order to understand how the form transformed from a productive address-form expression in EModE to a stigmatised construction in the eighteenth century.

12. ROYAL WE AND OTHER PRONOUNS OF SELF-REFERENCE[33]

The first-person singular pronoun *royal we* is a linguistic feature intrinsically connected to Elizabeth's accession. It appears in her idiolect after 1559 and serves self-referential functions specifically associated with her position as queen. In exploring how the self-reference pronouns distribute and function in QEIC, the discussion and analysis of the pronominal variable *royal we* and *I* cannot draw on comparative data from the CEEC macro-level baseline due to the highly specific nature of the self-reference form. Instead, the following discussion draws on precedents identified in historical and literary sources to establish if Elizabeth's usage conforms to or differs from the contemporary conventions of use. The final section of the chapter discusses other forms of pronominal self-reference that also develop after Elizabeth's accession, and considers their function alongside *royal we* in her idiolect.

12.1 *Background*

In the sixteenth century, *royal we* was firmly established as the official self-reference pronoun for the reigning monarch. Fisher, Richardson and Fisher (1984: 9) propose that the convention first emerged in the twelfth century,

[33] A version of this chapter first appeared in the *Journal of Historical Pragmatics* (2014), Issue 15.1. I am grateful to the editors and publishers for their permission to reproduce much of that content here.

and rapidly became the norm, modelled on European usage. In correspondence issued under the royal signet of Henry VIII, for example, *we*, rather than the conventional singular *I*, is used to consistently refer to the king:

(136) Right Reverende Fadre in God, right trusty and welbeloved, and trusty and right welbeloved, **We** grete you well. By a post of thEmperours, passing oute of Flaunders in Spayne by this waye, **We** wrote unto you **our** last letters (1525; Record Commission 1849: 476).

The practice continues into Elizabeth's reign. In the scribal letters produced by her administrative centre, many of which were signed and endorsed by Elizabeth, *royal we* is used consistently for first-person self reference:

(137) Elizabeth R. Trusty and wellbeloved, **we** greete you well. Understanding by a letter of **our** cousin, th'erle of Bedford to **our** Secretarie that he thinketh you to be not out of danger there by malice, in so much time as some pistles have ben shot into the howse where you lodge ; **we** have thoughte it meete, not only to advise you, if you fynde any such perrill, but also to lycence you to withdraw yourself for a tyme to Barwicke : pretending the same to be for your own pryvate busynesse, in sort, as you may returne to your charge upon occasion. Gyven under **our** signet at **our** Palais of Westminster, the third of October 1565 the seventh yere of **our** reign (3rd October 1565, Sir Thomas Randolph. BL MS Lansdowne 8 fol. 27. Scribal text with signature, my emphasis).

However, how this compares to the status of *royal we* in autograph texts by a king or queen is less clear, leading Katie Wales (1996: 64) to remark that the status of the pronoun in the language of monarchs before Queen Victoria 'is hard to tell'. Fisher, Richardson and Fisher make a curious observation when discussing a signet letter that they suggest was written by Henry V. In addition to the handwriting evidence—the script 'is firm and practiced, but not that of a professional scribe'—they cite as evidence of authorship that the letter is the only one in their collection 'which uses first person "I"; the majority all use royal we' (Fisher, Richardson & Fisher 1984: 12).[34] Perhaps unexpectedly, they put forward the absence of the royal pronoun as evidence for royal authorship. Thus, there is no reason that the conventions governing *royal we* in Elizabethan scribal correspondence will

---

[34] But cf. Benskin (2004: 12, fn.16), who suggests it could simply be a difference in hand 'between secretary and anglicana', rather than the non-professional hand of the King.

extend to Elizabeth's autograph writing. As the quotations from QEIC in previous chapters indicate, the presence of *I* suggests that different rules apply to her choice of first-person pronoun.

Speakers use pronouns to express 'social, political and rhetorical issues of culture, relationships and power' (Wales 1996: xii). The highly specialised social, political and rhetorical facets of *royal we* may explain its continued use from the Middle Ages into Elizabeth's reign, and indeed into PDE. In the sixteenth century, there is also an additional dimension to *royal we* that relates to the Tudor conception of kingship. The theory of the 'King's Two Bodies' was a legal stance designed to resolve the paradox that existed between the mortality of the sovereign and the perpetuity of the realm over which they reigned. The resolution was a 'twin-born majesty' made up of the body natural and the body politic (Kantorowicz 1957: 4–5). In the words of Elizabeth's contemporary, Edmund Plowden, the power of the crown, 'the office, government and Majesty royal', existed as the body politic—the immortal, invisible and infallible essence of kingship with governance over all his subjects. The body natural was the inferior body of the reigning sovereign, susceptible to frailty, weakness and death, yet it was nevertheless paramount in providing a suitable vessel (Kantorowicz 1957: 7). Together, these two components formed 'one unit indivisible, each being fully contained within the other' (Kantorowicz 1957: 9).

The investigation of *royal we* in Elizabeth's idiolect is one of the first analyses of the pronoun to use authentic monarchic language. The few discussions of the form in the Early Modern period have tended to focus on dramatic dialogue. These, however, offer valuable insight. The fictionalised, dramatised representation of *I* and *royal we* in a monarch's language reveals how the pronouns were understood by Elizabeth's contemporaries, and potentially by Elizabeth herself.

Angus McIntosh and Colin Williamson (1963) provide a detailed reading of the first-person pronouns in Shakespeare's *The Tragedie of King Lear*. Williamson, in his part of the article, focuses on Act 1, Scene 1, where Lear distributes his kingdom amongst his three daughters. He argues that the pronoun shifts between *I* and *royal we* are linguistic props designed to convey Lear's character and relationships to the audience. *Royal we* symbolises Lear's public, monarchic role and *I* the private, human man. Williamson concludes that as a pair the first-person pronouns function as 'an index' of Lear's attitude to his identity and emotional state (McIntosh & Williamson 1963: 57). Williamson's reading suggests that *royal we* was the linguistic equivalent of the royal crown or throne; a symbol of specifically monarchic power that dominated other facets of the speaker's identity.

Whilst Lear was first performed after Elizabeth's death (c. 1604), similar indexical associations are present in earlier Shakespearian dramas. *Richard II*, written c. 1595, is a particularly good example. The concurrent plots show the fall of Richard and the rise of Bolingbroke, highlighting the

Table 42. *Royal we* (%) in the dialogue of Richard
II and Henry IV—figures for Henry IV are taken
from Act 4, Scene 1 onwards, after his accession

	Total	*Royal we* (%)
Richard II	237	56.1
Henry IV (Bolingbroke)	54	27.8

differences between the two holders of the English crown. One such
difference is their use of first-person pronouns. *Royal we* is Richard II's
primary mode of self-reference (56.1%) (Table 42).

Critics such as Tillyard (1944: 262) have described Richard as a
'ceremonial' king: a 'king by unquestioned title and by his external graces
alone'. The frequency of *royal we* contributes to this characterisation,
highlighting the significance of kingship for his identity and outlook on
events. He uses *royal we* to demonstrate and ensure his authority over his
subjects:

> Richard II: Norfolk, for thee remains a heavier doom,
> Which **I** with some unwillingness pronounce:
> The sly slow hours shall not determinate
> The dateless limit of thy dear exile;
> The hopeless word of 'never to return'
> Breathe **I** against thee, upon pain of life.
>
> Mowbray: A heavy sentence, my most sovereign liege,
> And all unlook'd for from your Highness' mouth [...]
>
> Richard II: It boots thee not to be compassionate;
> After **our** sentence plaining comes too late (Act 1,
> Scene 3).

By contrast, Bolingbroke is presented as a 'man of action', and one less
obsessed with royal power. The lower frequency of *royal we* is a
contributing linguistic feature to his characterisation. Richard unwittingly
illustrates the difference between their attitudes to kingship, and its
manifestation in their linguistic self-representation, when he muses:

> How did he [Bolingbroke] seem to dive into their hearts
> With humble and familiar courtesy
> What reverence he did throw away on slaves [...]
> With 'Thanks, **my** countrymen, **my** loving friends'

As were **our** England in reversion his
And he **our** subjects' next degree in hope (Act 1, Scene 4).

The evidence from Richard II and Lear suggests that *royal we* was a key part of the idiolect of a fictionalised monarch. This may be partly due to the requirements of the stage, as the indexicality and significance of the pronoun are a means of conveying identity and character to the audience. Yet it seems unlikely that Shakespeare would entirely fabricate the contrastive difference between *I* and *royal we*. In the following analysis I consider how Elizabeth's usage of *royal we* and *I* compares to the dramatic representation.

12.2 *Results*

Table 43 provides the raw and normalised frequencies for both *I* and *we* in the QEIC correspondence, divided by decade. The table includes only *royal we* forms. *Inclusive* and *exclusive we* are discounted from the figures.

Perhaps the most striking, albeit expected feature of the distribution is that *royal we* does not occur in the pre-accession letters. The pronoun is a property of Elizabeth's post-accession idiolect, and arises directly from her accession.

Looking at the distribution in the post-accession correspondence, *royal we* is the less favoured pronoun, accounting for an average 7.5% of first-person forms. The relative infrequency reveals a key difference between the official letters written on Elizabeth's behalf, which use *royal we* continuously, and her autograph compositions—a contrast that may help to distinguish between the generic productions of the secretariat and the personal composition of the queen in authorship analysis.

The breakdown by decade shows that both pronoun forms occur more frequently in the 1560s than in subsequent decades. One explanation may be the dominance of postscripts as the material for this decade, which perhaps represents different stylistic conventions or interactive stance from

Table 43. Royal we (%) and normalised frequency out of *I* (*I, me, my*) and *royal we* (*we, us, our*) (QEIC correspondence)

	Total *I* and *royal we*	% *royal we*	*I*/1000 words	*Royal we*/ 1000 words
1540s	300	0	86.1	0
1550s	213	0	76.5	0
1560s	42	11.9	85.8	11.6
1570s	33	3.0	56.3	1.8
1580s	768	10.9	51.9	6.4
1590s	907	4.0	50.5	2.1
1600s	165	10.9	51.4	6.3

the main body of a letter. In the remaining decades, the percentage of *royal we* and the normalised frequencies for both forms show undulations over time, although within a relatively narrow range. The main diachronic distinction is therefore the post-accession acquisition of *royal we*, and the quantitative contrast between the two first-person pronouns in the later period.

12.3 *Interactive Factors*

In order to understand the factors that affect Elizabeth's selection of *royal we*, I have recalculated the data to show how *royal we* distributes across individual letters (Table 44). A third of the post-accession letters (28 letters) contain at least one instance of *royal we*; of these, only three letters contain continuous *royal we*, i.e. the pronoun is the only first-person form to occur in the letter. This clearly deviates from the distribution patterns in the scribal correspondence. In the majority of the 28 letters, *royal we* is sporadic and used as an alternative to the dominant first-person *I*. 11 recipients receive letters containing at least one instance of *royal we*, all of whom are male. They include Elizabeth's subjects, other monarchs, and individuals of close and distant acquaintance. The gender of the addressee is unlikely to be overly significant, as there are only four letters addressed to female recipients in the post-accession corpus; more data is needed for a proper assessment of this feature.

The dramatic index suggests that the use of *royal we* may be influenced by Elizabeth's relationship with the recipient of the letter. Continuous *royal we*, as the most forceful application of the official and distant first-person pronoun, would be theoretically more appropriate to addressees socially distant from Elizabeth. Yet this hypothesis finds no support in the three letters in QEIC, which are addressed to Robert Dudley, Earl of Leicester; Robert Devereux, Earl of Essex; and John Norris and Francis Drake (joint recipients) respectively. Robert Dudley was Elizabeth's closest friend and one time potential husband; Robert Devereux, Dudley's stepson, replaced

Table 44. *Royal we* (%) by letter and distribution (QEIC post-accession correspondence)

	Number of letters	%
Letters with *royal we*	28	29.8
Letter without *royal we*	66	70.2
Total	94	
Continuous *royal we*	3	10.7
Sporadic *royal we*	25	89.3

the latter as the Queen's favourite in the late 1580s. Only John Norris and Francis Drake could be described as lesser acquaintances of the Queen, although Elizabeth's support and favour (financial and otherwise) of their naval and pirating activities is well known. Thus the social distance between Elizabeth and the recipient does not appear to accurately predict the selection of *royal we*.

However, incorporating other interactive factors provides a more persuasive explanation for the pronoun choice. The three letters have similar contexts and functions, written after each recipient had disobeyed Elizabeth's orders. The selection of *royal we* is, therefore, related to her relationship with the recipient, but at a localised, context-specific level.[35] The letter to Devereux suggests that continuous *royal we* was as much connected to emotional attitude as it was to the letter's practical purpose. Elizabeth wrote the letter to Devereux after he joined a 'hit-and-run' naval assault, commanded by John Norris and Francis Drake, against Elizabeth's orders.[36] The letter commands him to return immediately, as Perry wryly describes it, 'telling him what she thought of him for leaving without her permission' (Perry 1990: 293). The letter concludes with a command that draws on all of Elizabeth's authority and status as ruling monarch:

(138) **We** do therefore charge and command you forthwith upon receipt of these **our** letters all excuses and delays set apart to make your present and immediate repair unto **us** to understand **our** further pleasure. Whereof see you fail not as you will be loath to incur **our** indignation and will answer for the contrary at your uttermost peril (15th April 1589, Robert Devereux, QEIC correspondence).

Continuous *royal we* reinforces the public, detached and explicitly monarchic aspects of her identity, correlating with Williamson's index. Importantly, the impact of the letter would be heightened by its contrast to Elizabeth's normal pronominal expression, *I*, used in other letters to her Court favourite (e.g. 15th April 1596, to Robert Devereux, QEIC correspondence). The switch to the first-person monarchic pronoun enables Elizabeth to re-define, quickly and emphatically, her relationship with the recipient, on her terms. Unlike other EModE pronominal pairs, such as *you/thou*, the first-person system is non-reciprocal. In her forms of self-reference, Elizabeth has complete control over the identity she presents to the recipient, and can dictate the relationship between herself and the recipient for that interaction.

The three letters which contain continuous *royal we* present a different 'self' to the majority of letters contained in QEIC, in part through the use of

---

[35] The finding again highlights the possible loss of detail that may result from classifying the author–recipient relationship using broad categories (i.e. family and non-family recipients).
[36] Devereux's desertion of the Court is also the topic of the letter to Norris and Drake.

the pronoun. This dimension is further explicated by their survival as drafts, rather than autograph sent copies. In writing these particular letters, which were presumably issued not in Elizabeth's hand but by a scribe, Elizabeth is working in tandem with her Council and secretariat to produce documents more official than personal. Admittedly, this presents a challenge for the determination of the contents' authenticity, although Elizabeth was known to be highly involved with the affairs of her favourite courtiers. The personal nature of the attack, e.g. 'How contemptuously we conceive ourself to have been used by you' (to Robert Dudley, February 1586, QEIC correspondence), further supports their inclusion within the corpus.

Nevertheless, although the continuous *royal we* letters hint at Elizabeth's conceptualisation of the pronouns and their social significance within the more official capacity, they are the least common type of *royal we* letter in the corpus. In the post-accession period, *royal we* is more typically used for sporadic, one-off instances within a letter as a switch from the dominant first-person *I*. Many of these examples of *royal we* occur with specific lexical collocates connected to the semantic field of sovereignty; for instance, the terms 'nation' or 'people' consistently take the possessive *our*, not *my*, in the QEIC correspondence:

(139) most of **our** nation (July 1563, to Nicholas Throckmorton, QEIC correspondence).

(140) the ears of **our** people (August 1580, to Edward Stafford, QEIC correspondence).

(141) out of **our** land (November 1585, to James VI, QEIC correspondence).

Vuorinen (2002) has also observed pronoun switches in Elizabeth's correspondence. The main purpose of her investigation was to compare features of Elizabeth's language with the language of three male and three female near-contemporaries. The discussion of *royal we* is thus in itself interesting, in that it is a deviation from her central thesis, but consequently her analysis does not consider Elizabeth's self-reference pronominal system in the way conducted here. Vuorinen's analysis was based on the CEEC letters written by Elizabeth, which for the CEEC post-accession file consists, with one exception, of letters to James VI. It is therefore significant that the pronoun switches also occur in letters to other recipients in the QEIC correspondence. This indicates the switches are not specific to James (perhaps connected to his own royal status), but rather representative of Elizabeth's general conception of her identity as queen when referring to political and sovereign matters.

The pronoun switches demonstrate, in my opinion, Elizabeth's recognition of the connection between the royal pronoun and the sovereign 'office, government and Majesty royal' within Tudor society. Elizabeth's adherence to this framework results in switches even in the most affectionate and personal letters. In a note to her godson John Harington, Elizabeth uses *I* throughout except in the final line:

(142) I do this because thy father was ready to serve and love **us** in trouble and thrall (1576, John Harington, QEIC correspondence).

The switch to *royal we* highlights the official context for the verbs 'serve and love', reflecting Harington's duty to his sovereign and nation.

The switch from *I* to *royal we* can also foreground or emphasise Elizabeth's topic, with the official connotations of the royal pronoun often used to aid her argument. One example occurs in the letter to Sir Amias Paulet, written in August 1586. Paulet was the keeper of Mary, Queen of Scots, in the months before her execution. In this letter, Elizabeth expresses her approval of his work after the discovery of the Casket Letters, and Mary's involvement in a conspiracy to assassinate Elizabeth. Throughout the letter, Elizabeth refers to herself using *I*, suggesting she had a high opinion of Paulet and respect for the personal and significant task he was performing for her. Only once does she switch to *royal we*:

(143) And **I** bid her from **me** ask God forgiveness for her treacherous dealing towards the saver of her life many a year, to the intolerable peril of **our** own (August 1586, Amias Paulet, QEIC correspondence).

In this extract, Elizabeth requests that Mary ('her') seeks forgiveness for the trespasses she has committed against her English cousin. The switch to *royal we* shifts the reference from Elizabeth as the letter-writer to Elizabeth the sovereign, in order to emphasise the significance of Mary's 'treacherous' behaviour. Mary has not simply put a woman's life in 'intolerable peril', but the life of the ruling, God-appointed queen. The switch helps to legitimise Elizabeth's orders to Paulet, over which she was highly conflicted.

Elizabeth's use of *I* and *royal we* in the letters to James VI of Scotland as part of their long-standing exchange warrants its own discussion. The correspondence between the two monarchs has proved a fascinating resource for historians, including recent studies by Mueller (2000), Doran (2005) and Allinson (2007). Mueller, in particular, offers an interpretation relevant to the current analysis. She describes the sustained nominal kinship terminology throughout the 20-plus years of correspondence and observes how it developed from 'friendship-in-kingship to kinship between these two, self and other self, equals as friends and monarchs' (Mueller 2000: 1066).

Mueller (2000: 1068) argues that address terms are key to this diplomatic correspondence: James addresses Elizabeth as 'Madame', 'dearest sister' and as the correspondence progresses refers to himself as 'son', whereas Elizabeth uses address-forms 'brother' and 'cousin'. Both make reference to

their shared roles as kings. Whilst these terms of address were part of the
formal conventions of sixteenth-century royal letters, Mueller believes that
Elizabeth and James endorsed these terms with significant meaning,
enabling the monarchs to build and comment upon their relationship and
its hierarchy, to embrace shared experiences, or to identify individual
transgressions, whilst adhering to the polite conventions befitting their
status.

Elizabeth's selection of first-person pronoun forms is another significant
linguistic feature used to construct and maintain the epistolary relationship
with the Scottish king. In Elizabeth's letters to James VI, *I* is the dominant
form, with the royal pronoun used in brief switches. Because she is writing
to another monarch, Elizabeth can exploit the different associations of
royal we to implicitly shape and construct her identity and their relationship
according to her needs at that time. For example, in the following extract,
Elizabeth uses *royal we* to carefully situate her 'care' for James within an
official monarchic context:

(144) Right dear brother the strangeness of hard accidents that are
    arrived here, of unlooked for or unsuspected attempts in Scotland
    even by some such as lately issued out of **our** land, constraineth **me**
    as well for the care **we** have of your person as of the discharge of
    our own honour and conscience to send you immediately this
    gentleman (November 1585, James VI, QEIC correspondence).

'Our own honour and conscience' is that of the office, government and
Majesty royal, and Elizabeth makes it clear that it is primarily a
statement of political affection rather than private concern. The pronoun
switch clearly demarcates the boundaries of their social relationship
and, once established, Elizabeth switches to *I* for the remainder of the
letter.

In other letters, Elizabeth exploits the potential ambiguity that arises
from the royal status of both recipient and addressee. Mueller (2000: 1066)
suggests that the diplomacy between Elizabeth and James originates in
'lexical markers of [...] friendship [including] frequent use of first-person-
plural constructions with conjoint predicates', through which Elizabeth can
express her care for James 'as for a second self' and vow to speak plainly
and honestly. Mueller is here referring to the use of *we* as an inclusive
pronoun, suggesting it is a marker of solidarity. However, when
contextualised within the broader significance of *royal we*, another reading
is that Elizabeth uses the indexical significance of *we* to implicitly persuade
her godson to do what she wants. In the following extract, Elizabeth
demands that James VI quash the Presbyterian threat in Scotland:

(145) Let **me** warn you that there is risen both in your realm and **mine** a
    sect of perilous consequence such as would have no kings but a

presbytery and take **our** place, while they enjoy **our** privilege, With a shade of God's word which none is judged to follow right without by their censure they be so deemed. Yea, look **we** well unto them when they have made in **our** people's hearts a doubt of **our** religion and that **we** err if they say so what perilous issue this may make, **I** rather think than mind to write (6th July 1590, to James VI, QEIC correspondence).

At first glance, it appears that the referents of the first-person plural are clearly set out—'your realm and mine'—and thus the pronoun operates as inclusive *we*: *I* (Elizabeth) + James. However, the topic refers to explicitly sovereign matters: 'our place', 'our Privilege', 'our people's hearts', 'our religion', terms that Elizabeth conventionally refers to using *royal we*. In this letter, the shared status of Elizabeth and James blurs the distinction between the two senses, constructing an inclusive *we* with royal emphasis: Elizabeth and James, as princes. Whilst Mueller might be inclined to see this self-reference as an act of friendship, I believe it has an underlying function of persuasion and authority. Elizabeth's status as the older, more experienced monarch enables her to impress her opinions and judgements onto James, through the illusion of shared experiences and the indexical strengths of the royal pronoun. James' usage of the first-person pronouns is discussed below.

12.4 *Stylistic Factors*

A comparison between Elizabeth's correspondence and her parliamentary speeches (there are no tokens in Elizabeth's translations) indicates that *royal we* is far less common in the latter genre, at only 0.5%. Furthermore, the absence of *royal we* is contrasted by the frequency of *I* (72.3 times per 1000 words), which is much higher than in her correspondence.[37] This indicates that the low figure for *royal we* is not attributable to a lack of possible contexts, but instead presumably reflects Elizabeth's selection of first-person *I* as her self-reference pronoun.

The two examples of *royal we* occur in a single speech dating from 1586. The context of this speech is particularly fraught. Elizabeth was reluctantly responding to parliament's petition for the death warrant of Mary, Queen of Scots. Throughout the events of the mid-1580s, Elizabeth was far less eager than her government to deal in any decisive manner with her cousin, despite Mary's attested involvement with numerous conspiracies to end her life. The context of the speech may explain why Elizabeth uses *royal*

---

[37] The difference between the speeches and post-accession correspondence is statistically highly significant (p > 0.001).

Table 45. *Royal we* (%) and normalised frequencies of *I* and *royal we* (QEIC speeches and post-accession correspondence)

	Total	% *royal we*	*I*/1000 words	*Royal we*/ 1000 words
Speeches	433	0.5	72.3	0.3
PostA correspondence	1915	7.5	51.9	4.2

we, in contrast to her normal preferences for the genre. The switch to *royal we* can be understood as a strategy to legitimise her hesitation over her decision by reinforcing her monarchic authority and ensuring her subjects are aware of the magnitude (holy, regal and political) of any decision that she makes.

(146) **I** think it very requisite with earnest prayer to beseech His Divine Majesty so to illuminate **mine** understanding and inspire **me** with His grace as **I** may do and determine that which shall serve to the establishment of His church, preservation of your estates, and prosperity of this commonwealth under **my** charge. Wherein for that **I** know delay is dangerous, you shall have with all conveniency **our** resolution delivered by **our** message (12th November 1586, QEIC speeches).

The fact that *royal we* appears in only one speech in the corpus indicates that there was a stylistic difference in Elizabeth's usage between the genres. One possible explanation is the difference in interactive contexts. Unlike the one-to-one communication of Elizabeth's letters, Elizabeth's speeches address her councillors and other individuals who are part of the state machine; men who, within the two bodies theory, are also part of the *royal we* reference. Elizabeth's decision to mainly use *I* in this genre may therefore reflect the tension that could arise from the use of *royal we* in speeches that instruct and authorise the actions of the same individuals who grant that authority. If the hypothesis is accurate, then the two instances of *royal we* in the 12th November speech indicate the gravity of Elizabeth's situation. By using *royal we*, Elizabeth is drawing explicitly on the ideology of English kingship, and her unique God-appointed position. In the final line of the extract, the contrast between the second-person address 'you' and the self-reference 'our message' constructs a distinction between the human authority behind Elizabeth's sovereignty (her parliament), and Elizabeth's lineage as the English monarch, appointed by God. *Royal we* makes it clear to Elizabeth's parliament that the significance of the decision relating to Mary, Queen of Scots, is a matter of the highest importance, one that those without royal blood cannot fully comprehend.

12.5 *Comparison With Other Royal Idiolects*

In the other investigations presented in this study, the analysis uses macro-level data to make a systematic comparison between Elizabeth's idiolect and the contemporary preferences of social groups. For *royal we*, this type of comparison is not possible. The defining property of the English monarch during the Tudor period was their singular and unique status as the God-appointed ruler. However, following the earlier exploration of contemporary dramatic depictions of the royal pronoun, it seems pertinent to establish the function of *royal we* in the language of Elizabeth's predecessors and contemporaries, first by consulting some existing studies that have examined *royal we*, before looking at the correspondence of Mary, Queen of Scots, and James VI of Scotland.

Nevalainen (2002) examines the CEEC sub-file for Elizabeth's father, Henry VIII. In her analysis of his language and letters, she notes that the king's most informal correspondence, the love letters to Anne Boleyn, do not use *royal we* but *I*:

(147) For **I** ensure yow, me thynkth the tyme lenger syns your departyng (Henry VIII 1528; HENRY8, 136) (Nevalainen 2002: 172).

Whilst there are no love letters by Elizabeth in QEIC, her selection of *I* in affectionate letters to Robert Dudley ((148)) and Robert Devereux is comparable to her father's preferences.

(148) Rob, **I** am afraid you will suppose by **my** wandering writings that a midsummer moon hath taken large possession of **my** brains this month (19th July 1586, to Robert Dudley, QEIC correspondence).

Excepting the letters to Anne Boleyn, Nevalainen reports only a few other non-*royal we* letters, such as early letters to Thomas Wolsey (Nevalainen 2002: 173). The prominence of *royal we* possibly reflects Henry VIII's lack of interest in letter writing. The king commissioned a stamp to replicate his signature, in order to avoid the laborious process of hand-signing royal documents (Goldberg 1990: 261)—a clear contrast with the continually lavish signature of his youngest daughter. It is feasible that Henry did not require or develop the more nuanced associations of *I* and *royal we* that occur in Elizabeth's autograph correspondence.

Another comparison can be found in sixteenth-century France. Dickerman and Walker (1999) discuss the correspondence of King Henri III of France (1574–1589), focusing on a letter dated from 1584, before the king's sudden dismissal of his entire advisory council in 1588. Henri's usage of first-person pronouns, they suggest, is revelatory of how the French king allocated blame and diffused responsibility for his actions. They suggest that:

[Henri] expanded the boundaries of self from the solitary 'I' to a collective 'we'. By including his advisers as agents, Henri III assigned responsibility for his reign's disasters not to himself alone but to a kind of corporate self. Here Henri distinguished between 'us', the corporate self comprising king and ministers, who had been agents of misgovernment, and 'I', the individual self, who perceived and commented on the action (Dickerman & Walker 1999: 82).

The correspondence contains the first-person singular *je* and the first-person plural *nous*. Importantly, Dickerman and Walker caution against interpreting the latter as a true *royal we*. In Henri's usage, he explicitly refers to his ministers to make them implicit in the mistakes of his reign—the 'corporate agents of misrule' (Dickerman & Walker 1999: 82). It is true that Elizabeth's usage of *royal we* makes a similar gesture towards the political foundation of her power, but the references to 'our subjects' or 'our land' typically confirm the unity between Elizabeth and those who sanction her rule. In Henri III's correspondence, the French King's *nous* is explicitly *I* and *you*. Thus, 'when Henri felt righteous or angry, he stood alone and used "I" consistently', disassociating himself from the actions he has assigned to the collective 'nous' of his ministers (Dickerman & Walker 1999: 84). Henri's usage of the first-person pronouns in his autograph letters differs from the English system, as he avoids *royal we* to use the first-person plural. Yet despite these differences, the correspondence of Henri III indicates the political and social significance of pronominal self-reference in royal idiolects in the pursuit of personal goals in the public gaze.

The correspondence of Mary, Queen of Scots, provides an interesting comparison with Elizabeth's usage. Mary's first language was French, and her autograph letters are predominantly written in this language. However, the scribal letters written after her arrival in Scotland as Queen in 1561 are written in Scots English. In the six letters consulted (Pollen 1904) from the 1560s, written before Mary's deposition in 1567, *I* and *royal we* follow the autograph/scribal distinction seen in Tudor English correspondence. In a scribal letter addressed to Queen Elizabeth on 5th January 1561–2, *royal we* occurs continuously. Given the content, it is possible that Mary elected to use a scribe for this letter to grant her argument the extra authority endowed by *royal we*:

(149) **We** know how neir **we** ar discendit of the blude of Ingland, and quhat devisis hes bene attempt to make **us** as it wer a strangear from it. **We** traist, being so neir zous cousine, ze wald be alith **we** suld ressave so manifest ane injurie, as awnterlie to be debarrit from that title, quhilk in possibilitie may fall unto **us** (Pollen 1904: 70).

In an autograph letter to Queen Elizabeth, written in French, Mary uses first-person *I* throughout, to discuss more personal and intimate matters ((150)). The letter lacks any lexical items that, in Elizabeth's idiolect, might have triggered a pronoun switch. The other autograph letters from this period do not contain any examples of *royal we*, which could indicate that Mary did not use the royal pronoun in her autograph letters.[38]

> (150) Vous voies ma bonne Sœur comme sellon lasuranse que maues
> *You see my good Sister like as to the assurance that*
> 'You see, my good sister, how, in accordance with the assurance that you
> donnee de le prandre en bonne part,
> *gave to take to take in good part*
> you have given me that you would take it in good part
> je parle franchemant aveques vous
> *I speak frankly with you,*
> I am speaking frankly with you
> me fiant encous de tout ce quit me touche,
> *trusting in you in all that touches me*
> trusting myself to you in all that concerns me'
> (Pollen 1904: 66–67—Pollen's translation).

In the correspondence of Mary's son, James VI of Scotland, the scribal/autograph distinction is also consistently upheld. In the 29 autograph letters to Elizabeth found in the Camden Society edition (Bruce 1849), James refers to himself using *I* throughout. Interestingly, he does not switch to *royal we* when referring to topics of the crown or state. The few occurrences of *we* are true first-person plurals ((153)). Autograph letters that James wrote to other recipients, such as Robert Cecil (see Bruce 1861), also use *I* and not *royal we*.

> (151) For this effect then have **I** sent yow this present, hereby to offer unto yow **my** forces, **my** person, and all that **I** may command, to be imployd agains yone strangearis (1st August 1588, to Elizabeth I) (Bruce 1849: 52).
> (152) **I** thocht goode [...] to assure you that the Spanische flete neuer entered uithin any roade or heauen within **my** dominion, nor neuer

---

[38] The nature of Mary's self-reference from her deposition onwards is an area too large for the present study, but deserves further analysis. The polemic and propaganda of the Scottish Queen was a battle of words, including the intercepted letters, forgeries and cyphers written by those directly involved, as well as in the literature of the period (see Shrank 2010). The distribution of *I* and *royal we* and other self-reference forms in Mary's scribal and autograph correspondence from this time may provide further insight into this period of Mary's life. As John Guy notes, Mary considered herself an 'absolute queen' until her execution in 1586 (2004: 488), and during her trial 'demanded to be judged only by her own words and writing' (2004: 483).

came uithin a kenning neere to any of **my** costis (September 1588, to Elizabeth I) (Bruce 1849: 55).

(153) For the further satisfaction quhairof to both **oure** honouris (7th December 1593, to Elizabeth I) (Bruce 1849: 98).

When compared with Elizabeth's correspondence, the egocentricity of phrases such as 'my dominion' and 'all that I may command' are striking. Plausibly, the contrast may reflect the strong Scottish tradition of absolute monarchy (the belief that a king answered to no one but God), which had been perpetuated by the long and unbroken descent of the Stewart line, and for which James would become a strong advocate (Gadja 2010: 90). Perhaps this tradition also resulted in autograph *I* in his correspondence, rather than the more cautious and political *royal we* found in Elizabeth's correspondence.

The evidence from the correspondence of Henry VIII, Henri III, Mary, Queen of Scots, and James VI of Scotland suggests that Elizabeth's use of *royal we* and *I* operates within the broad conventions of sixteenth-century royal correspondence. Like her father's letters, *royal we* is absent from her more intimate letters and is used continuously in the official documents. However, Elizabeth appears to have incorporated *royal we* into her post-accession idiolect more fully than her predecessors or contemporaries, using the scope of *I* and *royal we* to construct and redefine her relationships with her recipients. Her usage potentially reflects the ideology of the King's Two Bodies and shows respect for the powers invested in her by 'our subjects'. The scope for variation in a monarch's usage of *royal we* and *I* identified here highlights the need for further research into monarchic pronouns in English and elsewhere.

12.6 *Other Pronouns of Self-Reference*

Discussion has so far concentrated on the variation between *I* and *royal we*. However, this is not the only change in Elizabeth's self-reference to occur after her accession. In addition to *royal we*, Elizabeth's correspondence also contains examples of the first-person plural *we*. A small number of these can be discussed collectively as they refer to Elizabeth's membership within a group of monarchs. These instances of the first-person plural, termed *exclusive monarchic we*, present Elizabeth's royal authority differently to *royal we*. She is not referring to specific contemporary royals (with whom she had changeable political relations) but to the larger body politic of her immortal ancestry. There are four occurrences of this pronominal self-reference in the post-accession QEIC correspondence; two in a letter to Sir Thomas Heneage, and two in a letter to Catherine Knyvett, Lady Paget.

(154) **We** princes be wary enough of **our** bargains think you I will be bound by your speech to make no peace for mine own matters without their consent? [...] I am assured of your dutiful thoughts but I am utterly at squares with this childish dealing (27th April 1586, to Thomas Heneage, QEIC correspondence).

This rebuke to Heneage was written after he had deliberately withheld a message to Robert Dudley during the Netherlands campaign, much to Elizabeth's frustration. The letter makes clear her opinion on his transgression. She uses *I* throughout, except for the switch shown in (154). In the extract, *exclusive monarchic we* enables Elizabeth to foreground her authority and distinguished position, working within the ideology of Tudor kingship, but in a way that lacks the explicit distance and consciousness of office seen in letters containing continuous *royal we*. The gentleness of Elizabeth's criticism is evident in the final line, where she expresses her appreciation for Heneage's loyalty (using *I*) but frustration over his actions.

The letter to Lady Paget has a different function, but draws similarly on the greater benevolence of *exclusive monarchic we*. The short text conveys Elizabeth's condolences on the death of Paget's daughter, reassuring Paget that it is part of God's plan:

(155) Call to your mind good Kate how hardly **we** princes can brook a crossing of **our** commands. How ireful will the highest power may be you, be sure when murmur shall be made of his pleasing will. Let Nature therefore not hurt your self but give place to the Giver. And though this lesson be from a sely vicar yet is it sent from a loving Sovereign (c. 1570, to Catherine Knyvett, Lady Paget, QEIC correspondence).

The sensitivity of the topic, along with the affectionate address 'good Kate' and self-reference forms 'a loving sovereign', are indicative of a personal and intimate communication. The selection of *exclusive monarchic we* adds a regal authority to the letter, and provides a level of reassurance to the recipient, appropriate to the occasion, that is not accessible to ordinary individuals. Elizabeth, as the God-appointed sovereign, could write authoritatively of God's plan surrounding Paget's bereavement: 'give place to the Giver'. Katherine Duncan-Jones (2007: 33) writes that Elizabeth 'believed she could heal someone she loved simply with the power of her own concern and affection'. Within the context of this particular letter, we can see that this belief was not born out of mere vanity or self-importance, but from the ideology at the foundation of Elizabeth's royal identity as represented by her personal construction of *exclusive monarchic we*.

Exclusive monarchic we also occurs in Elizabeth's parliamentary speeches. Unlike *royal we*, the form allows Elizabeth to distinguish herself from her subjects (and addressees) at parliament by invoking her unique genealogy, and thus avoid the political conflict connected to the connotations of the royal pronoun. It needs to be noted that the examples are only found in the speeches from 1586, both of which relate to Mary, Queen of Scots, and one of which contains the only instances of *royal we* in this genre. The extremity of impending regicide appears to have necessitated different self-reference tactics than the subject-matter of earlier speeches, such as Elizabeth's marriage, offering linguistic support for Somerset's observation (1991: 555) that Elizabeth was 'in inner turmoil at the prospect of having to turn predator on one of her own kind' whilst subject to continual pressure from her councillors. In the following extract, Elizabeth uses *exclusive monarchic we* to explain (or excuse) her delayed response to the petitioned death warrant:

(156) And all little enough: for **we** princes, I tell you, are set on stages in the sight and view of all the world duly observed. The eyes of many behold **our** actions; a spot is soon spied on **our** garments, a blemish quickly noted in **our** doings. It behooveth **us** therefore to be careful that **our** proceedings be just and honourable. But I must tell you one thing more: that in this late Act of Parliament you have laid an hard hand on me, that I must give direction for her death, which cannot be but most grievous and an irksome burden to me (12th November 1586, QEIC speeches).

The switch to *I* marks the shift to a more personal topic, re-focusing her audience's attention through the direct assertion 'I must tell you one more thing' and providing her subjective evaluation of events: 'a hard hand on me', 'grievous and [...] irksome'. The contrast between *we* and *I* carefully delineates between Elizabeth's monarchic role and her more private self, thus enhancing the validity of both the public and private components of her argument.

Third-person pronouns also have a role in Elizabeth's post-accession self-reference system. The self-directed forms, *she* and *her*, are admittedly less frequent than true first-person pronouns, and occur only in the final three decades of the correspondence with the majority concentrated in the final 14 years, 1589–1603.

The following example demonstrates that Elizabeth uses the pronoun to differentiate between her role as queen and that of letter-writer, to a stronger degree than *royal we* and *I*. In the extract, she informs her cousin Charles Blount, Lord Mountjoy, that his service to her in Ireland has been appreciated:

Table 46. Third person self-reference
(QEIC post-accession)

	Third person (n.)	Third person/ 1000 words
1560s	0	0.0
1570s	0	0.0
1580s	5	0.37
1590s	18	1.0
1600s	3	1.0

(157) Comfort yourself therefore in this, that neither your careful endeavours nor dangerous travails, nor heedful regards to **our** service, without your own by-respects, could ever have been bestowed upon a prince that more esteems them, considers and regards them, than **she** for whom chiefly, **I** know, all this hath been done, and who keeps this verdict ever in store for you, that no vainglory nor popular fawning can ever advance your forward but true vow of duty and reverence of prince which two afore your life **I** see you do prefer (Charles Blount, 3rd December 1600, QEIC correspondence).

Here, Elizabeth switches from *I* to both *royal we* and *she*. *I* refers to Elizabeth-as-letter-writer, and the switch to *royal we* refers to Blount's commitment to Elizabeth as his sovereign: 'our service'. The reference *she* also refers to Elizabeth's royal position (indicated by the preceding noun 'a prince') but the third-person pronoun creates a temporary distinction between Elizabeth, the first-person letter-writer and her sovereign identity.

Elizabeth's motive for the pronoun switch may reflect the different indexical properties of royal self-reference pronouns. At this point in the letter, Elizabeth is thanking Blount for his service to her in a royal capacity. He is serving in Ireland on behalf of Elizabeth, as his queen, and as a representative of the government and royal office. The pronominal index for the first-person pronouns suggests that *royal we* would be the appropriate form of self-reference here; recall the pronoun switch in the letter to Harington, (142) above. However, the authoritative force of *royal we* may make this pronoun unsuitable for a letter written to convey gratitude, particularly when Elizabeth's default self-reference to her cousin is the more personal, intimate *I*. The indirect, third-person self-reference provides an alternative way for Elizabeth to construct her relationship with the recipient, allowing her to articulate the regal context of Blount's service—'she for whom chiefly [...] all this hath been done'—whilst at the same time expressing a personal and direct appreciation by continuing to use first-person I: 'I know'. The example provides further insight into how Elizabeth correlated the linguistic options available to her with the different and distinct aspects of her social position after her accession.

12.7 *Summary*

The function of first- and third-person pronouns in Elizabeth's correspondence and speeches clearly demonstrate Wales' assertion that pronouns express 'social, political and rhetorical issues of culture, relationships and power' (Wales 1996: xii). In Elizabeth's idiolect, the forms are acutely aligned with her unique social position and show an intrinsic connection to her accession. The acquisition of *royal we* was an inevitability, pre-determined by the social conventions and conceptualisation of kingship during the sixteenth century. However, the choice between the two pronouns (*royal we* and *I*) allows her to distinguish acts and decisions made in a state capacity from her personal opinions, and to identify herself to her subjects more or less explicitly as their queen. The other self-reference pronouns, *exclusive monarchic we* and *she*, suggest that the bipartite first-person system did not always allow Elizabeth the precision of self-reference that she desired, and the additional forms permit greater nuances in the identity she presents in her letters and speeches.

The first-person pronouns may prove a useful feature for authorship attribution. The specificity of the contexts in which Elizabeth selects *royal we* (e.g. lexical collocates), as well as her apparent idiosyncrasy when compared with her royal contemporaries, provide clear parameters for the analysis of any interactive texts (correspondence, speeches) written predominantly in *I*. The analysis of official correspondence, however, may be less productive. The role of continuous *royal we* in the three letters from QEIC offers no variables to explore, and suggests that determining the authorship of more official documents may not be possible based on this feature alone.

From one perspective, the idiosyncratic nature of *royal we* and *I* could limit their value for historical sociolinguistics and the insight provided by idiolectal data. The acquisition of the royal pronoun is a highly localised rather than macro-level process of language change. However, the distribution and function of the first-person pronouns in Elizabeth's idiolect provide valuable information about the indexical role of pronouns in communication. In particular, pronoun switches, as the deviation from the normal mode of expression, are a key component in Elizabeth's use of the variant. Further analysis of *royal we* in the idiolects of other English monarchs, and the interaction with other self-reference pronouns, will establish if her usage is typical. It is not clear, for instance, if the absence of political collocates in the letters by James VI is a curiosity of James' writing, or if the collocates are an idiosyncratic feature of Elizabeth's. Further study will also help us to understand the transmission process of the royal pronoun—the succession from monarch to monarch which survived the Early Modern period and now exists in a new guise as *presidential we* (Wales 1996: 64).

13. Spelling[39]

The methods and theories of Labovian variationist sociolinguistics underpin much of the historical sociolinguistic approach. As a consequence, the framework plays a significant role in how historical idiolects are also studied. An analysis of spelling variation may thus appear an incongruous inclusion amongst the otherwise expected researches into morphosyntactic variables. Conventionally, spelling has occupied a marginal position in sociolinguistics. The traditional promotion of spoken language, perhaps especially due to the focus on phonological change, has sidelined properties specific to the written mode such as spelling (Smith 1996: 55). However, for historical language studies it seems rather curious that spelling has not been considered to any significant extent by sociolinguists in the past, although a recent exception is Nevalainen (2012). Developing the historical sociolinguistic approach to incorporate such modal elements is arguably a natural progression for the field. Spelling occupies the mid-point between linguistic form and the material properties of a manuscript. For the QEIC corpus, spelling provides the means through which all the data on Elizabeth's idiolect is drawn.

The analysis of Elizabeth's spelling is thus not only the first systematic study of this facet of her writing, it is a means to test and explore the applicability of the sociolinguistic framework for the study of sixteenth-century spelling. The investigation of historical spelling practices is not without its difficulties, and many of the following interpretations require caution and caveats. What is clear is that spelling variation can be correlated and explained by social factors, in a comparable manner to many morphosyntactic features previously identified in Elizabeth's idiolect. Her spelling system offers another perspective on the relationship between her life and language.

[39] A version of this chapter first appeared in *Studies in Variation, Contacts and Change in English*: Volume 10: Outposts of Historical Corpus Linguistics: From the Helsinki Corpus to a Proliferation of Resources. I am grateful to the editors and publishers for their permission to reproduce parts of that content here.

13.1 *Background*

Until the fifteenth century, spelling conventions were largely regional. This has allowed scholars to trace the provenance of manuscripts based on a cross-reference of spelling forms, known as the fit technique (see McIntosh et al. 1986). In the sixteenth century, however, the regional systems gave way to a broader, countrywide arrangement. The conventions used by a writer were determined by that writer's personal preference and knowledge of different systems; these could include regional and international conventions, and their own idiosyncratic preferences. As D.G. Scragg (1974: 68) notes, 'variation between writers was considerable, but the spelling of well educated individuals, though it might be idiosyncratic, was rarely totally haphazard'. The adjective 'idiosyncratic' suggests that there is considerable scope for variation, and the development of idiolect-specific systems. This situation is largely contemporary with Elizabeth's life and reign. After the turn of the century, spelling becomes largely standardised with far less individual variation. The study of spelling in PDE is therefore a different process, perhaps with some limitations, due to the wide reach of standardised spelling. However, text messages (SMS) and other new media offer an exciting new dimension for this field, and the social significance of spelling remains prominent (see Grant 2010).

Elizabeth's spelling system has received sporadic scholarly attention. Pemberton, in the introduction to her edition of the Boethius translation, suggests the Queen's spelling is 'untrammelled by any rules whatever' (1899: xii), a statement that contradicts Scragg's careful description of the spelling of the period cited above. F.J. Furnivall, in the same volume, considers aspects of Elizabeth's spelling 'peculiar' when compared with the practices of some of her contemporaries (1899: xvi–vii). His remark could suggest that Elizabeth used a spelling system defined by particularly idiosyncratic spellings.

More recent comments on Elizabeth's spelling offer different, and contradictory, opinions. Salmon (1999: 30) considers the Queen to be 'reasonably consistent'. Her opinion is shared by Scragg (1974: 69), who notes that whilst her spelling 'is not stable, it is the most part predictable'. Scragg bases his statement on the spellings found in Elizabeth's letters to James VI.[40] Conversely, Blake suggests that 'Elizabeth's letters show an extraordinary range of spellings' (2000: 74), implying that her system is highly variable and thus inconsistent—the opposite of Salmon's assessment. Blake does not explain on which letters his interpretation is based.

---

[40] In a footnote, Scragg (1974: 69, fn.2) notes that there are occasionally 'curious errors' in Elizabeth's spelling. His description firstly places a modern sensibility upon spelling 'correctness', and, secondly, the example he gives to support his opinion is not, in fact, an error. He suggests that *signe Emanuel* for *sign manual* is a mistake. Yet, as Mueller notes (2000: 1067), this is not a spelling 'error' but rather a pun on the Hebrew *Emmanuel* meaning, 'God-with-us', and the *sign manual*, the autograph of the monarch.

There is thus a clear discrepancy in the opinions of scholars regarding Elizabeth's spelling system, a discrepancy that has presumably arisen because there has not yet been a detailed, systematic study of her spelling preferences. None of the scholars referred to above explain their methodology, and many do not specify the source material that they consulted. The original spelling corpus (QEISC) offers an opportunity to address these past limitations, and provide a transparent and replicable analysis of Elizabeth's spelling system using a sociolinguistic framework.

The analysis is necessarily experimental. There are few precedents for the study of idiolectal spelling variation. Previous studies of historical spelling practice have largely focused on the spelling conventions used within a particular text or texts (e.g. Blake 1965; Taavitsainen 2000; Caon 2002) or on the larger historical and political context of the historical period (e.g. Shrank 2000; Nevalainen 2012). These offer some useful guidelines, although certain methodological and interpretative challenges are specific to idiolectal data.

The existing studies conducted from a sociolinguistic perspective suggest the potential insight of an idiolectal analysis, although they are concerned with PDE and LModE systems. Sebba's monograph (2007) examines the sociolinguistics of spelling in modern contexts, such as the significance of graffitied forms in present-day Spain and their deviance from the standardised system. His analysis shows that the selection of spelling forms can have as much social significance as phonological or morphosyntactic variables. Osselton (1984) and Sairio (2009) discuss the distribution of abbreviated and full word forms in LModE, noting the association of the former with private correspondence. Sönmez (2000) provides an illuminating analysis of seventeenth-century spelling, using Lady Brilliana Harley and William Cavendish as a case study for the perceived and real 'gender divide' in historical 'irregular' spelling. Nevalainen (2012) provides a persuasive exploration of the fit between spelling developments and the stages of standardisation for the period 1400–1500. Her studies draw on the concept of focusing, 'the high level of agreement in a language community as to what does, and what does not, constitute "the language"' (2012: 127), to provide a useful conceptualisation of the narrowing and reduction of variation that occurred in the Middle English and Early Modern English periods, across public and private (printed and manuscript) texts. Her analysis explores regional and register-based practices, and her focus is very much on the macro-level, rather than the spelling preferences and developments at the site of the individual.

The relative scarcity of detailed sociolinguistic studies of sixteenth-century spelling is surprising, particularly given the retention of original spelling in corpora such as CEEC and HC. Yet, one reason for the omission may reflect the fragility of spelling in the transmission process of historical texts. N&R-B (2003: 44) suggest that the mixed origin of the transcriptions (apograph manuscripts, edited published collections) make CEEC un-suitable for a scrupulous study of spelling. The different editorial principles, the opportunity for transcription error, and the overall distance from the original text (which, in some cases, will in fact reflect the spelling of a scribe, not the named author) make data collection on a large scale a tricky and time-consuming enterprise. Indeed, the questionable authenticity of spelling in CEEC impedes the extent to which the corpus can be used as a comparative baseline in the present analysis, and presents another methodological challenge for the study of this feature in Elizabeth's idiolect.

The theoretical motivation for a sociolinguistic study of sixteenth century spelling is less problematic. Salmon (1999: 15, 17) suggests that age, class, and education all influence a writer's spelling practice during the sixteenth century; the same social factors investigated for the morphosyntactic variables in Elizabeth's idiolect. Salmon offers detailed scenarios to explain how these factors influence an individual's spelling system. She (1999: 30) finds that education was a key factor in the consistency of an individual's spelling system, as well as in their graph combination preferences. As a rule of thumb, she suggests that the less educated the individual, the less consistent their spelling. The relationship between education and spelling hinges on the connection between spelling and literacy; a higher level of education equates to more frequent and broader exposure to the spelling conventions of other writers and languages, as well as that individual's greater experience with producing their own written communication (Daybell 2001: 60–61). Familiarity with Latin or continental spelling conventions may result in their incorporation into that individual's English spelling, whereas a less educated individual may use regional conventions, such as the infamous and problematic 'dialect' spelling of Henry Machyn (see Wilson 1963).

A necessary addition to Salmon's observations is the proposition that, as education is not a static experience but one in which the pupil advances in over time, a writer's knowledge and familiarity with spelling conventions would similarly increase over time. It is perhaps reasonable to suggest that a spelling system will become more consistent as the writer gets older and their output becomes increasingly habitual.

Applying these theoretical correlates to Elizabeth, it is expected that she will show a high level of spelling consistency, reflecting the influence of her education, her exposure to texts and documents from a range of sources and languages, and her frequent written output (as evidenced by the autograph material collected in QEIC). The hypothesis for real time development is particularly relevant for the influence of Elizabeth's accession on her idiolect. Historians (Woudhuysen 2007: 13) have speculated that the volume of written documents received and produced by Elizabeth during her reign was much higher than her pre-accession output, offering a potential trigger for the modification of her spelling practice after her accession.

A discussion of spelling within a sociolinguistic framework also needs to consider the potential influence of contemporary attitudes to spelling. My analysis has found that Elizabeth is highly sensitive to the stylistic properties of morphosyntactic variables, and this may also be the case in her spelling. Based on a remark she made to James VI, written in 1598, she was certainly aware of the value judgements placed on spelling in her lifetime:

(158) The argument of my letter my dear brother if it should have the theme that your messenger's late embassade did chiefly treat of would yield such a terror to my hand that my pen should scarce afford a right orthography to the words it wrote unnaming therefore what it was (26th December 1598, to James VI, QEIC correspondence).

Elizabeth implies that her spelling may suffer as a result of James' actions, of course, rather than because of any inadequacies on her part.

The reference to a 'right orthography' reflects a growing contemporary awareness of spelling forms and consistency in the period. In the first decades of the sixteenth century there is little widespread concern for consistent English spelling, either in print or manuscript form (Salmon 1999: 25). However, from the 1540s onwards interest in spelling reform increases, part of a wider movement to 'enforce a national identity' through a process of linguistic standardisation (Shrank 2000: 180). The scholars involved were prominent educated men associated with the Court and the Universities, including Sir John Cheke and Roger Ascham (Salmon 1999: 20; Shrank 2000: 180). In the latter half of the century there are repeated attempts to push English spelling towards a regular, consistent system. Salmon (1999: 27) reports that such attempts failed, in the sense that the specific suggestions for graph combinations and sound representation were not adopted, although a standardised system was finally achieved in the seventeenth century.

The breadth of the reformist movement (for a succinct overview for the sixteenth century, see Nevalainen (2012)) means that it is necessary to focus the analysis on two reformists with whom Elizabeth had direct contact: Sir John Cheke and William Patten. Sir John Cheke tutored the young Prince Edward and Princess Elizabeth in 1544, and it is feasible that his opinions on spelling would have been impressed upon the young royal siblings. William Patten, a courtier, and colleague of William Cecil, Lord Burghley, and Sir Christopher Hatton, also devised a reformed system; whilst less well-known than Cheke, Patten is attributed with the transcription of a mock patent (in his spelling system) in 1591, which was issued by Elizabeth to William Cecil after the death of Cecil's wife. May (2004a: xxvii) suggests that Elizabeth was closely involved in its composition.

13.2 *Methodology*

In sociolinguistic investigations of PDE and LModE spelling the significance of spelling variation is identified as being derived predominantly from the contrast between standard and non-standard spelling systems. In EModE, the existence of a standard is difficult to discern, and any standard/non-standard distinction is better described as being at an embryonic stage. Scragg suggests that only by the end of the sixteenth century did a more standardised system emerge, located in the printed texts of the period (1974: 70). Until then, sixteenth-century printers actually had a destabilising effect on spelling, due to European printers conflating foreign graph conventions with existing English ones, and altering spelling to maximise the economy of the page (Salmon 1999: 19; Nevalainen 2012: 148). Consequently, the sociolinguistic analysis of Early Modern spelling from an idiolectal perspective requires a different approach, with different points for comparison, than those used in investigations of LModE and PDE.

Three components offer the best reference points for the period: consistency (i.e. the repeated use of a particular spelling; this does not have to be the rendering now found in Standard PDE), selection of graphs (the letter combinations) and the relationship to the nascent process of standardisation. The literature suggests that these components can be related back to different social factors.

The data for Elizabeth's spelling was gathered from QEISC and sorted manually. A word-list was generated using AntConc and transferred to a database. The word forms were organised according to their PDE standard spelling, with the frequency of each word type and the number of variant spellings for each type both recorded. Advances in software suggest that large-scale investigations of variable spelling will soon be far more plausible. The VARD program (see Baron, Rayson & Archer 2012) was developed to allow the spelling of historical texts to be modernised rapidly and semi-automatically, and the potential of this software is clear. However, at present the software cannot sort and rank different variants according to a head-word (spelling form), which is a crucial stage in the data-sorting process.

Perhaps as a result of the numerous methodological challenges of historical spelling there is not, to my knowledge, a macro-level database of sixteenth century spelling practice. Consequently, the comparative analytic element of the QEISC analysis cannot be made on a large scale, nor across the social spectrum. Instead, comparison between Elizabeth and her contemporaries is made, cautiously, on a case-by-case basis. The prevalence of particular graph combinations is assessed in PCEEC. Word-specific searches are conducted using the sub-files for the sixteenth century, which also includes a small number of letters from the decades either side of this period, to get a sense of the currency of the spelling forms used by Elizabeth and their diachronic distribution. This qualitative approach has been used profitably in analyses of ME spelling (e.g. Smith 1996: 74–75). Unfortunately, the results can only be taken as an indicator, and thus the full significance of Elizabeth's spelling data cannot be realised. It is hoped that technological advances (particularly VARD) and a growing recognition of the merits of spelling analysis will allow a macro-level corpus to come to fruition in the near future.

13.3 Results: Spelling Consistency

The contradictory statements about Elizabeth's spelling hinge on the level and extent of variation found in her writing. Thus the first stage of analysis is to establish, quantitatively, the degree of consistency in Elizabeth's spelling system. By excluding the type/tokens that occur only once in the corpus, it is possible to calculate the level of variation between word type (denoted by italics) and the token form (denoted by < >), e.g. the word type, *marvel*, and the two token forms <marvel> and <marveille>.

The results from QEISC (Table 47) indicate that many spellings are repeated throughout the corpus. 707 word types, occurring at least twice in QEISC, are spelt with only one spelling form. This accounts for over 50% of non-hapax logomena word types. Further evidence of consistency is indicated by the proportion of words being inverse to the level of variation: thus 523 words (37.7%) occur with two different spellings, 108 words (7.8%) with three variants and only 36 words (2.6%) with four variants. At

Table 47. Range of variation in word types that occur twice or more (QEISC)

Variants (n.)	Word types (n.)	%
9 Var	1	0.1
8 Var	0	0.0
7 Var	0	0.0
6 Var	5	0.4
5 Var	9	0.6
4 Var	36	2.6
3 Var	108	7.8
2 Var	523	37.7
1 Var	707	50.9
TOTAL	1389	

the upper reaches are a small number of words with five or more variants; one, *highness*, occurs with nine different forms.

It is unfortunate that there is no macro-level data for comparison to reveal if the figures represent a system more consistent than most. However, in lieu of this, the heavy weighting towards single variants is suggestive of overall spelling consistency, although how typical Elizabeth is of the period is not known. The figures lend support towards Salmon's verdict of 'reasonable consistency' in Elizabeth's spelling, although it is possible to appreciate how Blake may have reached his conclusion of Elizabeth's 'extraordinary range' of spelling, if his opinion was based on a qualitative rather than a quantitative assessment.

The data can be further refined (see Table 48). Currently, the figures represent the ratio of word types to the number of spelling forms. Yet frequency of use is also an important factor when discussing consistency. For example, the significance of the 707 words in the corpus with a single spelling form will be greater if Elizabeth spells these words identically 20 times over, rather than if she uses them only twice. Out of the words with only one variant spelling, 18 (2.5% of single forms) occur over 100 times each in the corpus. All of these words are grammatical, including prepositions (*to*, 783 occurrences; *of*, 623 occurrences), pronouns (*I*, 750 occurrences), and conjunctions (*and*, 638 occurrences). The high level of consistency may therefore be explained both by the qualities of these words—monosyllabic, Germanic—and their high frequency in Elizabeth's correspondence.

In the mid-range frequencies, 80 words occur between 11 and 100 times in QEISC with a single spelling form. This group is made up of a wider range of lexical categories, including proper names (*Elizabeth*, 50 occurrences), common nouns (*cousin*, 36 occurrences) and verbs (first-person present *make*, 84 occurrences). The diversity of the lexis continues in the least frequent 1-variant words, comprising 609 total forms, ranging from 2 to 10 tokens in the corpus: e.g. (*French*, 5 occurrences), (*death*, 7 occurrences), (*declared*, 6 occurrences).

Table 48. Number and % of words with 1-variant (QEISC)

Frequency of single variant spellings	Word forms (n.)	%
2 to 10	609	86.1
11 to 100	80	11.3
101 +	18	2.5
TOTAL	707	100

In the 2–10 occurrences group, 323 of the word types occur only twice in the corpus, equating to 54% of the words with one spelling form (45.6% of all 1-variant words). Interpreting these figures is difficult; on the one hand, the low frequency of the words could disguise variation, yet on the other it may also indicate that Elizabeth had a remarkably stable spelling system that was not restricted to high frequency items such as grammatical words.

13.4 Diachronic Consistency

In order to test the hypothesis that Elizabeth's spelling will show an increase in consistency over time, as a reflection of her education and written output, the spelling variation data is divided into the pre-accession and post-accession periods. The size and composition of the database means that a full-scale study would be highly complex, including interpretative difficulties relating to sparser lexical forms. As a resolution, the diachronic analysis uses a representative sample designed to provide a sufficient quantity of tokens and variants to chart the diachronic development. The sample contains all word types with four or more spelling forms, which have a combined token count of at least five in the corpus. Overall, the sample contains 37 word types that occur in both the pre- and post-accession period: *although, been, believe, conscience, council, councillor, country, doubt, English, even, evil, friends, friendship, honour, loving, might, mind, ought, perceive, persuasions, praying, receive, received, sovereign, subjects, thought, thoughts, through, truth, understand, upon, vain, which, will, willingly, with,* and *wax*. Each word in this group has at least four variant spellings listed in the OED (OED Online), suggesting that the range of variation—if not the actual forms—is not unique to Elizabeth's practice.

Contrary to the hypothesis, the data (Table 49) suggests the level of variation increases between the pre- and post-accession periods. However, the figures do not tell the whole story. One factor not yet accounted for is the weighting of the variant forms, i.e. Elizabeth's preference for one

Table 49. Number of variant spellings in the pre-accession and post-accession periods, based on sample of all words with 4+ variants, occurring 5 times or more (QEISC)

	Variants (n.)	%
PreA words with more variants	5	13.5
PostA words with more variants	25	67.6
Same number of variants in each periods	7	18.9
Total	37	100

variant over another. The (dis)continuity of preferred forms over time will provide a more accurate gauge of consistency in the two sub-periods. The notion of "preference" is defined, numerically and to a degree arbitrarily, as a variant that occurs at least three times more than other variant forms. This entails that some words do not have a preferred spelling and within the smaller pre-accession corpus there could be problems with token counts. However, the sample includes the most frequent word types in the corpus in order to minimise the problem.

The concept of preference is best illustrated with an example. The verb *might* has five variant spellings in QEISC (Table 50). In the pre-accession period, Elizabeth uses three variant forms. In the post-accession period, the word occurs in four variant forms with one variant maintained from the pre-accession period. At this level, the distribution implies that Elizabeth became less consistent in her spelling of this word between the two periods. However, Elizabeth does not use all variants equally. In the pre-accession period, the variant < migth > occurs 8 times, < might > twice and < mighte > once. Thus < migth > is the preferred spelling for this period.

By contrast < might > is the preferred form in Elizabeth's post-accession correspondence, occurring 24 times. The other three variants in this period occur only once each. Therefore, the findings for *might* indicate that Elizabeth has both an overall consistency in her spelling of this word (< might > accounts for 26 of the 38 occurrences in QEISC) and different preferences in each period of the corpus: PreA < migth > = 72.7%, PostA < might > = 88.9%. The percentages suggest that Elizabeth became more consistent in her use of the preferred form in the post-accession period. The difference in preference between the two periods is statistically significant (p > 0.001).

In the sample there is a clear difference in the distribution of preferred spellings in word types found in both sub-periods. Whilst 11 of the words (29.7%) have a preferred variant in the pre-accession part of the corpus, this increases to 24 of the words (64.9%) in the post-accession period, implying that Elizabeth's spelling system increased in consistency over time.

Table 50. Number and proportion (%) of spellings variants: *might* (QEISC)

	Pre-accession	Post-accession
< might >	2	24 (88.9%)
< mighte >	1	1
< migh >	0	1
< migth >	8 (72.7%)	0
< myght >	0	1
Total	11	27

Of the 37 word types that occur in both sub-periods of the corpus, eight have a preferred spelling form in both periods. However, only three of the word types (*been, which* and *with*) maintain a preferred spelling across both periods. Table 51 shows Elizabeth's usage of the preferred variant out of all the forms for that word type in each sub-period. The listed form for these three preferred spellings accounts for at least 80% of the tokens, indicating that Elizabeth is highly consistent in her usage. The three words are a stable element in her spelling system, and may prove useful for authorship assessment. Notably, the three words are grammatical and occur frequently in the corpus. The analysis has already indicated that this word class contributed to the level of consistency with single-variant forms, suggesting that frequency of use is an important factor in the development of Elizabeth's spelling system. The factor may also apply more generally to Early Modern English.

Discontinuous preferred variants, i.e. changes in preference between the pre- and post-accession periods, are more common in the sample taken

Table 51. Continuous variants, pre- and post-accession (QEISC)

	Pre-accession	Post-accession
< bine >	8 (80%)	22 (84.6%)
< wiche >	52 (91.2%)	85 (96.7%)
< with >	34 (100%)	140 (96.6%)

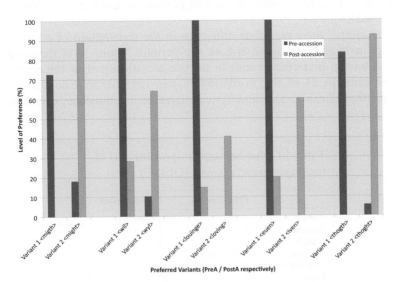

Figure 10: Discontinuous preferred variants (%) (QEISC)

from QEISC. Figure 10 represents this graphically for five different word types: *might, will, loving, even* and *thought*. Overall, the preferred variant from the pre-accession period (variant 1 on the graph) occurs infrequently, if at all, in the post-accession period. Conversely, the preferred variant in the post-accession part of the corpus (variant 2 on the graph) is often present (albeit infrequently) in Elizabeth's earlier writing. The progression from one form to another may indicate a process in which Elizabeth's spelling practice matured and stabilised, perhaps reflecting increased awareness of spelling conventions. The changes in preference, however, do not all move towards the PDE standard spelling: *might* and *loving* become standard, whereas < wyl >, < iven > and < thoght > do not. This suggests that Elizabeth's response to any nascent processes of standardisation was not consistent. Idiosyncratic variation, as noted by Scragg, appears the greater force in Elizabeth's spelling system.

Finally, the sample contains nine words (24%) which show no preferred spelling in either period. *English* has six variants, each form occurring once. The degree of variation for this word is interesting from an historical perspective, as it has obvious political and cultural significance for Elizabeth's position and to the recipients of her correspondence. Similarly, the terms *sovereign* and *councillors* also have no preferred variant in either sub-period. In the sample, these forms are marked for their inconsistency, and contrast with Elizabeth's tendency to have a preferred spelling form.

The results from QEISC indicate that Elizabeth's spelling system increases in consistency over time. Using a measure of preference, Elizabeth's spelling is more variable in the pre-accession period, with the post-accession containing a greater number of preferred forms. Only a few words show consistency throughout Elizabeth's life, and a similar number in the sample show no consistency at any time. The trend appears to support the hypothesis that, as an individual's education progressed, their spelling would develop and stabilise over time. The contrast between the pre- and post-accession periods may also be explained by the increase in Elizabeth's written output once she became queen. Whilst the connection is

Table 52. Variant spellings (number) for English (QEISC)

Variant spellings	Pre-accession (n.)	Post-accession (n.)
< english >	0	1
< englisch >	0	1
< englishe >	1	0
< inglas >	0	1
< inglische >	1	0
< inglis >	0	1

less explicit than the development of *royal we* or the changing function of superlatives, the trend is nevertheless suggestive of change connected to her accession.

Salmon (1999: 30) suggests that Elizabeth's spelling is 'noticeable' for being 'reasonably consistent', a description which appears to find quantitative support in the QEISC data. However, the definition of consistent must remain necessarily impressionistic at present because there is no comparative baseline to provide a definite measure. Hopefully, future investigations into spelling and social stratification can offer the means to support the analysis of Elizabeth's spelling preferences, and improve our understanding of the progression from idiosyncratic spelling systems to the adoption of a standard.

13.5 *Graph Combinations*

The analysis has so far focussed on the large-scale trends of variation and consistency in QEISC. The discussion now shifts to consider the graphs and graph combinations that constitute the cause of that variation. Eight graph combinations form the focus of discussion, selected because of their contribution to the patterns in Elizabeth's spelling practice, although there are many other graph combinations that can be considered representative of Elizabeth's orthographic system. The stabilisation of final < e > (due to standardisation) and the variability of < an/aun > in the spelling of Romance lexis reflect Elizabeth's participation in a general spelling trend. Other combinations show clear changes in preference over time, generally (but not always) towards the now-standard spelling: < sh >, < i/y/e > and < ght > and < gh >. Two graph combinations have a very narrow distribution in Elizabeth's spelling and are highly idiosyncratic, both for the time period and when compared to the trends for Elizabeth's own practice: final < s/z > and initial < wh/w >.

The discussion of graph combinations considers the written dimension only, working on the assumption that the written and spoken modes of language are distinct components of an inter-related system, and thus that one can be discussed without continuous reference to the other. This approach has previously been adopted in the discussion of ME spelling systems. The editors of *A Linguistic Atlas of Late Middle English* point out that 'it is only at one remove that spelling is evidence about spoken language, but it is direct evidence about written language [...] The written language can be studied in its own right' (McIntosh et al., vol. 1 1986: 5; see also Smith 1996). They caution that investigating the phonological dimension of spelling is a 'hazardous undertaking', and that interpretations of concrete written material soon become 'debatable derivative conjectures' when used for evidence of the spoken language (McIntosh et al., vol. 1 1986: 5). The relationship between the written graph and the spoken phoneme is inconsistent throughout the history of English, and focusing on written data as written data allows us to investigate variation that has no equivalent in spoken language (i.e. the interchangeability of <ʒ> and <y>), and treat such instances equally with those that may have a more tangible connection to the spoken word (McIntosh et al., vol. 1 1986: 6). This approach ensures a systematic, comparable and replicable account of the data.

13.6 *Final* <e>

Final <e> is a spelling remnant of the Old English inflection system, which initially represented word-final schwa before it was lost from this context (Caon 2002: 296–297). Writers in the Early Modern period use final <e> haphazardly, and Samuels (1991: 6) observes that, even in ME, scribes would often exercise their own preferences for final <e> when transcribing a text, rather than preserving the system of the exemplar. Scragg suggests that Elizabeth 'pays little heed to final <e> [...] and consequently her spelling is not consistent' (1974: 69). The QEISC data supports Scragg's statement at a general level. Final <e> contributes considerably to the variation in Elizabeth's spelling system, with almost 40% of all word types with two or more spelling forms including one spelling with a final <e>, although this is not necessarily the only point of variation. However, the corpus data can offer a more nuanced exploration of what Scragg means by Elizabeth's 'little heed'.

The following analysis concentrates on words with only two spelling variants. A spelling variant is identified as using final <e> only if the <e> is the exclusive point of difference in the two renderings of the word; for example *therefore* <therefor>, <therefore> is categorised as a final <e> variation, but *wit* <wit> and <witte> is not. For plural nouns, I have counted final <e> if the grapheme is inserted prior to the plural marker, and all other aspects remain equal (e.g. kings <kinges>, <kings>). This provides a focused account of the graph in Elizabeth's spelling.

The level of final <e> in words with only two variant forms is 23.9%. This is a considerable amount if we recall that this includes the words where <e> is the only point of variation, indicating the prominence of the convention within Elizabeth's spelling practice: e.g. *company* <company>, <companye>; *fruit* <fruit>, <fruite>; *would* <wold>, <wolde>. Yet, in the word types with two variants that occurred three times or more, final <e> was the preferred spelling in only 47 of the 125 words (37.6%). This indicates that the graph was, overall, not a preferred form in Elizabeth's practice.

Viewed diachronically, there is a decline over time from 58.2% in the pre-accession period to 31.1% in the post-accession correspondence (p > 0.001) (Table 53). For example, the past participle *were* occurs

Table 53. Preference in 2-word variants with a final < e > form, pre- and post-accession (QEISC) (not all words occur in both periods)

Pre-accession	Word Types (n.)	%
< e > favoured	57	58.2
< e > not favoured	35	35.7
Tied	6	6.1
Total	98	

Post-accession	Word Types (n.)	%
< e > favoured	37	31.1
< e > not favoured	74	62.2
Tied	8	6.7
Total	119	

54 times in QEISC, but the six tokens with final < e > (< were >) are all located in the pre-accession part of the corpus. For the remaining 48 instances in the post-accession correspondence, Elizabeth consistently uses the non- < e > form < wer >. The change in preference may support the hypothesis that the increase in Elizabeth's written output after her accession would affect her spelling; the omission of superfluous graphs such as final < e > would potentially increase speed and productivity. It is worth noting that the characteristics of lower-case < e > in Elizabeth's post-accession hand are themselves very distinctive. Elizabeth uses the secretarial form, but often the two inked dashes are loosely connected and barely legible; indicative, perhaps, of haste (see also Woudhuysen 2007). Alternatively (or relatedly), Salmon (1999: 42) posits that 'educated men were in the process of rejecting unnecessary [...] final < e >s in the early decades of the seventeenth century', citing a letter by Robert Cecil, Lord Burghley as an example. Therefore this may be a case of the queen anticipating a later trend.

To gain some insight into how Elizabeth's use of final < e > compares with contemporary trends, the spelling variants for *thing* and *see* were identified in PCEEC (with the appropriate caution surrounding the accuracy of the data). In QEISC both words show a change from pre-accession final < e > to non-final < e > in the post-accession period. PCEEC informants share Elizabeth's later preference for non-final < e > for *thing*, with more than two-thirds of the tokens occurring without the graph, although there is no clear connection with a particular decade. However, < se > is less common than the now standard < see >. The PCEEC informants who use Elizabeth's preferred spelling < se > include numerous fifteenth-century writers from the Paston and Plumpton correspondence, plus writers from the early sixteenth century including

Henry VIII's sister, Mary Tudor, Queen of France. Robert Dudley, writing in the 1580s, also uses <se>. Thus, neither form is particularly idiosyncratic, although non-final <e> *thing* perhaps shows greater conformity to the norm, whereas Elizabeth's preference for *see* is a move in the opposite direction, away from the form that would become the standard spelling.

13.7 *<an>* and *<aun>*

Blake's (1965) study of spelling evolution within English versions of *Reynard the Fox* found that the use of <au> began to replace single <a> before <n>, 'particularly in words of Romance origin' (1965: 67) in the late fifteenth century, e.g. <penaunce>. In QEISC, Elizabeth's normal practice is to spell the majority of words in this group using <an>, e.g. <continuance>, <assurance>. However, for a select group of 11 words Elizabeth also uses <aun> (see Table 54). Whilst <aun> is sometimes a sporadic variant in these word types, in others Elizabeth uses it repeatedly as the preferred variant. However, establishing a motive for the use of <aun> is problematic, as there is little coherence across the group. For instance, Elizabeth uses the <aun> form in the verb *command*, whereas other words with the same lemma such as past tense *commanded* and the noun *commandment* use only the <an> combination. This would appear to support Scragg's description of the idiosyncratic nature of spelling in the sixteenth century and Elizabeth's habits in particular.

Notably, Elizabeth's use of the <aun> spelling is restricted to words of Latinate (Romance) etymology, e.g. <perchaunce>, <demaunde>, <countenaunce>, suggesting that the use of this grapheme may reflect her familiarity with and exposure to the contemporary association between graph combination and lexical origin (see Blake 1965: 67). Yet this does not explain why many other words of similar heritage lack the <aun> spelling,

Table 54. Words with <aun> and <an> graph combinations

Word	Variants	Total (n.)	% <aun>
danger	danger, dangier, daunger, daungier	14	28.6
command	commande, commaud, commaunde	3	66.7
grant	graunt, grant	13	84.6
dangerous	dangerous, daungerous	8	37.5
repentance	repentance, repentaunce	3	33.3
demand	demande, demaunde	2	50.0
perchance	perchance, perchaunce	2	50.0
arrant	araunte	1	100.0
countenance	countenaunce	1	100.0
countermanded	countermaunded	1	100.0
grants	grauntz	1	100.0
Total		49	55.1

revealing a degree of inconsistency in Elizabeth's practice. Diachronic analysis shows that Elizabeth's use of <aun> became more variable over time. Whilst all tokens in the sample occur with <aun> in the pre-accession data, the graph combination accounts for only 45% (18 out of 40) tokens in the post-accession period. This suggests that Elizabeth became more consistent in spelling these words with the dominant <an> form, paralleling the standardisation of <an> now used in PDE spelling. It is not clear if this shift reflects Elizabeth's personal preference for the graph combination and her inclination towards consistency, or if she was influenced by the nascent developments of a spelling standard within the texts of the period.

In PCEEC, *danger* rendered using <aun> occurs predominantly in letters written in the first half of the sixteenth century, including correspondence by Thomas Cromwell, Thomas Boleyn and Stephen Gardiner. The social status of these men suggests that Elizabeth's early preference may reflect her education, if not the personal preferences of her educators. William Cecil uses both <daunger> and <danger> in his correspondence from the 1580s. This perhaps shows that Elizabeth's use of <aun> in these particular words coheres with the spelling preferences of her contemporaries of similar rank and educational background, potentially reflecting their shared familiarity with the Romance writing systems.

13.8 <sh> Combinations

Elizabeth uses five graph combinations for <sh>: <s>, <ss>, <sch>, <sh> and <ssh>, and the connection between graph combination and word form is relatively stable. 62 words (91%) use one graph combination (36 of these word types are hapax logomena), three word types occur with three combinations, and three words with two combinations. Overall <sh>—now the generalised form in PDE—is the dominant form, accounting for 81.9% of all tokens: e.g. <shortar>, <shewed>, <sonshine>.

Table 55. <sch> combinations by word position (QEISC)

	Initial position	Medial position	Final position
<s>	0 (0%)	2 (3.4%)	4 (10.3%)
<ss>	0 (0%)	1 (1.7%)	1 (2.6%)
<sch>	1 (0.4%)	23 (39%)	31 (79.5%)
<sh>	276 (99.6%)	28 (47.5%)	3 (7.7%)
<ssh>	0 (0%)	5 (8.5%)	0 (0%)
Total	277	59	39

Closer examination shows that Elizabeth uses the graph combinations systematically, with her preference dependent upon the graphs' position within the word. Table 55 shows that < sh > is Elizabeth's preferred combination in initial position at 99.6%: e.g. < shuld >, < shall >, < shameful >, < shadowe >. The alternative < sch > occurs in a single instance of sharply < scharpely > found in a pre-accession letter to Edward VI (29th April 1551, to Edward VI, QEISC).

For medial positions, there is a greater range of variants with all five combinations used by Elizabeth: < sch > and < sh > are the preferred graphs. The preferred combination for final position is also < sch >, e.g. < perische >, < blusche >, < rasche >. The second most frequent graph, < s >, is used in < skottis > and one of two variants for *punish* < punis >. However, the majority of non- < sch > final combinations are attributable to Elizabeth's spelling of *English*: < english >, < englas >, < inglas > as well as < inglische/englisch >. This further suggests that Elizabeth's spelling of *English* is contrary to her general practice.

Diachronic analysis shows that Elizabeth's preferences between the pre- and post-accession periods are similar (see Appendix, Table 74). The dominance of < sh > in initial positions is the case for both periods, at 99% in the pre-accession correspondence and 100% in the post-accession letters. In medial positions, Elizabeth's preferences become less consistent, with < sh > decreasing from 55.2% to 40% across the two periods, and < sch > increasing. Elizabeth's preferences are clearer for final position spellings, with the pre-accession preferred form < sch > (66.7%) becoming even more dominant in the later correspondence (85.2%).

Three words representative of Elizabeth's practice, *short*, *ashamed* and *English*, were examined in PCEEC. There are five variant spellings for *short*. < sh > in initial position accounts for 90.5% (143 of 158 tokens) of all spellings. However, the remaining 9.5% is attributable to the combination < sch >. The informants who use this variant are predominantly members of the Paston family writing in the latter decades of the fifteenth century, suggesting that as a word-initial graph combination, it was perhaps slightly archaic by Elizabeth's lifetime.

The PCEEC informants use only two forms for *ashamed* (n = 29): < sh > (93.1%) and < ssh > (6.9%) graphs respectively. Interestingly, no informants use the < sch > combination preferred by Elizabeth for this word, suggesting that this may have been a less usual spelling.

Finally, PCEEC informants use seven variant spellings for *English*. This indicates that the variation seen in QEISC for this word type parallels the macro-level variation of the word in the Early Modern period. However, only three of the variant forms that occur in PCEEC correspond with Elizabeth's preferences. When assessed for their frequency, < sh > is by far the dominant form occurring in 96.4% of all variants (135 of 140 tokens). The other combinations include < ssh > (used by Anne Boleyn) and a single example containing final <s>. The lack of <sch> in final position is surprising, and provides further evidence that this graph is an idiosyncratic feature of Elizabeth's spelling system. Further consultation of the PCEEC shows that <sch> is quite rare in any word position. However, two notable users of <sch> are Catherine Parr and Henry VIII (see (159)).

> (159) I can no les do then to sende her [Anne Boleyn] summe **flesche** representyng my name, whyche is hart **flesche** for Henry (1528, Henry VIII; Henry8, 128).

A letter (not in PCEEC) written by Elizabeth's governess Kat Ashley shows that <sch> was also her preferred spelling: *she* <sche>, *punishment* <ponysschment>, <ponyschment> and *Ashley* <aschyly>, with only one <sh> form, <shame> (Kat Ashley 1549, in Cusack 1998: 236–238). Elizabeth uses <sch> to spell Ashley's name, possibly copying the practice of her governess: <aschilye, aschiley, aschylye>. The distribution of <sch> thus appears to be localised, firstly to individuals writing in the early sixteenth century, and secondly to those associated with the Court and with Elizabeth.

Although caution is necessary when interpreting the PCEEC data, the currency of <sch> in the writing of influential and prominent individuals in Elizabeth's adolescence may explain the presence of the graph combination in her spelling system and suggests that spelling is susceptible to the same social factors as other linguistic variables. The concept of spelling contact (analogous with dialect contact) can be speculatively used to describe the evidence for <sch>. Sebba (2007: 60) notes that spelling contact is significant to English spelling at the macro level, describing the transmission of international conventions via scribes and printers from the continent. The QEISC findings suggest that the phenomenon also occurs at a localised level, with conventions shared between members of different groups. However, more evidence is needed to establish if Elizabeth's spelling system was extensively influenced by the preferences of her peers, or whether <sch> is a one-off example. The consistency of her spelling practice may have ensured that <sch> was then maintained in her spelling system throughout her life, despite its seeming decline at the macro-level. This distinctive element may prove useful for authorship assessment.

13.9 *<i>, <y> and <e>*

Another key area of variation in Elizabeth's spelling system is her use of <i>, <y> and <e> in initial and final positions of a word. During the sixteenth century, the three graphs were largely interchangeable, although there is some evidence that <y> was perceived as the more archaic spelling in the latter half of the decade. Salmon (1999: 42) reports differences between the manuscript version of a translation by John Harington and the later printed text prepared by Richard Field, with the latter changing <y> to <i> in some instances. The analysis of Elizabeth's spelling practice considers initial and final contexts, and excludes forms with grammatical morphemes such as *–ing* and *–ed*. Overall, the dataset yields six graph combinations: initial positions use three graphs, <i>, <e> and <y>, with final position contexts using the same three, plus a further three options <ie>, <ye> and <ey>.

In initial contexts, <i> is Elizabeth's preferred graph. It is used in 11 of the 14 word types in the sample (78.6%), and in absolute frequency terms it is by far the most dominant, accounting for 667 of the 739 tokens (91.6%). This is mostly due to its usage in high frequency grammatical items, such as *it*, *if* and *is*. However, only *increase* <increas, increase> and *inward* <inward, inwarde> have <i> throughout QEISC. Elsewhere, Elizabeth alternates <i> with other graphs. Of the six spellings for *English*, for example, initial <i> and <e> account for half each. The graph <y> occurs the least in initial position, found in only four word types and accounting for only 9 of the 739 tokens, e.g. <ynough>. For initial position contexts, there is no change in the dominance of <i> between the pre- and post-accession periods.

Final position contexts contain a greater range of variation, with six graph combinations used across 35 word types. The graph <y> occurs in 32 of the word types, making it Elizabeth's preferred form for this position, e.g. *greatly* <greatly, gretly>. The diachronic distribution indicates that Elizabeth becomes more consistent over time. In the pre-accession period, <y> accounts for 68% of final position tokens. By the post-accession period, her spelling practice has stabilised, with <y> the dominant graph at 94% (Table 56).

The data provides evidence in favour of the hypothesis that an individual's spelling system is likely to become more consistent over time. Salmon (1999: 28) notes that final <y> appears to be a preferred spelling in printed texts throughout the sixteenth century, and it is possible that Elizabeth's exposure to printed norms may have contributed to the increase

Table 56. Final position <y, i, e>,
pre- and post-accession, QEISC

	PreA (%)	PostA (%)
<i>	2 (1%)	1 (0.2%)
<e>	0 (0%)	1 (0.2%)
<y>	134 (68%)	389 (94%)
<ie>	28 (14.2%)	11 (2.7%)
<ye>	30 (15.2%)	11 (2.7%)
<ey>	3 (1.5%)	1 (0.2%)
Total	197	414

in consistency of the graph in her spelling system. Her preferences, whilst idiosyncratic, do show a movement towards many forms that would later become the standard.

Unfortunately, analysis of medial position <i, y and e> is not practical due to the difficulties of establishing consistent criteria for analysis; 'medial' can refer to many different positions according to the syllable count of the word, for example. However, there are some notable changes in specific words that warrant brief discussion. Between the pre-accession and post-accession periods, Elizabeth's preferred rendering of *will* shifts from medial <i> (86.7%) to medial <y> (69.2%). The change also applies to the spellings of *mine* and *mind*. It is not clear if there is a rationale behind these particular changes; <i> to <y> does not appear to increase productivity, for example, and it goes against the trend of standardisation.

The PCEEC comparison considers two words characteristic of Elizabeth's practice for the graph combination: *if* and *day*. The PCEEC data for *if* suggests that Elizabeth's preference for initial <i> fits with the general trends of the period; <if> occurs more than 3000 times in the PCEEC sample and is by far the most frequent spelling. The alternative variant used by Elizabeth, <yf> (which occurs twice in QEISC) is second most common in the PCEEC sample, with more than 1000 tokens.

The PCEEC informants also share Elizabeth's preference for <y> in final position, with <day> accounting for over three quarters of the forms. The form characteristic of Elizabeth's pre-accession spelling <daye> is the second most frequent variant in the PCEEC sample. William Cecil and Robert Dudley use the <y> and <ye> variants interchangeably in correspondence from the 1580s.

13.10 *<gh> and <ght>*

During Elizabeth's lifetime, the range of graph combinations for <gh> and <ght> was extensive. The spellings recorded by the OED for *ought* (v.), for example, number over 100 (OED Online). Consequently, the word types in QEISC were selected on the basis of PDE standardised spelling

Table 57. <gh> word types (QEISC)

	Word types (n.)	Word types (%)
1 Var	5	31.3
2 Var	7	43.8
3 Var	1	6.3
4 Var	3	18.8

(e.g. *thought* = < ght >), and this means a number of spelling variants in the sample lack the actual < gh(t) > combination.

The results for < gh > are some of the most variable identified in QEISC, with 10 different graph combinations. Some graphs are word-specific, for example < w > and < we > occur only in *through* < throw >, < throwe >, and the combinations < ie > and < y > are found only in final position monosyllables *weigh* and *high*, suggesting an overlap with Elizabeth's < i >, < y > and < e > spelling habits.[41] There are also diachronic differences (see Appendix, Table 75). The pre-accession correspondence shows the greatest range of combinations, using seven of the ten identified in the corpus, with < gth > being the dominant or preferred form in this period (43.6%). The < gh > graph occupies second spot (41%), with the other variants less frequent. Two words in the pre-accession data show a particularly high level of variation: *although* with variants < gh, ght, gth, ghe >, and *highness* with < gh, gth, g, th >. I have already commented on the variable spellings of the latter word, and it appears that the instability of < gh > is a key contributing factor. Interestingly, the digraph < th > occurs only in the 1540s correspondence ((160)), after which Elizabeth shows an increased preference for variants with < g > ((162)). Example (161) represents what might be described as an intermediate form.

(160) at your **hithnis** hande (June 1548, to Catherine Parr, QEISC).

(161) but made worthy for your **higthnes** request (15th May 1551, to Edward VI, QEISC).

(162) Your **highnes** most faithful subiect (17th March 1554, to Mary I, QEISC).

In the post-accession period, Elizabeth develops a more consistent system. < gh > accounts for 71.6% of all tokens in the sample, and the preferred pre-accession spelling < gth > has declined to 2.7%, found only in < length > and < strength > and thus anticipating the PDE standard spelling.

Overall, the diachronic patterns for < gh > show that Elizabeth's consistency increased between the pre- and post-accession periods, further supporting the hypothesis that her spelling system would stabilise over time. What is not clear from this data is if Elizabeth's inconsistency in her pre-accession writing is representative of a broader macro-level variation for the < gh > graphs in the mid-sixteenth century, or whether it reflects her young age, inexperience or idiolectal preference.

PCEEC contains seven different graph combinations for < gh > in *highness*, including the four used by Elizabeth. The < gh > combination is the most common, and is found in letters written in the 1530s and the 1580s.

---

[41] < w(e) > appears to have been a widespread rendering of *through* at least in ME, documented in the manuscripts of southern scribes (McIntosh et al., vol. 2 1986: 225–229.).

Elizabeth's preferred variant for the pre-accession period <gth> is also present in the PCEEC sample but occurs only twice: <highthnesse> and <hygthness>. Curiously, both examples occur in Paston letters written in 1461, which may indicate that the spelling was somewhat archaic by the time of Elizabeth's correspondence and suggests that the level of spelling variation for this word, and possibly the <gth> combination in general, is an idiosyncratic property of her pre-accession spelling system. The PCEEC informants also use the <ie> and <y> graph combinations that Elizabeth restricts to *high*, *highest* and *weigh*. There is also an additional <h> form not used at all by the Queen: <hyhnes> found in the correspondence of Thomas Wolsey.

Turning to the counterpart graph combination <ght>, it is notable that the 21 words for <ght> extracted from the QEISC database show a higher level of consistency, with 16 words (76.2%) using only one variant. The number of graph combinations is also reduced, with Elizabeth using 3 different forms rather than the 10 found in the <gh> sample (Table 58). <gth> dominates the pre-accession forms (e.g. <sigth>, <thogth>) and <ght> in the post-accession period (e.g. <sight>, <thought>). The switch to <ght> in the post-accession period is dramatic with over 99% of all tokens using this form. A similar, if less striking diachronic shift was also identified in the <gh> data, providing further evidence of the progression towards stability and consistency in Elizabeth's spelling system.

The level of variation in Early Modern spellings of <ght>, as represented by the OED Online entry for *ought*, is also illustrated by the range of combinations for *might* in PCEEC, including fifteenth-century <myt3> and sixteenth-century <miht>. It thus appears significant that the <gth> combination preferred by Elizabeth in her pre-accession correspondence is not found in the macro-level corpus. Even allowing for editorial interference in the corpus transcriptions, it appears that <gth> is an idiosyncratic feature of Elizabeth's pre-accession spelling system for both <gh> and <ght> contexts. The OED does record <gth> in the definition for *might*, but it is dated to the fifteenth, not sixteenth, century (may, v.1 form 4); (OED Online).

Table 58. Distribution of <ght> graph combinations, pre- and post-accession (QEISC)

Forms	PreA	PostA
<ght>	11 (34.4%)	123 (99.2%)
<gth>	21 (65.6%)	0 (0.0%)
<gh>	0 (0.0%)	1 (0.8%)

How might <gth> have been incorporated into the spelling system of the adolescent Elizabeth? LALME sheds some light on the provenance of this graph combination. Only in *strength* (McIntosh et al., vol. 2 1586: 183–188) is <gth> frequent across different regions; in *might* (1986: 219–224) <gth> occurs only (and rarely) in Somerset, Surrey and Suffolk; <gth> in *though* (1986: 141–146) occurs in Surrey, collectively suggesting that <gth> was more typical in Surrey than elsewhere in the ME period. It is possible, therefore, that the graph convention was transmitted the relatively short distance north into London by the mid-sixteenth century. Yet the marginality of <gth> in LALME (and also PCEEC) is striking. The geographical proximity between the attested examples and London may be theoretically persuasive, but it cannot explain why Elizabeth used this graph so extensively, rather than the more common renderings, in her pre-accession writings, or its subsequent decline in the post-accession period.

13.11 *<s>* and *<z>*

In PDE standard spelling, <s> is used to mark plural and genitive word endings. However, Early Modern writers had greater freedom, and in QEISC Elizabeth uses both <s> and <z> graphs to mark the plural or genitive:

(163) the bloudy invention of **traitors handz** (1st February 1587, to James VI, QEISC).

(164) nor els worthy to come, in youre **graces handes**, but rather all vnperfytte and vncorecte (1544, to Catherine Parr, QEISC).

In the pre-accession period, <s> is the only graph. The alternative <z> emerges in Elizabeth's post-accession spelling, accounting for 24.3% of all plural and genitive tokens.[42] The change suggests that Early Modern spelling systems were receptive to new conventions in adulthood, a trait also evident in the more conventional linguistic properties such as lexis and morphosyntax. But the development of <z> also contradicts the hypothesis that Elizabeth's spelling system would become more consistent over time. However, examining the data more closely reveals that Elizabeth restricts the <z> graph to words terminating in <t>, <d>, <l> and <ng>. The use of <z> is not exclusive, and Elizabeth continues to use <s> in these contexts, but the distribution of the <z> graph demonstrates consistency and something resembling an underlying system for these graphs (see Table 59).

---

[42] The change also applies to other word ending. *Else* <elz> becomes the preferred spelling in the post-accession correspondence with 5 tokens, replacing <els>, the preferred form in the pre-accession correspondence.

Table 59. < z > in four word-final contexts (%)
post-accession (QEISC)

Word ending	Total < s > and < z >	% < z >
Final -d	73	42.5
Final -t	97	60.8
Final -l	23	65.2
Final -ng	25	4

Analysis of the spelling of *hearts*, *councils* and *Godz* in PCEEC suggests that Elizabeth's use of < z > is not typical of the period; for instance, of the thirteen variant spellings of *heart*, only one form uses the < z > graph to mark the genitive, found in the Paston correspondence (there were no examples of heart, pl. using < z >):

(165) graunt you euer youre **hertez** desyre (John Russe, 1462; Paston II, 276).

However, the data for the < z > graph is potentially very precarious, as the distinction between < s > and < z > was not always clear in sixteenth-century hands, and is thus liable to different editorial interpretations. With the necessary caveats, the presence of < z > in post- < t/d/l/ng > contexts appears to be a highly idiosyncratic feature of Elizabeth's spelling system.

13.12 < wh > and < w >

The variation between initial < wh > and < w > is restricted to a very small group of words. On the whole Elizabeth uses < wh > and < w > consistently, and her selection of the graphs mostly conforms to PDE standards (e.g. *what* < what >, *wind* < winde >). Only four words in the corpus show variation between both < w > and < wh >: *whereas*, *whether*, *which* and *witsafe* (the latter occurs in the post-accession data only). In the pre-accession period, initial < w > is the preferred graph (Table 60). In the post-accession period, < w > is used consistently only for *which*. The high frequency of *which* in the corpus makes this a notable property of

Table 60. Non-standard < wh > and < w > initial graphs (QEISC)

	Variant	PreA	PostA
whereas	weras, wheras	< w > 1, < wh > 2	< wh > 1
whether	wether, wither, whather, whither	< w > 3	< wh > 3, < w > 2
which	which, whiche, wich, wiche	< w > 57	< w > 85, < wh > 3

Elizabeth's spelling system, one that deviates from her general conformity to the later PDE standard for this graph combination, and with potential significance for authorship analysis.

PCEEC data suggests that < w > -initial *which* is an idiosyncratic spelling trait. Although the form occurs just over 300 times in PCEEC, < wh > -*which* occurs over 5000 times. Furthermore, the < w > -initial *which* forms are concentrated in the late fifteenth century and the first half of the sixteenth century, used by writers such as Thomas Darcy (1500s) and Thomas Wyatt and Henry Clifford (1530s), whereas < wh > *which* is more evenly distributed across the 1540s to 1650s.

Curiously, two informants who do use < w > -initial *which* are Elizabeth's stepmother, Catherine Parr, and half-brother, Edward VI, writing in the 1540s and 1550s respectively. This suggests that Elizabeth's preferred spelling < wich(e) > may have been another feature of a shared spelling system, offering further evidence that spelling contact could also apply to small, localised community groups (such as within families) as well as at an international scale (cf. Sebba 2007: 60). The consistency of < w > -initial *which* throughout her reign, even when the majority of Elizabeth's contemporaries were using < wh > forms, is further testament to the consistency of Elizabeth's spelling system. Had Parr and Edward VI survived beyond the mid-sixteenth century, we may have seen a similar continuation of the form in their spelling systems.

13.13 *Idiosyncrasies and Spelling Reform*

The preceding analysis has highlighted a range of idiosyncratic spellings that either deviate from Elizabeth's general preferences or from the contemporary norms. One potential source for these idiosyncratic spellings is Elizabeth's exposure to the reformed systems of Cheke and Patten.

Evidence for Cheke's spelling system is drawn from published transcripts of two letters. The first was included in the publication of Sir Thomas Hoby's translation of Castiglione's *The Courtier* (1561), in which Cheke outlines his thoughts on the purity of English. The second letter is taken from Strype's (1821) biography of Cheke. Strype (1821: 99) explains that he has transcribed the letter 'word for word, (according to his way of reforming the spelling of English)'. Cheke endeavoured to remove superfluous letter forms and improve consistency; for example, the removal of final < e > in words such as *excuse, give, deceive*, whereas the double graph < ee > was to be used in words where we today find < y >, e.g. *necessity*. Indeed, one of the most characteristic traits of Cheke's system was his dislike of < y >, which he 'wholly threw [...] out of the alphabet' (Strype 1821: 162), preferring to use the graph < i >: e.g. < mi >, < sai >.

The two letters date from 1556 (to Cecil) and 1557 (to Hoby). Yet Cheke's scholarly achievements (such as his appointment as the king's scholar in Greek) mainly occurred in the preceding decades. It is likely that his thoughts on English spelling had been consolidated by the time he taught Elizabeth in 1544, and that some of the more unusual or idiosyncratic properties of her spelling, particularly those of the pre-accession period, may reflect Cheke's influence.

Despite the plausibility of the hypothesis, a comparison of Cheke and Elizabeth's spelling systems finds few similarities. Cheke's suggestions for < e > and < y > may be reflected in Elizabeth's preferred rendering of *they* as < the > and possibly *are* < ar >, although < are > also occurs in the pre-accession data, but these forms are outweighed by many counter-examples, such as the consistent < e > in *give* and *have*. The shortening of *were* from < were > in the pre-accession period to < wer > in the post-accession period could exemplify Cheke's thoughts on superfluity, although I would find this more persuasive if the pre-accession data also contained the < e >-less spelling. As it stands, Cheke spells *were* < weer >, indicating that Elizabeth probably did not follow Cheke in either principle or in form in this case.

There are also clear differences in Elizabeth and Cheke's spellings for < ght >. Cheke does not use the form Elizabeth prefers in the pre-accession period, < gth >, as his letters contain the now standard < ght >: < might > and < overstraight >. Similarly, Cheke uses the now standard < sh > for < wish > and < wishing >, rather than Elizabeth's consistent use of < sch > for the same words, and there is no indication that Elizabeth derived her idiosyncratic and highly consistent < wich(e) > from her one-time tutor, Cheke using the < wh > form. The differences are also apparent in < i/e/y > graphs, with Elizabeth showing a propensity for < y > in final position, such as < my >, < wherby > throughout her life, contrary to Cheke's reformist opinion of the graph. Overall, there is no clear or persuasive evidence that Sir John Cheke's spelling system influenced Elizabeth's spelling.

William Patten's spelling system can be found in a 1591 mock patent addressed to Sir William Cecil, which represented the queen's desire that her 'hermite' find 'solace' after the death of his wife.[43] The most striking feature is the presence of < z > for plurals and genitives, suggesting that his system may have contributed to Elizabeth's post-accession adoption of the graph. However, a word-by-word comparison indicates that the distribution of < z > in the systems of Elizabeth and Patten is dissimilar (see Table 61); < s >, on the other hand, does match both authors' renderings of *seas*, *wonders* and *years*, but this is the conventional spelling of the period and is less significant.

---

[43] The text is taken from Strype (1738: 77–78). For a modern spelling version, see May (2004a: 186–189).

Table 61. <s> and <z> spellings: Elizabeth I (post-accession) and Patten

Word	Elizabeth	Patten
causes	< causes >	< causez >
deserts	< desartz >	< deserts >
friends	< frendes, frends, frindes, frendz, frindz >	< frends >
seas	< seas >	< seas >
services	< services >	< servicez >
wonders	< wondars >	< woonders >
years	< yeres, yeares, years >	< yeerz, years >

Comparing other spelling forms, there is minimal evidence to suggest that Patten influenced Elizabeth's post-accession spelling. Elizabeth's consistent use of < wich(e) >, for example, contrasts with Patten's usage of (the now standard) < which >. Other characteristic traits of Elizabeth's spelling that contrast with Patten's reformed system include Elizabeth's < the > to Patten's < they > and Elizabeth's < commaund(e) > to Patten's < command >.

Nevertheless, the presence of Patten's spelling system in the patent is intriguing. Elizabeth was almost certainly involved in the text's composition, with the patent containing her nickname 'sprite' for Cecil (see May 2004a: xxvi–xxvii), and this suggests that she may also have approved the transcription before it was issued. The presence of the reformed spelling system in the mock patent suggests apathy towards reformist matters on Elizabeth's part, if not an endorsement of Patten's system. I would find the latter interpretation more persuasive, however, if the spelling data bore out further similarities between Patten and the queen. It may be that Elizabeth adopted or developed the practice of plural and genitive < z > independently. The comparative analysis suggests that the idiosyncratic characteristics of her spelling system are a product of her personal preferences, rather than conceding to external influences.

A spelling system that has not yet been discussed is the Chancery Standard, the localised spelling system that emerged within the administrative centre of the king in the fifteenth century. The documents that preserve the Chancery language are some of the earliest to use English for official writing. In the introduction to their *Anthology* the editors, Fisher, Richardson and Fisher, suggest that

> [t]he Chancery clerks fairly consistently preferred the spellings which have since become standard [...] At the very least, we can say that they were trying to limit choices among spellings, and that by the 1440's and 1450's they have achieved a comparative regularization (1984: 27).

However, Smith (1996) suggests that 'Chancery Standard' requires careful definition, as the term 'standard' does not denote a unified system as we would understand it in PDE, but rather represents a 'standardised system' with the scribes using a smaller degree of variation than seen in the ME spelling system at large (Smith 1996: 70–71). Furthermore, Smith (1996: 71) suggests that the texts collated in the Fisher et al. *Anthology* do 'not necessarily form a coherent body of texts representing the Chancery Standard' because the scribes would often copy manuscripts and preserve the regional spelling of the original (*literatim* transcription). Michael Benskin (2004) provides a detailed (and somewhat devastating) evaluation of the editorial principles of the *Anthology*. He finds irregularities in the provenance of texts (2004: 8), errors in attribution (2004: 5) and, most importantly for the present analysis, errors in the editors' transcriptions (e.g. 2004: 7, fn.7) and documentation (e.g. 2004: 20). Thus, whilst the glossary of spelling forms at the back of the collection offers an appealing resource in principle, at present a graph/form comparison with Elizabeth's spelling is ill-advised. Benskin (2004: 21) concludes that the *Anthology* 'reports an ideology, rather than its texts. The Signet Clerks' diversities of usage are represented as mere incidentals in an implied uniformity'.

There is perhaps a more abstract connection to be made between Elizabeth's spelling and the Chancery Standard. As the 'direct ancestor of the modern written standard' (Benskin 2004: 1), Chancery contributes significantly to PDE standard spelling forms, although the process was not simply a case of the system's prestige leading to widespread, autonomous replication (see Smith 1996: 73–75 for data). Re-calculating the QEISC data, the proportion of word types that include the PDE standard spelling as a variant is 42.5%. More research is necessary to establish if the degree of 'modernity' in Elizabeth's spelling system was typical of the educated upper-ranks during the sixteenth century. Currently, without a comparative baseline, there is no way to establish the meaningfulness of Elizabeth's standard spellings, nor their significance in regards to the Chancery Standard and her position at the Court.

13.14 *Summary*

The QEISC findings are in favour of Salmon and Scragg's opinion that Elizabeth's spelling was 'reasonably consistent' (Salmon 1999: 30). The quantitative approach shows considerable merits over those of the qualitative readings of previous investigations and importantly can be replicated in the study of other spelling systems to allow comparison between idiolectal systems. This is a necessary step if the assessment of Elizabeth's consistency is to be verified against the macro-level trends.

The influence of Elizabeth's education, her age, and the effect of her accession upon her written output can be identified in the development of her spelling, appearing to support the application of a sociolinguistic framework to orthographic variation. The influence of nascent standardisation, however, is more difficult to determine. Certainly, not all developments in Elizabeth's spelling move towards the PDE standard form, e.g. <even> to <iven>, and the lack of any consistent spelling for politically significant words such as *English, sovereign* and *councillors* is also striking. It is worth pointing out that Benskin (2004: 21) cites the seven variant spellings for *England* used by the scribes writing in the 'Chancery Standard' as indicative that the scribes were not concerned with 'institutional spelling norms'. Such a significant word, he suggests, 'would surely have been a prime candidate for fixity' (2004: 21). It is curious that Elizabeth, writing around a century later, shows no intention of establishing a consistent spelling of *English* in her spelling system, nor—based on the results from PCEEC—providing a standardised form to be used by her subjects.

Elizabeth's idiosyncratic spellings may be (partly) explained by a factor already found to have considerable influence upon her morphosyntactic choices: stylistic prestige. Taavitsainen's (2000) study of spelling in fifteenth-century scientific texts found that the genre showed greater variation, and used less variant forms from the standard emerging in London, than administrative or literary works of the period. She proposes that the prestige of science, as an intellectual pursuit, had a distinct kind of power, one that would conflict socially with the administrative standard and thus affected the implementation of spelling standards in the genre (2000: 146–147). The principles of Taavitsainen's hypothesis may also apply to Elizabeth's idiosyncratic spellings. Tacitly or explicitly, the consistent use of <sch>, <wich(e)>, the introduction of <z> and <the> for *they*, for example, are small but distinguishing features that demarcate Elizabeth's spelling—the written form of her idiolect—from the spellings of her contemporaries in PCEEC, including many of her courtiers and councillors. As such, they serve to mark out her unique social position.

If this is the case, then it suggests that even prior to the emergence of a standardised spelling (such as that analysed by Sebba (2007) or Sairio (2009)) social significance was attached to spelling forms. The meanings of conformity and difference operated instead at a localised level (i.e. within the Court, or between family members) rather than being nationally recognised. Nevalainen (2002: 178) makes a similar observation about the spelling of Henry VIII, who 'did not feel compelled to revise his spelling habits in accordance with the public trends of the time'.

The range of these idiosyncratic forms would also appear to provide a rich resource for authorship analysis. However, the fragility of spelling in historical documents means, with the exception of autograph manuscripts, it is perhaps unlikely that her spelling—were it originally present—would be preserved by a copyist. In texts produced by scribes, such as those based on dictation, there is no opportunity for Elizabeth's spelling system to be recorded at all. Only for texts that have a questionable palaeographic status, such as the manuscript of the Azores prayer (1597), is spelling likely to be truly profitable for authorship attribution. An analysis of the prayer can be found in Part III.

The methodological and comparative aspects of variationist socio-linguistics prove highly applicable for the analysis of spelling variation. Yet, it is not as clear how the sociolinguistic concepts of progressiveness and conservativeness translate to the study of spelling. Most occurrences of language change are thought to progress without the conscious awareness of the speakers (Nevalainen et al. 2011: 26), whereas the implementation of spelling standardisation is a high profile, explicit affair. That said, the evidence for localised spelling contact suggests that, at least in the sixteenth century, there were trends and developments in spelling that diffused across social networks, and that linguistic leaders within those networks were presumably involved in establishing these trends. To take one example, we might say that Elizabeth's adoption of <z>, although failing to become the standard in the seventeenth century, may represent an innovation amongst her contemporaries. To speculate more wildly, perhaps the presence of the graph in the spelling system of Patten is indicative, not of his influence upon her, but rather of the queen's influence upon him. Only further research of sixteenth-century spelling practices can shed light on the distribution of spelling variation across communities and social groups. The significance of Elizabeth's education, age and writing habits suggest that a larger sociolinguistic analysis of spelling variation may help us to understand the processes that shaped this intermediary stage in English spelling, and enable us to better appreciate the social significance of the written mode in EModE.

PART III

RESEARCH QUESTIONS

14. RESEARCH QUESTION 1: DOES ELIZABETH'S IDIOLECT CHANGE IN RESPONSE TO HER ACCESSION?

The survey of linguistic features in QEIC clearly demonstrates the complexity of idiolectal data, and the relation to individual identity, biographical experience, and macro-level trends of language change. Throughout the study, the analysis has sought to respond to three research questions that represent the diverse theoretical, methodological and socio-historical facets of the investigation. To further explore these questions, I now evaluate the findings from the analyses collectively in regards to each question, to draw more conclusive, broad-ranging interpretations and highlight key areas for future research.

The short answer to the first research question is: to some extent. The studies in Part II examined 10 linguistic features in total, but only two showed persuasive evidence of a change that correlated with Elizabeth's accession: the acquisition of *royal we* and the decrease in periphrastic superlative adjectives, although the increasing consistency of Elizabeth's spelling system may also reflect the rise in written output after her accession. These three features play an explicit role in the interpersonal dimension of language use, making them most sensitive to the social changes that resulted from Elizabeth's accession. The seven remaining linguistic features, affirmative *do*, negative *do*, *ye/you*, single negation, possessive determiners, animacy and marker and *(the)which* showed no clear relationship with Elizabeth's accession, suggesting that the emphasis placed on this event by biographers and historians is too simplistic an approach for an analysis of Elizabeth's idiolect. Instead, many of the developments that occur in her idiolect can be traced to other elements of her biography—both long-term social factors and specific short-term events.

The results suggest that a key social factor contributing to the development of Elizabeth's idiolect is her age, or more precisely the correlation between her youth and the stage of the change at the macro-level. During her adolescence, and as a member of the younger generation, she is more receptive to the incoming variants than older speakers. In the morphosyntactic variables at the early stages of change, including affirmative *do*, the generalisation of *you*, possessive determiners, the emergence of single negation and the rise of *who*, her usage of the incoming variants is higher than the macro-level average and that of the older generations (where the data is available). Elizabeth's age is a persuasive factor to explain her position as a leader in these changes.

Interrelated with Elizabeth's age is another significant social factor: her education, and, by implication, her social rank which granted access to an advanced level of schooling. Historians have frequently lauded Elizabeth's education for its influence upon her appreciation and solicitation of learning and the arts during her reign (Somerset 1991: 15, 469–474; Shenk 2007) and, as a result, it was anticipated that education would be an important factor in the developmental patterns and characteristics of her idiolect.

That said, the influence of Elizabeth's education is striking, seen in the diachronic reach throughout her life and in the diverse ways that her learning shaped her use of language. Her education can explain why Elizabeth repeatedly led in changes that entered the language 'from above' through literary and learned channels, e.g. the rise of *who*, the dehumanisation of *(the)which*, and the emergence of single negation. CEEC investigations show that the upper ranks tend to lead changes with prestigious associations, and Elizabeth's uptake of these variants therefore fits with her biographical background. However, for the changes occurring during the pre-accession period, Elizabeth uses the incoming variants more frequently than many of her contemporaries of a similar education and rank. It is plausible that her education made her acutely aware of the prestigious and learned connotations of these linguistic features and led to her high uptake of the variants—perhaps she desired to use language in a way that would please her superiors or educators, or in a way that she felt was appropriate to her social position. Her usage often exceeds that of her social contemporaries, a pattern that fits the sociolinguistic concept of hypercorrection (see the discussion of research question 3, below).

The influence of Elizabeth's education can also explain the stylistic sensitivity identified in the cross-genre comparison of many of the linguistic variants. In the pre-accession period, for example, Elizabeth uses the long determiner forms (*mine/thine*) in her more formal writing, anticipating the later stylistic trend. The different functions of affirmative *do*, the usage of the ME pronoun system *ye/you*, and the increased frequency of multiple negation in Elizabeth's pre-accession translations offer further evidence for the influence Elizabeth's education had on her understanding of style. Similar evidence was found in her post-accession writing. The data for affirmative and negative declarative *do* showed a dip in the post-accession period that was attributed to Elizabeth's stylistic re-evaluation of the variant.

Shenk (2003: 80) suggests that Elizabeth's education was an important facet of her identity during her reign, allowing Elizabeth 'to carve out a space for herself specifically as a learned queen'. She cites Elizabeth's university orations as key examples. In her speech to Cambridge (1564), for instance, Elizabeth uses her knowledge of Classical themes to establish points of similarity between herself and her audience (allusions to Alexander the Great) whilst simultaneously selecting specific examples that 'distinguish her position as monarch' (Shenk 2003: 81). Shenk's observations are significant for the interpretation of the linguistic data. The context proffered by Shenk leads me to suggest that Elizabeth does not attend to the linguistic stylistic trends in the post-accession period tacitly, because her education makes her more aware of them but rather her stylistic sensitivity is something that she crafts and pursues as part of her identity as a 'learned queen'. Frye's (1993: 4) proposition that Elizabeth perceived monarchs to be created through language gains an additional dimension, as it appears that such a perception may have been created by and enacted through the knowledge acquired in her Humanist education. The academic and literary profiles of her earliest educators, such as Roger Ascham and Sir John Cheke, may have further impressed upon her the import and prestige of language, in addition to the curriculum itself.

The social factors of age and education have a sustained influence on Elizabeth's idiolect throughout her life, and provide explanations for her participation in linguistic change. Alongside the conventional social factors considered in macro-level sociolinguistic studies, specific biographical events also have idiolectal ramifications. Her accession, which was the focus of the diachronic analysis, influenced three linguistic features and I have discussed the probable reason for their connection to this event above. More importantly, the analysis highlights other biographical events that are associated with the variation and developments in her idiolect.

One event concerns Elizabeth's changing social experiences in the late 1540s and early 1550s. In Part II, I hypothesised that the sudden drop of *the which* after 1549 was connected to Elizabeth's new role at the Court alongside her brother, Edward VI, which prompted her to moderate her language to that of her new peers. Re-evaluating the data of other linguistic features finds further changes that support the interpretation of the importance of this period. In the analysis of affirmative *do*, for example, I found that discursive *do* was a notable feature of Elizabeth's letters to Edward Seymour in 1549, but that, curiously, the form was absent in the 1554 "Tide" letter to Mary which was written in a comparable context. The distribution of negative *do* also divides along this period; all of the pre-accession examples of negative *do* are concentrated in the 1540s correspondence, with Elizabeth shifting to her favoured post-verbal *not* after this time. In the analysis of the dehumanisation of *which*, it is likely that the change developed rapidly in her adolescence, based on the examples of animate *which* in her translations and non-animate examples in her 1550s correspondence. There are also spelling changes that show a temporal correlation: *highness* changes from < th > in the 1540s to a < gh > graph combination in the 1550s. Further investigation—working within the limitations of the pre-accession data—may well reveal additional contrasts.

The linguistic significance of the crossover between the 1540s and 1550s most likely reflects a combination of social factors, including Elizabeth's advancing age and the progress she made in her education. Yet her move from the household of her stepmother, Catherine Parr, to the royal Court may be most significant; as a diplomat at the time noted, Elizabeth was favourably received by the King and his councillors, who had 'a higher opinion of her for conforming with the others and observing the new decrees' (Borman 2009: 124). Whilst the diplomat's statement refers to Elizabeth's conformity to the new religion, it seems plausible that she may have also modified her linguistic behaviour to accommodate to the new set of norms to which she was now exposed. The social changes in the 1550s were perhaps not as politically and historically striking as Elizabeth's accession, but it appears that her move to Court was an important event for her personal development, and hence for her idiolect.

Re-evaluating the data using diachronic splits other than the pre- and post-accession divide may well reveal other biographical events of significance. The events of the late 1580s are a case in point. In these years, the Queen eliminated her closest rival to the throne, Mary, Queen of Scots (in 1586), and successfully repelled the Spanish armada two years later. There were also domestic changes at the Court. Elizabeth's lifelong friend Robert Dudley died in 1586, Francis Walsingham in 1590, and a new generation of Court favourites emerged, including Robert Devereux, Earl of Essex, and Sir Walter Ralegh, who upset the old guard (and each other) with their new ideas (Somerset 1991: 597–604, 651; Guy 1995: 2). The period also saw a new royal iconography, with Elizabeth increasingly idealised as an 'invincible majesty' (Borman 2009: 331). Gadja (2010) suggests that ideologies of kingship were more avidly debated during the latter decades of Elizabeth's reign, with outspoken proponents for both mixed and absolute monarchy. Collectively, the significance of the changes from the mid-1580s has led John Guy to describe the subsequent period as the 'second reign' of Elizabeth I (Guy 1995; see also Gadja 2010).

Re-analysing the QEIC data indicates that the events of the late 1580s may well have had linguistic repercussions, with a number of forms and functions occurring for the first time in Elizabeth's idiolect. For example, the first occurrence of the double superlative is found in a letter written in 1588:

(166) Your **most assurest** sister and cousin (1st July 1588, to James VI, QEIC correspondence).

Elizabeth also modifies her self-reference repertoire, increasing her usage of the third person pronoun and decreasing her use of *royal we*; changes that suggest Elizabeth felt it necessary to modify and refresh the forms used to construct and maintain her social identity. In Elizabeth's spelling, plural and genitive <z> emerges at the end of the 1580s. Other variants show a change in distribution: negative *do* increases slightly in the 1590s after the drop in the previous decade, a rise that correlates with the literary trends of Ellegård's (1953) corpus.

Admittedly these changes are slight, but they could plausibly reflect the developments at Court after the mid-1580s. The emergence of new variants (form and function) indicates that Elizabeth remained responsive to linguistic changes throughout her life and receptive to new means of expression. The idiolectal data enriches the quantitative findings of Raumolin-Brunberg (2005, 2006) who makes a persuasive case for morphosyntactic change in adulthood.

The QEIC data permits speculation as to possible biographical triggers for the idiolectal developments of the 1580s. Interestingly, many biographers have commented on Elizabeth's vanity in this late period as she resorted to heavy make-up, flirted with men more than 20 years her junior, and required constant flattery from all visitors in her attempt to maintain the illusion of 'an eternally youthful Goddess ruling over her adoring subjects' (Borman 2009: 333). Set against this background, it is conceivable that the development of linguistic features, aligning her with the practice of the younger generation and the innovative, literary usage of her courtiers, is a further means to deny the advances of old age and embody the new iconography of her 'second reign'.

14.1 *The Gender Question*

The debate over Elizabeth's self-representation in gendered terms has not been the primary focus of the idiolectal analysis, although it is an undeniable facet of any study that considers the queen's self-representation and identity. The linguistic data provides a new perspective on the juxtaposition between her sex and her role in Early Modern society, and the claims that she established herself as an honorary male during her reign.

The comparative analysis found that Elizabeth aligns with both male and female informants in her usage of different variants. In broad strokes, her usage of first- and second-person possessive determiners, the replacement of *ye* by *you*, and the lag in the replacement of *the which* by *which* correlate best with the preferences of CEEC female informants. Elizabeth's infrequent usage of positive and negative declarative *do* also shows a greater (if less convincing) similarity to the trends for women than those for men. Conversely, her uptake of single negation, relative marker *who*, and the dehumanization of *which* is closer to the preferences of male informants. Elizabeth's consistent spelling may also be classified as a male correlate, based on qualitative assessments of gender differences which attest to the greater inconsistency of female writers (e.g. Salmon 1999: 30). No data is available for the social stratification for superlative adjectives, and the specialised function of *royal we* makes a gender comparison inapplicable. For the nine features, therefore, Elizabeth's usage correlates with five female trends, and four male trends; a near-equal division that provides no explicit support for the honorary male label in sociolinguistic terms. The distribution of male and female-led changes in Elizabeth's idiolect concurs with the interpretation of Elizabeth's progressiveness in five linguistic changes put forward by Nevalainen et al. (2011). The authors propose that the queen's prominent social position in both male and female domains is a plausible explanation for her participation in changes from above (male-led changes) and below (female-led changes), and the QEIC data appears to confirm this across a wider spectrum of linguistic features. Yet the stylistic and diachronic data from QEIC offers a more nuanced picture of Elizabeth's alignment with male and female linguistic trends, and suggests that this explanation can be developed further.

Firstly, it should be noted that the correlation between Elizabeth's use of positive and negative declarative *do* and the CEEC female informants is not robust, and the QEIC patterns show a better fit with Ellegård's literary corpus; significantly, a corpus comprising only male-authored texts. The persuasive evidence of stylistic variation in the three genres leads me to align Elizabeth's usage with that of the more literary, stylistically sensitive male writers of the period, rather than women.

Another important nuance of the data is that the three remaining linguistic features for which Elizabeth's usage correlates with female informants are diachronically biased, with the changes concentrated in the pre-accession period. Female informants led the pronominal changes (the generalisation of *you* and short-form first- and second-person possessive determiners) in the early to mid-sixteenth century. The rapid advance of both of these changes means that they were either near-completion or completed by the 1580s, at which point there are negligible differences in usage between genders. In the replacement of *the which*, Elizabeth's lag concords with the slow uptake of other female informants in the early sixteenth century, but very quickly 'corrects' itself in the 1550s. Gender difference is negligible for these changes at the macro-level in the latter half of the century (N&R-B 2003: 118–120, 129–130). The strength of the female correlations in the pre-accession period is further diluted by the overlap with Elizabeth's youth at this time, which also plays a significant role in shaping her early usage of many variants. The changes that correlate with female informants are notably restricted to the earlier period of Elizabeth's life, with no correlation found after her adolescence and accession.

The fit between Elizabeth and male informants applies to changes that took place throughout the sixteenth century. The dehumanisation of *which* has been traced over the sixteenth and seventeenth centuries (Dekeyser 1984; N&R-B 2002: 118) and the uptake of single negation continues beyond Elizabeth's lifetime (Nevalainen 2000: 51–52), despite Elizabeth's early adoption of both variants in her youth. The stylistic re-evaluation of positive and negative declarative *do* occurred in the latter decades of the sixteenth century in literary data (Ellegård 1953), and again Elizabeth was in the vanguard of this change, anticipating the trends in correspondence some 20 years later. For these linguistic features, Elizabeth's preferences consistently show best fit with the leading male informants. There is thus a diachronic contrast in Elizabeth's correlation with the different genders. Once out of childhood and early adolescence, her linguistic preferences repeatedly align her with her male contemporaries.

Could this be linguistic evidence that Elizabeth became an honorary male? Such an interpretation is most likely too simplistic, and gives short shrift to the complexities of idiolectal data. Sociolinguistics, both historical and modern, has repeatedly shown that language change is the product of a combination of factors (Bayley 2002: 118), and this plausibly applies as much to idiolectal preferences as it does to macro-level trends. It is important to contextualise gender as a social factor within the socio-historical context of the sixteenth century. Being born male or female had a considerable influence on that speaker's (potential) social rank, domicile and certainly their education.

In macro-level changes in the Early Modern period, women show a tendency to lead 'from below', a trend attributed to the lesser educational opportunities available to Tudor women and thus demonstrating the precept that, for an individual to participate in a language change, they have to be exposed to the linguistic variants involved (N&R-B 2003: 116, 131). Elizabeth's unique social position freed her from the social limitations experienced by the majority of her gender, granting her more in common, socially, with male informants. Thus, she shares her linguistic preferences with other female informants (from the mid- and upper-ranks) in the pre-accession period only, feasibly reflecting the greater influence of women in her life at this time (e.g. her early caregivers).

The uptake and usage of linguistic features with male correlates is seen across Elizabeth's lifetime because this was the gender of the individuals and groups with whom she had the most contact and shared the most experiences (either literally or at a more abstract level). Her humanist education was predominantly a masculine domain, and her high rank granted her a level of power more typical of male contemporaries; indeed, Elizabeth's closest political advisors throughout her life were men, with women restricted to private, domestic affairs. In light of these trends, it is important to emphasise that the sociolinguistic perspective does not provide evidence that suggests that Elizabeth consciously sought to align her language with male contemporaries because they were male. The greater number of correlates with male informants is a by-product of the social factor's overlap with other biographical elements.

14.2 *Summary*

The sociolinguistic analysis of aspects of Elizabeth's idiolect has shed new light on the relationship between Elizabeth's writings, her social self, and the key components, long-term and specific, which have greatest impact upon her language and arguably her life. The exploratory re-analysis of the 1550s and the 1590s indicates that sociolinguistic analysis can offer still more information, and that a number of time periods and events, not just her accession, can be connected to changes in Elizabeth's idiolect. The approach helps to foreground events that may not necessarily be considered biographically significant. Placing idiolectal data at the centre enables the analysis to cut through the complex layers of fact, myth and memory that constitute our understanding of Elizabeth, and re-evaluate the factors that shaped her language and, by extension, her sense of self.

Further research into the language of other women at the Elizabethan Court, especially Elizabeth's gentlewomen Kat Ashley, Blanche Parry and Bess of Hardwick, would advance our understanding of the different socio-historical pressures operating at the Court, and the relevance of gender in this domicile as a social factor. Indeed, further work on the linguistic behaviours of various Court personnel, following a comparable method to that applied here, would help to clarify the role of language in the lives of men and women in contact with the queen, and hence provide insight into the patterns and preferences of Elizabeth herself. For example, such data may help to illuminate the contrasting picture of linguistic preferences identified among Elizabeth's closest councillors, such as William Cecil and Francis Walsingham, who seem immune to many of the influences affecting Elizabeth and show generally conservative behaviour (Nevalainen et al. 2011). Establishing the import of the social factors (education, age) and biographical events in the idiolects of these individuals will further enrich our understanding of language and identity in Early Modern society.

15. RESEARCH QUESTION 2: CAN A SOCIOLINGUISTIC ANALYSIS OF ELIZABETH'S IDIOLECT PROVIDE A USEFUL MEANS FOR ASSESSING AUTHORSHIP?

In the process of conducting an idiolectal comparative analysis, the collected data appears to offer a potentially valuable baseline for the investigation of authorship in texts of unknown provenance. Convention-ally, the linguistic analysis of authorship is the preserve of FORENSIC LINGUISTICS, where the properties of an idiolect are considered distinctive enough from others within a speech community to allow accurate identification. Although influenced by the variationist framework, forensic studies do not usually account for sociolinguistic or stylistic dimensions— primarily because the data used is drawn from contemporary sources, and amassing a comparative corpus that would permit the 'linguistic fingerprint' of a speaker or social group to be identified is presently unrealisable due to technological and practical constraints: 'no one has even begun to speculate about how much and what kind of data would be needed to uniquely characterize an *idiolect*' (Coulthard & Johnson 2007: 161; emphasis in the original).

One of the frustrating constraints of historical data is that the quantity of material is pre-determined; yet in some ways this feature provides a helpful focus for how the available data can be exercised and implemented. The sociolinguistic treatment of the QEIC data, for example, has not only established whether Elizabeth does or does not use a form (e.g. *mine/thine*, subject *ye*, *royal we*, the spelling forms < gth > and < sch >) but potentially allows a linguistic feature to be evaluated according to:

- a particular time period, e.g. the analysis of *(the)which* showed that the form became highly marginal after 1550;
- a particular social correlate, e.g. Elizabeth's consistent spelling aligns with upper-ranking, highly educated contemporaries and, in her spelling of < wiche > for instance, a highly localised group;
- a particular systemic context, e.g. the study of animacy and marker found that *who* had generalised across deity and human antecedents in non-formulaic contexts;
- an interactive context, e.g. Elizabeth's preference for elative superlatives in address-forms was a notable feature of her correspondence, with a clear change in function in the pre- and post-accession texts; and
- a stylistic context, e.g. near-continuous usage of affirmative declarative *do* in her pre-accession translations vs. the infrequency of the form in the post-accession texts.

The data presented in Part II is by no means a complete or definitive account of Elizabeth's idiolect (her linguistic fingerprint). However, it does provide the investigator with a choice of features as a starting point for authorship assessment, which can be explored and evaluated from a number of perspectives. The technique, which I term CONTEXTUAL LIKELIHOOD, draws meaning from the different factors operating on the features in a text, rather than simply documenting the presence or absence of a form. The evidence for different facets of usage—interactive, stylistic, social—allows the external evidence, either for or against Elizabeth's authorship, to be considered in a qualitative fashion; for example, if a hypothetical literary text, dated to the 1590s, contains no examples of affirmative *do*, then an explanation can be offered for why this may support a case for authorship, drawing on the diachronic patterns for the variant and stylistic preferences in Elizabeth's 1590s writing. Theoretically, therefore, the results have merit for the assessment of authorship. However, the real test is in its practical application.

There are a number of scenarios for which linguistic authorship analysis may prove relevant. The multifarious processes of Early Modern text production, and the subsequent transmission and preservation for the present century, means that manuscripts may represent copies of autograph originals, the scribal transcription of dictated content, or the careful emulation of a particular hand. The following case studies explore how successful the contextual likelihood approach can be in four different contexts.

15.1 *Case Study 1: The Seymour Letters*

The Seymour letters are a valuable resource, not only for our historical appreciation of Elizabeth's attitude and actions during her house arrest in 1549, but also for the rich linguistic data they provide for her adolescence. However, contrary to popular belief, Steven W. May (p.c.) has expressed uncertainty regarding their authorship, and suggests that they are not the result of Elizabeth's sole compositional effort, as is conventionally believed, but a collaborative work between the young princess and members of her household. To assess the accuracy of this hypothesis the contextual likelihood approach may offer some insight. The analysis will indicate the fit of these letters with Elizabeth's idiolectal preferences based on the data collected for QEIC. Instances of deviant usage may be indicative of third-party involvement during composition, although analysis will also consider other plausible explanations.

The Seymour letters contain some of the highest frequencies of affirmative declarative *do* in the QEIC correspondence caused by frequent discursive *do* clusters. Clustering does not occur as extensively in the other letters in the corpus. The Seymour letters also contain the only examples of negative *do* in the pre-accession correspondence, and only one example of Elizabeth's preferred variant, post-verbal *not*. The patterning of periphrastic *do* could therefore be the result of third-party interference during the composition process, since it deviates from the patterns in the pre-accession correspondence. However, cross-genre analysis shows that periphrastic declarative *do* occurred in similar contexts, and in even higher frequencies, in Elizabeth's pre-accession translations. Potentially, she received assistance in the composition of her earliest translations, too, but the results of declarative *do* cannot be interpreted as conclusive evidence of interference in the Seymour letters.

The distribution of relative marker *the which* is relevant to the question of authorship. The 1549 letters to Edward Seymour contain the majority of the tokens recorded in Elizabeth's correspondence, which could indicate that *the which* is evidence of third-party interference. However, cross-genre analysis reveals a similar distribution in the pre-accession translations, in both frequency and the influence of systemic factors. The examples in the letter to Catherine Parr also reduce the authorial value of the variant. Consequently, the presence of *the which* alone is not definitive evidence of third-party interference and collaboration in these letters.

Another potential anomaly is the presence of a multiple negation construction, the only such example in the pre-accession correspondence:

(167) Kat Ashley she never advised me unto it but said always (when any talked of my marriage) that she would **never** have me marry **neither** in England **nor** out of England without the consent of the King's Majesty, your Grace's and the Council's (28th January 1549, to Edward Seymour, QEIC correspondence).

However, the value of this token is reduced when we consider that (a) it occurs in indirect reported speech, which may influence the choice of wording and (b) multiple negation is (again) a variant found more frequently in Elizabeth's pre-accession translations. The repeated overlap between the aforementioned features of the Seymour letters and the translations suggests there are perhaps similarities in the interactive and stylistic factors shaping the production of the texts.

Other linguistic features show less deviant patterning. The Seymour letters contain periphrastic superlatives in address-forms, comparable with Elizabeth's other pre-accession letters, and the pronoun *you* and the short possessive determiners in pre-vocalic contexts also fit the general patterns of Elizabeth's pre-accession usage. The spelling data shows no signs of interference, with her spelling characteristic of other letters from this pre-accession period. To a degree, the importance of spelling is limited in the analysis of the Seymour letters. May's hypothesis does not contest that the letters are in Elizabeth's hand; instead, he suggests that Elizabeth may have reproduced dictated or drafted content.

Collectively, the linguistic features provide no definitive evidence that Elizabeth wrote the letters from dictation, rather than composing them herself. Yet, May's questioning of the authorship of these particular letters is wholly appreciable, as there are clear disparities between their linguistic properties and other examples of Elizabeth's correspondence. The discourse situation is the most likely explanation. The earlier discussion of these texts found some linguistic trends were shared with those found in trial depositions from the period (affirmative *do*, negative *do*), and it is perhaps more likely that the distinctiveness of these letters is a consequence of their testimonial stance rather than third-party interference.

The distinction between the Seymour letters and those to Edward VI or Catherine Parr may even reflect institutionalised differences in the types of Early Modern epistolary writing. Lynne Magnusson (2011) has examined letters written in the middle to late sixteenth century by children of the

Herrick family, originally from Leicester. She identifies two different styles of letter-writing used by the children: the vernacular letter, which uses simple, conjoined sentence structures, and the Ciceronian letter, which has more complex syntax and incorporates rhetorical devices, such as parenthetical remarks. Her results show that the son with a grammar school education uses each type to different recipients. The vernacular style is used in letters to his less-educated brother, and the Ciceronian style to his father, presumably to impress and demonstrate his learning. The other brother, who remained in Leicester on an apprenticeship, uses only the vernacular style.

Magnusson's distinction is very significant for the analysis of Elizabeth's pre-accession letters. The contrast between the Seymour letters and those to other recipients in the pre-accession period may in fact reflect a conscious stylistic decision to use the vernacular style of letter to Seymour, and the Ciceronian style to her sibling and stepmother. If the hypothesis is correct, then it further demonstrates Elizabeth's stylistic sensitivity. Indeed, Magnusson's vernacular and Ciceronian categorisation has broader implications for historical sociolinguistic studies. If educated individuals moderated their epistolary writing style as distinctly as the evidence for the Herrick family (and Elizabeth) suggests, then the macro-level linguistic trends for the upper-ranks in CEEC may show an inaccurate picture of their usage. Documenting language change for educated informants would need to account for the style of letter, a point that supports a case for the greater incorporation of stylistic variation into sociolinguistic studies (see the discussion of research question 3, below).

Overall, on the basis of the linguistic evidence presently available for the pre-accession period, the Seymour letters should retain their place in the canon.

15.2 *Case Study 2: 1576 Parliamentary Speech*

The second case study examines the 1576 parliamentary speech. This is an apograph text included in QEIC due to Elizabeth's endorsement of the original manuscript, although I was aware of the potential complications that may arise from including a text so many steps removed from the original document. The findings reported for *who* and *which* suggest that these concerns were justified, as, unlike Elizabeth's other post-accession writing, relative marker *who* is limited to deity antecedents, and *which* is used for human antecedents in this speech. However, further analysis indicates that this is the main deviation from Elizabeth's linguistic preferences in the text. For instance, whilst there are no tokens for multiple or single negation, the speech contains two instances of post-verbal *not*, and none of negative *do*, fitting with the patterns identified in QEIC as a whole. The results for superlatives are similarly reassuring. The frequency of this feature in the speech is greater than other examples of the genre but the actual trend (inflection for non-address-form superlatives) accords with the norm. The only other linguistic feature present in the speech that may show evidence of interference is positive declarative *do*. In the 1576 speech, *do* occurs once, at a normalised frequency of 1.1 times per 1000 words. This is lower than the average for Elizabeth's speeches, at 2.3 times per 1000 words. By contrast, the frequency of non-*do* declarative contexts is higher than the average: 35.9 times per 1000 words vs. the average 25.5 times. It is possible that these figures reflect the omission of periphrastic *do* during the transmission process. On reflection, the possibility of scribal interference in this text cannot be ruled out, but it is seemingly limited to two morphosyntactic forms (for which there is data). The majority conform to Elizabeth's idiolectal preferences.

If the results are accurate, then they also shed valuable light on the relationship between Elizabeth's scribes and copyists and the royal source text. In her letter to Harington that enclosed the speech, Elizabeth remarks that she has had a clerk 'write fair my poor words for thine use' (to Harington, 1976, QEIC correspondence). It would appear that the scribe was primarily charged with the visual clarity of the document (which unfortunately has not survived), and not a re-writing of its linguistic expression. Studies into scribal practice have provided a contradictory picture of a writer's fidelity to their source text (e.g. Samuels 1991; Daybell 1999; Williams 2010), and there is much potential in exploring this area, both for our understanding of the processes of manuscript production and Early Modern perceptions of authorship.

15.3 *Case Study 3: The CEEC Hoby Letter*

The third case study examines a text that represents another aspect of the author/scribe relationship. The letter, written in 1566 to Lady Margaret Hoby to express Elizabeth's sympathy and condolences regarding the recent death of Lady Hoby's husband, Sir Thomas Hoby, is included in the CEEC sub-file for Elizabeth. However, it was omitted from QEIC on the grounds that it bears the hallmarks of a conventional scribal letter, i.e. closing conventions 'given under our signet', and thus Elizabeth's involvement in its composition is difficult to determine. The text is also not included in the recent publications of Elizabeth's autograph correspondence (e.g. Mueller & Marcus 2003; May 2004a). It is now appropriate to revisit the letter (168) to see if Elizabeth's participation in its composition is detectable, and thus whether the decision to omit it from QEIC was the correct one.

(168) Madam Although we heare that since the death of your husband, our late Ambassador, S = r = Thomas Hoby, you have received, in France, great and comfortable courtesyes from the French King,

the Queen Mother, the Queen of Navarre and sundry others, yet we made accompt that all these layd together cannot so satisfye you as some testimony and sparke of our favour, with the application of the late service of your Husband, and of your own demeanour there: wherefore though you shall receive it somewhat lately in time, yet we assure you the same proceedeth only of the late knowledge of your return. And therefore we let you know that the service of your Husband was to us so acceptable, as next yourself and your children we have not the meanest loss of so able a Servant in that calling. And yet since it hath so pleased God to call him in the entry of this our Service, we take it in the better part, seeing it hath appeared to be Gods pleasure to call him away, so favourably to the service of him, especially in the constancy of his duty towards God, wherein, we hear say, he dyed very commendably. And for your self, we cannot but let you know that we hear out of France such singular good reports of your duty well accomplished towards your husband, both living and dead, with other your sober, wise, and discreet behaviour in that Court and Country, that we think it a part of great contentation to us, and commendation of our Country, that such a Gentlewoman hath given so manifest a testimony of virtue in such hard times of adversity. And therefore though we thought very well of you before, yet shall we hereafter make a more assured account of your virtues and gifts, and wherein soever we may conveniantly do you pleasure, you may be thereof assured. And so we would have you to rest yourself in quietness, with a firm opinion of our especiall favour towards you. Given under our Signet at our City of Oxford the [...] of September 1566: the eight year of our Reign. Your loving friend, Elizabeth R. (Elizabeth Tudor, 1566; Origin2, 230).

Royal we occurs continually throughout the letter, an uncharacteristic feature in the majority of Elizabeth's post-accession correspondence. The letters with continuous *royal we* were notable both for their function (written to express Elizabeth's dissatisfaction with the recipient) and their more ambiguous manuscript status, surviving only in draft form. The presence of *royal we* in this letter suggests a similar provenance, more closely affiliated with the official scribal documents issued in Elizabeth's name than the personal autograph letters included in QEIC. However, the involvement of a scribe does not mean that Elizabeth could not have composed the letter via dictation, or written it as a draft prior to its scribal transcription.

The other pronouns in the letters fit the patterns in QEIC. *You* occurs throughout, with no examples of *ye* or *thou*, which are unusual forms in her correspondence. The letter contains no examples of affirmative declarative *do*, a property that also fits with the infrequency of the variant in Elizabeth's post-accession correspondence. There is one example of an inflected superlative, the elative adjective *mean*. The use of inflection with a monosyllable accords with Elizabeth's practice, although it also fits with that of many of her contemporaries. More interesting is the lack of any address-form superlatives in either the opening or closing formulae. The letter opens simply with 'Madam', and has no subscription, except for the closing formula 'under our signet'. These epistolary features differ from the norm in Elizabeth's QEIC correspondence, but are not wholly without precedent (e.g. letter to Throckmorton, 1563, QEIC correspondence). Elizabeth only began to use superlatives in her closing formula in the 1580s, based on the QEIC evidence, and thus we cannot take the lack of examples in the Hoby letter (composed 1566) as conclusive evidence against her authorship. The letter contains no negative declarative contexts, no examples of multiple or single negation, and no instances of *wh-* relatives, which prevents the examination of these features for authorship assessment. Although the absence of these features may in itself be significant, it is difficult to make any conclusive intepretations without a greater knowledge of the linguistic practices of Elizabeth's scribes.

The spelling of the letter mostly uses PDE standard forms, but there are two non-standard forms that provide a point of comparison with QEISC. Whilst no examples of < layd > and < dyed > occur in the spelling corpus, it is possible to compare the components. In the verb *displayed*, Elizabeth uses < i > for both occurrences: < displaied > and < displaid >, whereas for present tense *die*, Elizabeth uses < dy > and < dye >. The results are inconclusive, and spelling has a limited applicability for the analysis of Elizabeth's authorship in this particular case. This is not because it is an unworkable feature but because of the greater likelihood of interference with the spelling in the transmission of the text. The value of spelling may lie in the assessment of contemporary manuscripts of a dubious hand, rather than scribal texts that are potentially the product of dictated content rather than copying.

Of the linguistic features analysed, four provide some guidance in the assessment of the letter to Margaret Hoby, and give some support for the hypothesis of dictation. However, the findings are far from conclusive, and the limited examples of features for which I have linguistic data greatly restrict the success of the analysis. The unpredictable content and the relatively short length of the Hoby letter are problems that are likely to apply to other questionable texts. It is clear that the approach would benefit from a greater number of linguistic features available for analysis. More generally, research into the characteristics of scribal letters would allow us to establish the features that characterise Elizabeth's involvement, and potentially those associated with different scribes, and thus enrich our understanding of the production of royal scribal correspondence.

15.4 *Case Study 4: 1597 Prayer*

The final case study tests the applicability of the approach and data for a genre not represented in QEIC; a plausible scenario given Elizabeth's wide-ranging and literary output. The text is known as the Azores Prayer, dated to 1597 ((169)). Woudhuysen (2007: 18) discusses the palaeography of the surviving manuscript, and finds he is 'almost, but not quite willing to believe' that the beautiful italic script is Elizabeth's.

(169) O God all-maker, keeper, and guider: Surement of thy rare-seene, unused and seeld-heard-of goodnes, powred in so plentifull sort upon us full oft; breeds now this boldnes, to craue with bowed knees, and heartes of humility thy large hand of helping power, to assist with wonder oure iust cause, not founded on Prides-motion nor begun on Malice-Stock; But as thou best knowest, to whome nought is hid meanes thou hast imparted to saue that thou hast given, by enioying such a people, as scornes their bloodshed, where suretie ours is one : Fortifie (dear God) such heartes in such sort as their best part may be worst, that to the truest part meant worst with least losse to such a nation, as despise their liues for their Cuntryes good That al Forrene Landes may laud and admire the Omnipotency of thy Worke : a fact alone for thee only to performe. So shall thy name be spread for wonders wrought and the faithfull encouraged, to repose in thy unfellowed grace: And wee that mynded nought but right, inchained in thy bondes for perpetuall slauery, and liue and dye the sacrificers of oure soules for such obtayned fauoure. Warrant, Dear Lorde, all this with thy command. Amen (BL MS Harley 6986 fol. 58).

The potential autograph status of the manuscript suggests that the spelling data may be able to shed immediate light on whether the palaeography is Elizabeth's or that of another individual. Firstly, the spelling of this text is relatively consistent, with a number of spellings using the PDE standard—a property typical of Elizabeth's post-accession spelling. The non-standard forms are also similar to those found in post-accession QEISC, e.g. <ght> in <nought> and <wrought>, <mynd> with medial <y> (Elizabeth's preferred spelling in QEISC) and the final <s> in <boldnes> (the only spelling in QEISC). The spelling of foreign <forrene> in the prayer differs from the form in QEISC, <foraine>, but shows similarity with Elizabeth's spelling of foreigners <foreners>, arguably congruent with her preferences.

There are a few spelling forms that are less typical of Elizabeth's system. The variation between single and double final <l> is found in QEISC, e.g. <all> and <al>, but <ll> is slightly too dominant in the prayer for Elizabeth's more variable practice. The spelling <cuntryes> is present in QEISC, but the diachronic data indicates that it occurs only in the pre-accession period, with medial <oun> or <on> the preferred forms in the post-accession correspondence. The final <ie> in <fortifie> and <suretie> is also less typical of Elizabeth's practice, as final-position <y> accounts for 94% of all spellings in the post-accession QEISC, including the five instances of *surety*. Moreover, first-person pronoun <wee> is highly unusual, with the 12 instances in QEISC rendered <we>. Similarly, *seld* uses a double <ee> in the prayer, whereas only <seld> and <sild> occur in QEISC.

The spelling evidence suggests that the existing manuscript is not the original autograph but rather a careful attempt to replicate a now-lost original. The similarity to Elizabeth's hand (Woudhuysen 2007) and the presence of many of Elizabeth's spelling forms suggests that a copyist worked closely from another (possibly the autograph) manuscript, even attempting to replicate the spelling in most cases. The extra final <ll> and the double <ee> may therefore represent the scribe's practice, reflecting a reversion to their own spelling system. If this is the case, the other linguistic features in the text should show a high level of conformity to the QEIC patterns. As the prayer is a more formal and deferential text, it may share its properties with the more literary traits of Elizabeth's translations, rather than the less formal style of her post-accession correspondence.

The absence of affirmative declarative *do* accords with Elizabeth's preferences (both correspondence and translations) for this period, although the prayer only contains one declarative context. There are no negative declaratives, but there is an example of coordinate multiple negation: 'not founded [...] nor begun'. Although this deviates from Elizabeth's typical practice in her correspondence, multiple negation was more common in her translations. Looking at other morphosyntactic features, the use of *whom* with an animate antecedent (rather than *which*) fits Elizabeth's post-accession preferences. The consistent use of the short form *thy* in consonant-initial and vowel-initial contexts conforms to QEIC trends, as does the inflected superlative for monosyllabic adjective *true*.

In sum, the linguistic features analysed in the 1597 prayer show a good fit with Elizabeth's practice, and support the hypothesis, based on the spelling, that the manuscript is a copy of her original composition. The number of morphosyntactic features available for analysis was limited, but there are no linguistic features that show a deviant usage and therefore argue against her authorship of the prayer.

15.5 *Summary*

The case studies illustrate that idiolectal data can offer a linguistic resource for authorship assessment, with the contextual likelihood method allowing the nuances of genre and date to be incorporated in the analysis. There is undoubted scope for expansion and improvement. Additional morphosyntactic data is desirable, and lexical data may also be a productive addition to the morphosyntactic results. Expanding spelling to include Elizabeth's punctuation practice could also be beneficial for works with a suspected autograph provenance. The analysis also highlights the limits of current knowledge concerning scribal practices at the court. The complex composition processes of Early Modern documents warrant greater exploration, and building up a picture of scribal linguistic preferences would greatly enhance authorship analysis. Despite these caveats, the sociolinguistic data provides a workable and valuable addition to the existing techniques (manuscript analysis, palaeography) already used in the field.

16. Research question 3: what can idiolectal analysis contribute to historical sociolinguistics?

The application of a historical sociolinguistic framework to Elizabeth's idiolectal data has provided new insights into the monarch's language, writing, and social identity, complementing the traditional literary and historical approaches. In this final section, I consider the potential contributions that idiolectal data could offer to theoretical and methodological aspects of variationist sociolinguistics, both historical and modern. Overall, the key findings of the investigation provide evidence in support of a number of central tenets the field, which I discuss in more detail below. The data also permits other facets of sociolinguistics to be evaluated afresh, and I consider three areas in particular. Firstly, the QEIC data provides a rich basis to evaluate the descriptions of linguistic leadership, such as the categories of Innovator and Early Adopter; secondly, the historical idiolect illustrates the strength of Communities of Practice as a theoretical construct to explain linguistic variation; and thirdly, the evidence highlights the significance of stylistic variation in the analysis of variation and change.

16.1 *Idiolects and Idiosyncrasy*

Despite Elizabeth's unique social position, the analysis of her morphosyntactic choices, self-reference pronouns and orthography reveal that the queen's language shares many of its characteristics with the patterns and preferences of other Early Modern speakers. The finding supports Chambers' argument that linguistic uniqueness is a theoretical possibility and not a feature of real-life speakers. He notes (2003: 114) that 'truly idiosyncratic speakers have never emerged from our [sociolinguistic] researches. If they exist, they are so rare that no sample population to date seems to have included one'. Even though Elizabeth is socially distinct from her contemporaries, particularly in the post-accession period, her linguistic preferences show a degree of fit with her contemporaries. She is more like those with whom she shared (literally and abstractly) her experiences, less like those with whom she did not. This patterning correlates with the findings from modern sociolinguistic studies. Even speakers on the edge of the bell-curve, a leader or a lagger, 'relate to the people who surround them in well-defined ways' (Chambers 2003: 114).

16.2 Adolescence and Adulthood

The diachronic dimension of the study provides a historical perspective on another core variationist hypothesis: the significance of adolescence in the progression of language change. There is a strong consensus in the literature that 'the vernacular people learn in adolescence remains the basic vernacular that they use throughout their lives' (Bayley 2002: 320). Thus it is the adolescents, as the second-youngest generation, who play a crucial role in advancing change within a community. The significance of adolescents as a social group in language change has been identified in numerous present-day studies, with the relationship between linguistic differentiation and social identity providing a persuasive social explanation for their linguistic behaviour (e.g. Eckert 2000; Meyerhoff 2002; D'Arcy & Tagliamonte 2009).

Although the emphasis of the present analysis is on Elizabeth's idiolectal development in relation to her accession, the data can be seen to provide support for adolescence as a significant period. In the pre-accession data, which represents Elizabeth's linguistic preferences between the ages of 11 and 24, there is considerable morphosyntactic variation both diachronically and synchronically (i.e. stylistically). Declarative *do* offers the best example of such variation, as does the rapid obsolescence of *the which*, although Elizabeth's progressiveness in this period is notable across the majority of variables studied. The spelling analysis offers an insight into the possible written dimension of adolescent linguistic instability, although one that is perhaps particular to the sixteenth century.

However, the data also suggests, quite persuasively, that Elizabeth's idiolect is not completely fixed and invariant once she reaches her mid-twenties. Variation occurs throughout her life, across a number of linguistic levels, and adds to a growing body of research indicating that language change also occurs in adulthood (Raumolin-Brunberg 2005, 2006;

Sankoff & Blondeau 2007). Some of the developments show Elizabeth's continued participation in an ongoing linguistic change, such as the use of *which* with non-animate antecedents, and the expansion of short-form possessive determiners across phonological contexts, fitting what Sankoff and Blondeau (2007: 582) call a 'lifespan change'. In these two morphosyntactic changes, Elizabeth's adulthood acquisition of the incoming forms occurs at a far more moderate rate than in her pre-accession developments. This fits with contemporary sociolinguistic studies (of phonological variation) in which older speakers contribute less dramatically than younger speakers to a change, but—importantly—they do contribute (Sankoff & Blondeau 2007: 581).

In evaluating the variation in Elizabeth's adolescence and adulthood, it becomes clear that there is another dimension to consider. Among the more striking aspects of the QEIC data are the prevalence of stylistic variation and Elizabeth's sensitivity to (or even establishment of) changes in linguistic fashions. The decline in negative *do* is an excellent example of variation that has no macro-level diachronic implications, in the sense that Elizabeth is not advancing the linguistic change: from a historical perspective, it is a minor deviation from the generalisation of *do* in the negative declarative context. Yet, at the idiolectal level, it is a notable characteristic of Elizabeth's language in the 1580s and 1590s, and clear evidence of variation in adulthood (i.e. instability).

Micro-level variation of this kind is perhaps overlooked in sociolinguistic studies: partly because it does not lead to macro-level language change; partly because it is located within the individual speaker, not social groups; and partly because variationist work traditionally uses speech-based evidence, and not the data in QEIC which is taken from across the vernacular-literary spectrum. Yet this type of idiolect instability is significant, I believe, precisely because it represents variation that does not lead to change—the crux of the actuation problem (Weinreich et al. 1968).

Such examples of variation in adulthood, as part of or separate from a macro-level change, can potentially offer a fine-grained perspective on the sociolinguistic pressures that act on speakers. The relationship between adulthood idiolectal variation and the generational progression of language change is one that requires further investigation. Elizabeth's language gives only a snapshot of the possible influences (literary fashions, contact with younger generations) that can trigger variation. In the case of negative *do*, for example, it may be that the shift in stylistic evaluation at the upper strata was not socially prominent or significant enough to stop the progression of the change in the language of other social groups, which was likely further propagated through internal factors (e.g. analogy with interrogatives).

The rising number of panel- and trend-studies in contemporary sociolinguistics (e.g. Nahkola & Saanilahti 2004; Sankoff & Blondeau 2007) highlights a growing appreciation of intra-speaker diachronic variation. But this is also an area of study ideally suited to the resources and methodologies of historical sociolinguistics, where diachronic data for multiple individuals can be rapidly amassed, and systematically compared. The work of Raumolin-Brunberg (2005, 2006) and Nevalainen et al. (2011) demonstrate how quantitative methods can illuminate speaker roles in change against the background of macro-level norms. The QEIC findings suggest that there is rich future potential for combined quantitative and qualitative approaches to explore variation at the idiolectal level and establish its relationship with contemporary macro-level trends.

16.3 *Linguistic Leadership*

Elizabeth's general preference for innovative variants suggests she is a linguistic leader. The QEIC data shows that, in seven of eight morpho-syntactic changes, Elizabeth's uptake started earlier and occurred more rapidly than for many of her contemporaries. Only the data for *(the) which* showed evidence of a lag. Thus the study reveals that Elizabeth is mostly a leader of linguistic change in the variables I have analysed, but we cannot say she is always a leader. Linguistic leadership, even in the most striking of cases, is not a uniform property of an individual speaker. The evidence from Nevalainen et al. (2011) suggests that Elizabeth is in fact highly unusual in her progressiveness across this many morphosyntactic variants when compared with her contemporaries.

As a further caveat, we should also not overlook the fact that Elizabeth's progressiveness, as identified in this study, is based on a select number of features chosen because of their development at the idiolectal level. There are many variables (morphosyntactic, lexical, discursive) that have not been analysed in Elizabeth's idiolect, and that may show very different traits. To give one example, Elizabeth's formation of adjectival comparatives was found to be highly consistent and stable, unlike the data for superlatives (discussed in Chapter 11). Due to space restrictions and the over-arching goals of the study, the data was omitted from discussion. My decision also reflects the conventional focus of diachronic linguistics more generally, as Milroy (1992: 10) remarks: 'historical linguists do not generally describe patterns of maintenance'. Yet language change always occurs in a space where the pressures for stability and divergence collide. The actuation problem (Weinreich et al. 1968), when viewed from an idiolectal perspective, asks why an individual speaker participates in one change but not another. Why do they shift their usage in this way, but not in that way? Idiolectal maintenance, against which the variable elements can be compared, may provide an important perspective on patterns of maintenance, variation and change.

Returning to the features that do show change in Elizabeth's idiolect, it is significant that the social factors that seem to contribute to Elizabeth's linguistic leadership are not uniform across the variables. For instance, Elizabeth's education appears to be a key factor in her uptake of *who*, the dehumanisation of *(the)which* and use of single negation; three changes that emerged 'from above'. Conversely, Elizabeth led a different type of change in the uptake of *my/thy* (excepting *own/nown*) and the generalisation of *you*; both of these changes emerged 'from below', through the lower social ranks. This diversity may well be a reflection of Elizabeth's unusual social position, as Nevalainen et al. (2011: 28-9) also suggest. However, the results for the morphosyntactic variables nevertheless suggest that, firstly, an individual's participation in language change is not uniform–a speaker can be both a leader and a lagger–and, secondly, an individual's linguistic behaviour in a change can also be prompted by different social factors, even if the result (i.e. as the leader of a change) is the same.

Elizabeth's progressiveness therefore provides an exemplary case to explore the different speaker roles proposed in relation to the innovation and diffusion of language change.

16.4 *Innovators, Early Adopters and Networks*

Within the sociolinguistic literature, there are two distinct models of speaker roles in language change. The first argues that linguistic leaders are individuals located at the centre of their social networks (e.g. Labov 1972). These leaders, which Labov terms Innovators, have a higher status and prestige than their peers, which grants them influence (not solely linguistic) over other speakers in their network. As centrally-located members, Innovators have direct (first-order) and indirect (second-order) network connections, and it is the diversity of their contacts which allows them to be exposed to and incorporate variant forms into their vernacular. Their social standing subsequently endorses these forms and ensures their diffusion within the social group.

The second model posits that it is peripheral members of the network who are responsible for innovation. Milroy (1992; see also Milroy & Milroy 1985) argues that linguistic innovations are spread via weak ties, rather than the strong contacts specified in Labov's definition. Milroy's Innovator is characterised by a peripheral involvement in speech communities, as the weak ties allow them to act as 'a bridge between groups', with little import in the centre of a group (1992: 184).

The two models appear to offer competing realisations for the same process. As Fagyal et al. (2010: 2065) remark: 'How can both roles be legitimate alternatives?' In fact, the role of central and peripheral speakers in language change may prove to be equally significant. The results of computational simulations run by Fagyal et al. (2010) reveal that Labov's Innovator and Milroy's Innovator are two key facets in the process of language change. Simulations of networks that lacked any peripheral members (referred to as *loners* by Fagyal et al.) resulted in a speech community that 'converges very quickly to a norm, which then stays fixed', indicating that *loners* serve 'as either sources of new variants, or repositories of past norms' (2010: 2071–2072). Conversely, in a social network simulation without leaders (the highly central members known as *hubs*) no norms emerged as a majority. Furthermore, the simulations suggested that the *hub's* prestige within their network is a third significant facet; a network simulation that lacked any collectively popular individuals also resulted in the absence of norms. In summary: 'the cumulative adoption of novel variants by centrally-connected, hyper-influential individuals is crucial for a successful diffusion process' (2010: 2072).

Milroy (1992: 185) has previously posited comparable dual roles in the diffusion of change, based on his study of phonological variation in Belfast. In addition to the peripheral Innovator, characterised by weak ties, he suggests the Labovian Innovator can be better described as an 'Early Adopter': speakers who 'are relatively central to the group and relatively conforming to the group norms'. They help the variant to diffuse throughout the group to reach the mid-point stage of a change, due to their strong contacts and social status amongst their peers—a description that is clearly comparable with what Fagyal et al. term a *hub*.

It is difficult to see how Elizabeth's linguistic leadership could be identified as originating from a peripheral network membership, given her central and prestigious position at the Court. Viewed in the above terms, Elizabeth's linguistic behaviour bears a strong resemblance to the *hubs* or Early Adopter (Labov's Innovator). In their investigation of progressive and conservative language users in sixteenth-century England, Nevalainen et al. (2011) suggest that, for many Early Modern changes, it is crucial that the incoming variant is adopted by 'the topmost strata' in society. Elizabeth's role, in this sense, is paramount. They suggest that 'Elizabeth's central role in her social networks most likely promoted the diffusion of the variants she adopted in their new and vigorous phrase, as with the individuals Labov found to be leaders in Philadelphia' (2011: 29).

The interplay between *hubs* and *loners* modelled by Fagyal et al. (2010) provides a persuasive means of accounting for Elizabeth's linguistic behaviour, its relation to (and apparent impact on) her contemporaries, and the complex and changeable qualities of the Tudor Court networks. Historians emphasise the ever-changing make-up of peripheral courtiers, each seeking favour from the queen and the men at its centre. May (1991: 19) suggests that there was 'a politically active class'—hundreds of men who held no official office but came to the Court and 'associated personally with the Queen'. It is unlikely that Elizabeth's contact with these peripheral members can be labelled strong, relative to her decades-long connection with the members of her Privy Council and gentlewomen, but they do ensure a constant influx of and exposure to variation (linguistic, social or otherwise). Thus we have a configuration of a large, multi-network model in which Elizabeth is central and has strong ties, with additional contact through weak ties with more peripheral individuals at Court. The advances in archival research and digital humanities will hopefully enable these networks to be empirically modelled and explored in more detail.

However, there is a further (and important) distinction to be made regarding the main role of the *hub*. In their computer simulations, Fagyal et al. found that, regardless of the point of innovation, whether from peripheral or central speakers, the *hubs* would always be the means through which a variant would be propagated. As they astutely note:

> Highly-influential centers can, of course, also introduce novel variants, copy innovations from other leaders and their cohorts. Calling them *innovators*, however, obscures their essential function of spreading, rather than inventing or introducing the most socially prestigious variants. Thus our results lend support to the view that the dynamics underlying the propagation phase should be examined separately from constraints motivating the innovation process (Fagyal et al. 2010: 2074).

The use of the term Innovator (Labov 1972) is therefore somewhat misleading. Elizabeth's position is better characterised as a leader-propagator; an individual who plays a crucial part in the diffusion of change in their network. For Elizabeth, the reach of that network is vast and may well explain the connection Nevalainen et al. (2011) identify between the adoption of a variant at the Court, by Elizabeth, and the subsequent uptake by the general populace.

Turning to the issue of innovation, specifically in relation to Elizabeth's linguistic leadership, there is no reason why Elizabeth, as a *hub*, could not also innovate through coinage (form or function) as well as through the contact method, and subsequently impress that innovation on her peers; it seems reasonable to assume that all speakers can innovate, that is, use language creatively for their individual communicative purposes. However, identifying and classifying innovation is difficult. Milroy (1992: 184) notes that 'there seems to be no easy way [...] to identify in the data the crucial distinction between innovators and early adopters', and, despite the insights provided by historical material, there is presently no palpable means to determine if Elizabeth is using a particular variant for the first time, either in her idiolect or amongst her peers, nor whether it is one of her own devising or one that arose through contact with other speakers. The process of innovation and the process of diffusion would seem to require different methodological approaches. At present, the idiolectal data offers insight only into the latter.

Overall, Elizabeth's linguistic position finds a surprisingly good fit with the bi-part diffusion model posited by Milroy (1992) and computationally simulated by Fagyal et al. (2010). Thus, the idiolectal data provides empirical support for theoretical speaker categories, attesting that the uniformitarian principle operates as effectively for the individual speaker as it does for social groups. Whilst the details of Elizabeth's biography are undoubtedly very different to the speakers studied in contemporary sociolinguistics, it appears that the influences from various social factors and their interaction at the site of an individual have comparable linguistic effects. Yet there is a lingering sense that Elizabeth is not simply a normal *hub* or Early Adopter, of the kind identified in Harlem, New York or Belfast, Northern Ireland. The extent of her progressiveness, as a characteristic feature of her idiolect, is striking and an unusual property among her contemporaries (Nevalainen et al. 2011). I explore why this might be the case in the following section.

16.5 *Explaining Progressiveness: Communities of Practice*

At present, the sociolinguistic models of leader-propagators (Labov's Innovator or Milroy's Early Adopter) do not fully explain how such a speaker's social facets (their social background, social prestige, their network ties) translate to the progressive use of incoming variants by that particular individual. One argument for idiolectal analysis is the insight it offers into the 'socio-psychological underpinnings' of variation (Schreier 2006: 28), and, by drawing on recent work on the relationship between identity and language, it is possible to speculate how Elizabeth's social context feeds into, and is part of, her linguistic behaviour. In the following discussion, I use the material gathered on Elizabeth's idiolect to suggest how the descriptive leader-propagator (Early Adopter) category might become an explanatory one. If Elizabeth is not the one innovating the change, but rather identifying and utilising the incoming variants as a positive linguistic feature (tacitly and/or explicitly) from a very early stage, then it is important to identify the social and linguistic needs that create and drive her behaviour.

One means of developing the account of Elizabeth's involvement and status in language change is to relate her linguistic behaviour to her membership in different COMMUNITIES OF PRACTICE (henceforth CofP). A CofP is a construct denoting 'a group of people who over time share in the same set of social [including linguistic] practices with a common purpose' (Charlebois 2009: 238). Individuals can be members of multiple CofPs— such as the local football team or the PTA— and their position within the group can also vary from highly involved central membership to peripheral participation. The important distinction between a CofP and the main-stream definition of 'community' is the emphasis placed upon the practice of membership. The enactment of certain behaviours, including language, 'structures forms of participation within the group and relations to the social world around them' (Eckert 2005: 95). One of the claimed benefits of the CofP concept, therefore, is its focus

> on the linguistic and social practices of actual groups of people. It helps to avoid making generalizations about abstract categories such as age, ethnicity, gender, and social class. A focus on CofPs allows us to see how people experience and decipher the social order on a personal basis (Charlebois 2009: 238).

CofPs allow us to appreciate identity as a fluid, complex and dynamic construct, 'pulling us away from a tendency to "pigeon-hole" speakers' (Eckert 2000: 39) and provide 'a framework for understanding both the social and the linguistic facets of sociolinguistic variation' (Meyerhoff 2002: 526). The richness of the CofP model has been an emergent theme in sociolinguistic investigations over the last decade, perhaps most famously exemplified by Eckert's (2000) study of adolescents at Belten High. Its currency in historical sociolinguistic studies is less established and Meyerhoff (2002: 542) questions how much insight can be gathered 'when researchers are restricted to using archival materials'. Elizabeth's idiolect offers an indication of how CofP can be productively applied to historical social and linguistic data.

I am not suggesting, however, that CofP should replace the social categories approach in sociolinguistic (idiolectal) analysis. The structured data provided by the categories has contextualised Elizabeth's linguistic preferences, and established the points of similarity and difference with the macro-level trends. However, the CofP approach provides a finer-grained account of Elizabeth's position, linguistically and socially, and offers an opportunity to explore how sociolinguistic meanings 'emerge, are some-times contested and sometimes maintained, through the actions of individuals' (Meyerhoff 2002: 534).

In the pre-accession period, Elizabeth was a leader in several morpho-syntactic changes. These changes can be collated into two groups. The first group is affiliated with educated usage and includes changes 'from above'; Elizabeth's leadership contrasts with the early (incipient) stage of the change at the macro-level. The second group is associated with female speech, and the changes emerge 'from below'; these are at a fairly established (new and vigorous) stage at the macro-level. In the preceding analysis, the two types of change were correlated with Elizabeth's contact with two social groups. I hypothesised that the first linguistic set are related to Elizabeth's tutelage under the esteemed scholars of the universities, as well as the influence of her learned stepmother, Catherine Parr, and second group to Elizabeth's earliest childhood experiences with her caregivers and other women in her household.

However, connecting Elizabeth's language to these socio-biographical groups does not explain why Elizabeth is a leader of these changes. To do so, we should return to a key concept of sociolinguistics: the social significance of the linguistic variable. Scholars have suggested that speakers adopt variants to benefit from the social associations; for instance, a speaker can be associated with a particular group known to use the linguistic feature (Labov 2001: 191). More recently, some variationists have argued that individuals use particular linguistic properties as an act of identity, to consciously construct a particular persona to reflect their wishes for that context (see Johnstone 2000). Podesva's (2007) work on falsetto voice properties is one study that adopts this approach to linguistic variation.

Within a CofP, particular linguistic variants can become markers of membership, signifying and constructing an individual's position and identity within the group, whereas in other CofPs the same linguistic variant may have far less significance. Eckert carefully points out that the systems that demarcate different CofPs can also operate within a group:

> [T]he community of practice is the nexus between the individual and the wider social world, making individual and group identity work inseparable. It stands to reason, then, that the very oppositions that distinguish a given community of practice from others will function within the community as well. If a group distinguishes itself with respect to others along the lines of, for example, toughness or race or intelligence, there will be differentiation within the group along the same lines (Eckert 2005: 95–96).

Recall that a leader-propagator occupies a central position within the group, and this is key to their linguistic leadership. In CofP terms, the leader is a key participant in the group. Relating this to Elizabeth, her social position as princess in the pre-accession period places her at the centre of the CofP involving her caregivers, and also at the centre of the CofP with her educators. It is therefore conceivable that Elizabeth felt pressured by her position to be the exemplary model for the group—to be the humanist scholar, for instance, or to be the young princess—and this offers one explanation for her linguistic behaviour.[44]

For example, the variants 'from above', animate *who* and single negation, were not well established at the macro-level in EModE during Elizabeth's childhood. However, it is reasonable to assume that within the CofP

---

[44] Goldberg (1990: 42–44) hints at the possible pressures Elizabeth may have experienced. He suggests that Roger Ascham used Elizabeth's scholarly achievements to indirectly demonstrate his own abilities as a tutor, repeatedly reporting on the princess' academic progress in letters to his intellectual peers on the continent.

containing Elizabeth and her educators these variants were current, and had positive associations because of the high education level of those members. As a key member of the CofP, Elizabeth needs to correlate her linguistic practice with her status to allow her to construct and maintain her goals for her identity in that context. In the proffered scenario, this would lead to her rapid uptake of the positively marked variants such as *who* and single negation. The same scenario can also explain Elizabeth's linguistic leadership in another CofP involving Elizabeth's caregivers. Elizabeth adopts the variants emerging 'from below' in order to indicate her membership with the women who were early adopters of the incoming forms. Elizabeth's behaviour and participation within the different CofPs exemplifies how individual practices intersect with the macro-level social categories, such as social rank and gender. Elizabeth's correlation with others of her educational level (social rank) or gender reflects her participation within smaller communities that enact and define the (linguistic) behaviours that are subsequently associated with broader social categories at the macro-level.

The above examples help us to understand Elizabeth's pre-accession idiolectal development, in part because this period offers the clearest examples of Elizabeth's linguistic leadership. However, it is possible to apply the CofP framework to the post-accession data, with similar interpretative insights. For instance, Elizabeth's acquisition of *royal we* reflects her new membership within a 'royal' CofP—working with the precedents established by her ancestors, as well as the conventions of Court administration. By incorporating the self-reference term into her idiolect, Elizabeth is both signalling her social position, and sustaining the pronoun's significance within the CofP. She is meeting the expectations of the group, whilst simultaneously constructing her own position within it.

I do not wish to suggest that Elizabeth adopted the variants because she wanted to be (or her CofPs expected her to be) a linguistic leader. An individual's perspective of their language is predominantly synchronic, not diachronic. Elizabeth's interpretations of the communicative context, her knowledge of cultural conventions, the elements significant to her position within a CofP, her personal preferences of use for an interactive context based on prior experience: all inform her choice of the available linguistic variants. As Mira Ariel notes more generally:

> There is nothing special or different that the speaker does when she's participating in language change (and she always is). The speaker always does the same thing, which is use her language in context in an effective way for whatever local purposes she may have (Ariel 2008: 114).

In Elizabeth's case, the 'effective way' for 'local purposes' often happens to be the use of the incoming variants, a consequence of her membership in particular CofPs, and her central position within the groups. Her linguistic leadership is the product of the intricate relationship between social experience and language.

16.6 *Hypercorrection and Linguistic Leadership*

The distinctiveness of Elizabeth's linguistic leadership, that is the level of progressiveness she displays in comparison to her contemporaries, is evocative of the sociolinguistic phenomenon HYPERCORRECTION. In essence, hypercorrection is a form of accommodation. A speaker uses a linguistic form because its qualities signify, or relate to, membership with a particular group. Rather than accommodating within accepted parameters, however, 'in their zeal to adopt the linguistic norms of the more prestigious group, the adopters [outdo] their models' (Chambers 2003: 67). Labov identifies the phenomenon in the speech of lower-middle-class speakers in New York (Labov 1972), as does Trudgill (1974) in his Norwich study. Subsequent research suggests that higher social classes also hypercorrect (see Tang Boyland 2001), with geographical mobility a further trigger (Chambers 2003: 67). The analysis of Elizabeth's idiolect suggests that hypercorrection can be discussed as part of the construction and practice of local groups, as well as in terms of broad social categories. It is her position within different CofPs that promotes the excessive use of particular linguistic variants, as part of the mutual development of the linguistic practices associated with the different domains.

The relationship between Elizabeth's 'hypercorrect' adoption of linguistic variants and the explanation offered based on the CofP construct has further implications for the understanding of language change. In Chambers' survey of speaker categories and language change, he makes an intriguing proposition regarding hypercorrection. He suggests that

> if a noticeable proportion of the population uses variants at a frequency beyond the norms of their social cohort—that is, hypercorrectly—in successive generations, then it seems likely that the norms themselves will come to be altered in that direction (2003: 64).

Chambers' prediction refers to twentieth/twenty-first century speakers. Yet the analysis of Elizabeth's idiolect finds evidence in favour of his proposition for the development of EModE. Elizabeth's linguistic leadership is characterised by her early adoption of a variant at a level 'beyond the norms' of others in her social category. As a result, it is plausible that her position in Tudor society, as a central member of the influential upper ranks and the Court, subsequently influenced the linguistic patterns of her contemporaries. Her participation in different CofPs will have influenced the linguistic behaviour of other individuals, who themselves have membership in other communities. In this way, the social significance of a variant is transmitted across society, and could indeed become the norm.

The present analysis suggests Elizabeth's idiolect, specifically, may play an important role in endorsing a variant that later becomes the norm. This interpretation, which offers a new dimension to our understanding of Elizabeth's social import and historical legacy, can be plausibly justified at the micro-level (through her central position within various CofPs), at the meso-level (through the different social networks and ties she developed during her lifetime) and at the macro-level (through the opportunities and experiences offered by her social rank, age, education, etc.). Consequently, the investigation of Elizabeth's idiolect confirms the suspicions of modern sociolinguists such as Podesva (2007) and Schreier (2006) that the value of idiolectal analysis lies in the detail—the 'socio-psychological underpinnings of variation' (Schreier 2006: 28). However, I would contest Schreier's view that idiolectal analyses cannot contribute to sociolinguistic theories of language change. The preceding discussion has demonstrated how theoretical categories and approaches can be tested against idiolectal data, and conceptual approaches such as CofP, which were designed for contemporary sociological contexts, can be successfully applied to historical data.

16.7 *Stylistic Variation and Historical Sociolinguistics*

The analysis of Elizabeth's idiolectal data repeatedly foregrounded the role of style, and stylistic variation, as a contributing factor to the patterns identified over time and across different genres. The importance of style has implications for the position of this factor in sociolinguistic studies, particularly in historical investigations. As Eckert and Rickford (2001: 1) observe, sociolinguistics has conventionally 'focused on the relation between variation and the speaker's place in the world, at the expense of the speaker's strategies with respect to this place'. However, the importance of style and style-shifting in idiolectal and group analysis is being increasingly recognised in modern sociolinguistic studies. Eckert (2000), Coupland (2007), Podesva (2007) and Moore (2012), for example, all demonstrate the important role stylistic variation plays in the day-to-day construction of individual identity, with their analyses based on a diverse range of speakers, linguistic features and social contexts.

Labov (2010), too, acknowledges the important role of style at the site of the individual speaker. He emphasises the need for the comparative study of idiolectal variation across different situations:

> Much is to be learned from the study of individual variation [...] To make the case strongly, we have to go beyond the description of

individual acts and observe how a person changes from one social situation to another (2010: 189).

The evidence from QEIC adds empirical weight to Labov's proposition and indicates that studying stylistic variation in historical data can offer a complementary perspective to modern studies with a stylistic focus. As the findings presented in Part II demonstrate, Elizabeth's idiolect shows a considerable stylistic range. The multi-genre corpus, which incorporates more literary writing than is typical for sociolinguistic analyses, allows for the impact of social conventions of genre and 'literariness' to be considered in the description and interpretation of Elizabeth's linguistic preferences. This proves to be highly beneficial. In the investigation of affirmative and negative *do*, for instance, the decrease in *do* in the 1580s would have been less transparent if only the correspondence data had been considered. Only by collating the diachronic trends in Elizabeth's translations with those identified in her less literary writing, and then interpreting the idiolectal results against the macro-level social data in CEEC, could I argue for what now appears to be a striking feature of Elizabeth's idiolect. The interface of social and stylistic elements was crucial to the process of description and interpretation.

The analysis also suggests that interactive variation, as the second dimension of style, is equally insightful. By carefully documenting the context surrounding each individual text, the analysis could consider the influence of the communicative scenario on Elizabeth's linguistic decisions. The contrast between the Seymour letters and other pre-accession correspondence is perhaps the most striking example, foregrounding Elizabeth's association of particular linguistic variants (in terms of both frequency and function) with particular communicative styles, and revealing how these associations could explain the quantitative trends identified in the corpus as a whole. The self-reference pronouns in the 1586 parliamentary speeches, discussing Mary, Queen of Scots are another case in point. The particularities of the scenario necessitated the use of linguistic resources (*royal we* and *exclusive monarchic we*) that Elizabeth would usually reserve for other contexts, such as her correspondence.

The importance of style variation in the analysis of Elizabeth's idiolect suggests that this dimension should be more broadly incorporated into historical sociolinguistic studies of language change. The function of a variable, such as the stylistic role of *my/mine* or affirmative *do*, was found to be as important a dimension of her linguistic leadership as the quantitative comparison. These qualities could only be fully appreciated through the cross-genre analysis of her letters, speeches and translations. Collectively, the significance of stylistic range for the understanding of variation suggests that the current historical sociolinguistic focus on single genre analysis may be a cause for concern, and in particular the central position of letters as the preferred linguistic resource. It was the comparison between Elizabeth's letters and other genres of her writing that produced some of the most interesting data for analysis.

Notably, Sharma (2011) has recently critiqued the conventional methods for evaluating stylistic variation in contemporary sociolinguistics. Her investigation of generational patterns in the use of Indian and British English phonological variables found that the social meaning of each variant could only be properly recognised when a range of stylistic contexts were taken into account. The style-shifting behaviour of her informants, which reflected the interactive properties (addressee, topic) of the communicative context, was not evident in data she gathered from the same informants in traditional sociolinguistic interviews. Moreover, the range of style-shifting was not homogenous amongst her informants, but rather reflected the social experiences and communicative needs of different speakers: older male speakers and younger female speakers showed greater variation in their use of British and Indian phonological variables due to their more diverse social networks. Engaging with the breadth and diverse contexts in which speakers interact, Sharma argues (2011: 487), is the best means to understand speaker agency in sound change, identified through the study of 'repertoire "portraits"'. There are clear similarities between Sharma's methodology and that implemented in the present investigation, despite the different modes (speech versus written language) and data constraints. This suggests that both contemporary and historical studies can benefit from the shift towards the individual speaker and the greater consideration of style in their linguistic practice in pursuit of advancing our understanding of language variation and change.

The single-style focus on letters in historical investigations arose in part because the genre is considered the best written evidence of spoken language, so valued because modern sociolinguistic analysis cites spoken language as the locus of language change (Labov 1972: 208). Current scholarly interest in correspondence of course extends beyond the field of historical sociolinguistics, and I do not wish to suggest that the genre is not a fascinating and rich resource for historical and linguistic study. Yet, surely, a distinctive attribute of historical sociolinguistics compared to its modern counterpart is the element of hindsight and the ability to retrospectively analyse and explore language change, which therefore permits a more detailed study of the progress from one form or function to another. The present study demonstrates that historical idiolectal analysis can make the important connection between the language choices of the individual (encompassing the interactive, stylistic, and social dimensions of a communicative act), and the macro-level trends of variation and change.

On a related point, Elizabeth's idiolectal data also makes a case for the greater role of literary or more formal language in the study of variation and change. Schneider (2002: 71) suggests that 'formal and literary writing [...] maybe of marginal interest [for variationists because] [...] being shaped by prescriptive traditions and conventions, they normally display categorical, invariant usage'. But this bias may lead to an under-appreciation of the data, just as Sharma (2011) argues that the sociolinguistic interview may limit recognition of linguistic variation and generational change in phonological variables. Similarly, Schilling-Estes (2002: 395) suggests that 'self-conscious speech, even overtly performative speech seems essential' when considering how individuals use language 'as a resource for creating and projecting one's persona', and the intersection with macro-level developments in language change. For the Early Modern period, particularly for an individual such as Elizabeth, participation in written networks and an awareness of literary fashions can be considered an important component of the upper ranks' social experiences. Although written, rather than spoken, Elizabeth's literary writing surely captures the more performative and self-conscious dimension that Schilling-Estes argues for. This quality is perhaps best exemplified by Elizabeth's pre-accession translations, which offer a strong counter to Schneider's assertion that literary texts are categorical or invariant. These works are characterised by a distinctive distribution of linguistic variants that contrast with Elizabeth's preferences in other stylistic contexts; for example the prolific use of declarative *do*, the implementation of an archaic pronoun system, the use of conservative variants for possessive determiners and the presence of multiple negation.

   The linguistic make-up of the translations undoubtedly reflects Elizabeth's understanding of the genre conventions of the period; the attribute that Schneider appears to consider uninteresting for variationist studies. Yet the influence of genre conventions is a crucial factor shaping the linguistic identity that Elizabeth wished to construct and present to the intended reader, her stepmother Catherine Parr (and perhaps others of Parr's household). Notably, previous studies of the translations (e.g. Mueller & Scodel 2009) do not appear to comment on these stylistic properties, perhaps because they can only be recognised when compared with Elizabeth's preferences in other contexts. The stylistic qualities of the translations serve to emphasise the precociousness of Elizabeth's linguistic and literary ambition. Furthermore, the early establishment of her stylistic sensitivity may well be a crucial factor in understanding Elizabeth's linguistic leadership throughout her life. The HC was developed for macro-level analysis of genre and linguistic variation, but the lack of cohesion across the corpus means that an individual's stylistic shifts cannot be traced and documented against other social and internal variables. Idiolectal data, perhaps what we might call a 'corpus of idiolects', offers the best means of capturing the intersections between style and social factors, between micro and macro.

The importance of cross-genre comparison for the understanding of Elizabeth's linguistic behaviour and her participation in language variation and change also suggests that the conventional approach to written language in sociolinguistics may require revision. Schneider (2002: 81) suggests that 'the validity of written texts for speech analysis largely depends on the writer: his or her willingness to render speech forms, and his or her ability to do so'. In this study, Elizabeth's language has been used and interpreted specifically as written language, shaped by its mode of transmission. This stance has allowed the different facets of text production to be considered in analysis, and the study of Elizabeth's spelling directly exploits the written dimension of the data, with fascinating results. This seems a profitable direction for future work on variation in EModE; one that surely makes 'best use' of the 'bad data' we have available.

In conclusion, the patterns identified in Elizabeth's idiolect and their relation to systemic, social, interactive and stylistic factors make a strong case for a fresh emphasis on the individual speaker: a new appreciation of their role as designer, manipulator and user of the linguistic system in pursuit of their communicative goals. As Chambers eloquently summarises (2003: 370):

> We express who we are with fine nuance and no little grace, selecting linguistic variants contingent upon the setting in which we are speaking and on not only our own class, sex, age, ethnicity, style and much more, but also contingent upon all those things in the people we are speaking to. Human beings have apparently always done so, and it is safe to say they always will.

Queen Elizabeth I exemplifies Chambers' statement. Her linguistic choices show an acute awareness of the relationship between language and the communicative context, self-representation and interpersonal relationships. The findings from QEIC provide valuable insights into the relationship between an idiolect and the speaker's identity, and between an idiolect and the progression of language variation and change.

17. Final word

In his investigation of the 'representation' of Queen Elizabeth I, Montrose (2006) stresses the value of cross-disciplinary analysis. Describing himself as '[f]ormally a literary scholar', Montrose (2006: 4–8) argues that expanding the literary-historical approach to less literary documents, such as letters or patents, is an important step in the study of Early Modern culture. I wish to emphasise the value of cross-disciplinary analysis that has emerged in this study of Elizabeth's idiolect. Bridging the gap between different disciplines is an important pursuit, one that allows us to corroborate or re-assess existing concepts with new evidence. By treating Elizabeth's writing with fresh, linguistic eyes, I have argued for an historical approach that considers the language in its socio-historical context, alongside the more conventional reading of the semantic content. The findings have enhanced our understanding of her writings, her idiolect, and her social identity, and provided a substantial new resource for authorship analysis. At the same time, the study has allowed me to test and develop the sociolinguistic approach, and to contribute to our understanding of the individual in language change. My hope is that scholars from both disciplines find value in my interdisciplinary approach, not only on Elizabeth I and EModE, but as an example of how we might further our understanding more generally of history, language and the individuals involved in their creation.

Department of English
Arts Building
University of Birmingham
Edgbaston
United Kingdom
B15 2TT
m.evans@bham.ac.uk

PART IV

APPENDIX

18. Tabular Data

Table 62. Affirmative *do* and non-*do* (QEIC translations)

Translation	Total *do*/non-*do*	% *do*	*Do*/1000 words	Non-*do*/1000 words
Navarre (1544)	358	43	14.9	19.7
Calvin (1545)	447	64.7	22.9	12.5
Cicero (1592)	122	12.3	3.9	28.0
Boethius (1593)	310	11.9	8.2	60.8

Table 63. Affirmative *do* (%) by syntactic contexts, *do* tokens only (QEIC pre-accession translations)

	Do (n.)	% *do*
Adverbial	31	7.0
Verb final	4	0.9
Inversion	19	4.3
Intervening material	55	12.4
Second person	35	7.9
No context	299	67.5
Total	443	

Table 64. Affirmative *do* by syntactic contexts (%) out of *do* and non-*do* (QEIC pre-accession translations)

	Do and non-*do* (n.)	% *do*
Adverbial	39	79.5
Verb final	16	25.0
Inversion	23	82.6
Intervening material	101	54.5
Second person	58	60.3
No context	568	52.6
Total	805	

Table 65. Affirmative *do* by syntactic context (%), *do* tokens only (QEIC post-accession translations)

	Do (n.)	% *do*
Adverbial	4	7.7
Verb final	29	55.8
Inversion	9	17.3
Intervening material	2	3.8
Second person	0	0.0
No context	8	15.4
Total	52	

Table 66. Affirmative *do* by syntactic contexts (%), *do* and non-*do* tokens (QEIC post-accession translations)

	Do and non-*do* (n.)	% *do*
Adverbial	20	20.0
Verb final	106	27.4
Inversion	20	45.0
Intervening material	42	4.8
Second person	7	0.0
No context	237	3.4
Total	432	

Table 67. Affirmative *do* (%) in syntactic context, *do* tokens only (QEIC speeches)

	Do (n.)	% *do*
Adverbial	4	28.6
Verb final	1	7.1
Inversion	3	21.4
Intervening material	3	21.4
Second person	0	0.0
No context	3	21.4
Total	14	

Table 68. Affirmative *do* (%) in syntactic contexts, *do* and non-*do* tokens (QEIC speeches)

	Do and non-*do* (n.)	% *do*
Adverbial	13	30.8
Verb final	6	16.7
Inversion	4	75
Intervening material	22	13.6
Second person	0	0
No context	115	2.6
Total	160	

Table 69. Single negation (%) in noncoordinate and coordinate constructions (QEIC correspondence)

	Total	% single negation
Noncoordinate	48	97.9
Coordinate	19	78.9

Table 70. Single negation (%) in noncoordinate and coordinate constructions, upper-ranking letter writers for the period 1525–1599 (adapted from Kallel (2007: 33–4))

	Total	% single negation
Noncoordinate	504	82.7
Coordinate	203	65.0

Table 71. Animate *who* (%) out of *who/which* by syntactic category (QEIC correspondence)

	Total (*who/which*)	% *who*
Proper name/title	24	100
Common noun	14	93
Pronoun	17	82

Table 72. *Which* and *the which* in five systemic contexts (%), duplicate tokens in each category (QEIC correspondence)

	% *the which*	% *which*
Pre-accession		
Non-restrictive	100	63.3
Continuative	60	20.4
Sentential	20	32.7
Determiner	40	16
Prepositional	60	6.1
Total forms (n.)	10	49
Post-accession		
Non-restrictive	100	87.6
Continuative	0	15.3
Sentential	0	22.7
Determiner	0	2.5
Prepositional	66.7	22.1
Total forms (n.)	3	163

Table 73. *Which* and *the which* tokens in five systemic contexts (%) (QEIC pre-accession translations)

	% *the which*	% *which*
Non-restrictive	90.1	66.3
Continuative	39.4	5.1
Sentential	15.5	5.6
Determiner	22.5	4.6
Prepositional clause	33.8	1.5
Total forms (n.)	71	197

Table 74. Distribution of < sch > by word position (pre- and post-accession QEISC)

	PreA initial position	PreA medial position	PreA final position
< s >	0 (0%)	0 (0%)	1 (8.3%)
< ss >	0 (0%)	1 (3.4%)	1 (8.3%)
< sch >	1 (1%)	10 (34.5%)	8 (66.7%)
< sh >	98 (99%)	16 (55.2%)	2 (16.7%)
< ssh >	0 (0%)	2 (6.9%)	0 (0%)
Total	99	29	12

	PostA initial position	PostA medial position	PostA final position
< s >	0 (0%)	2 (6.7%)	3 (11.1%)
< ss >	0 (0%)	0 (0%)	0 (0%)
< sch >	0 (0%)	13 (43.3%)	23 (85.2%)
< sh >	178 (100%)	12 (40%)	1 (3.7%)
< ssh >	0 (0%)	3 (10%)	0 (0%)
Total	178	30	27

Table 75. Distribution of < gh > variants (QEISC)

Forms	PreA	PostA
< gh >	16 (41.0%)	53 (71.6%)
< gth >	17 (43.6%)	2 (2.7%)
< ght >	2 (5.1%)	1 (1.4%)
< ie >	1 (2.6%)	5 (6.8%)
< ye >	0 (0%)	2 (2.7%)
< w >	0 (0%)	3 (4.1%)
< we >	0 (0%)	2 (2.7%)
< y >	1 (2.6%)	5 (6.8%)
< g >	1 (2.6%)	1 (1.4%)
< ghe >	1 (2.6%)	0 (0%)

19. The queen elizabeth i corpus (qeic)

The following discussion provides details about the Queen Elizabeth I Corpus, explaining my reasoning behind the texts included, and the difficulties encountered during the compilation process. My initial goal was to compile a corpus of Elizabeth's writing, transcribing only autograph manuscripts.[45] Documents written in the author's own hand have a high level of authenticity (Nevalainen 2002; see also Daybell 2009), both as historical documents and for the accuracy of the linguistic features, making them highly suited to idiolectal analysis. However, the number of surviving autographs was insufficient for diachronic and cross-genre comparison. Consequently, I conceded the original autograph-only ambition, and the final QEIC corpus, mainly in the correspondence sub-section used for the greater part of analysis, now includes a number of apographs (scribal copies). The discussion that follows describes the different procedures used to collate the most suitable texts for each sub-section of the corpus. A list of all texts and their sources can be found at the end of this section.

19.1 *Correspondence*

The impression given by historians (Harrison 1935: x; Doran 2000: 701) is that there is a large body of correspondence attributed to Elizabeth, of more than 3000 letters. However, when researching these texts I found that the majority survive in the hand of scribes (many with questions over Elizabeth's involvement) or as apographs. The queen simply did not write as many letters as she signed, as the mechanisms of the Elizabethan government were too vast and complex (Doran 2000: 700–701), which leads to an uneven diachronic distribution of autograph material.

When compiling the texts for QEIC, whenever possible I made a transcription directly from the autograph manuscript; many of these texts, particularly Elizabeth's correspondence with James VI (BL MS Add. 23240) and Edward Seymour (BL MS Lansdowne 1236), are kept at the British Library. These initial transcripts recorded the original spelling of the letters, as well as any errors or corrections, with additional notes made about the circumstances of composition. These autograph transcriptions are the basis for QEISC.

When modernising the spelling for QEIC, I checked my transcriptions of Elizabeth's writing with the recent published editions (e.g. Mueller & Marcus 2003; May 2004a). The heavy elisions and amendments in some of Elizabeth's later letters, for instance, are quite difficult to read and I wanted to ensure the transcriptions were accurate. Interestingly, I found the occasional discre-

---

[45] I use the term *autograph* following its etymological sense, 'in the hand of the author' (viz. *manuscript*), the definition endorsed by Peter Beal (2008: 29–30). The term *holograph* is occasionally used with the same meaning (e.g. May 2004a).

pancy where the edited publications differed in their reading of a sentence or word; for example Marcus, Mueller and Rose (2000: 358) transcribe one phrase as 'at lenth [length]', where May (2004a: 182) has 'at large'. In the manuscript (BL MS Add. 23240, fol.77) the word is poorly formed, but in my opinion May's reading is the better fit, and the same reading is found in Harrison (1935: 194). Although the differences between the most recent published editions were relatively minor, they demonstrate the impact intermediate parties can have on the accuracy of a transcription.

Nevertheless, the correspondence sub-section required a greater number of texts than Elizabeth's autograph manuscripts could provide, and I had to look to other types of document. I decided to transcribe a select number of apograph manuscripts, either contemporary to the original letter, or a copy made at a later date, e.g. the letter to Thomas Heneage, dated 27th April 1586, which was copied by the recipient and is preserved in BL MS. Galba C. IX, fol.197b.

The apograph manuscripts that I include in QEIC follow May's (2004a: xxvi) reasoning that 'certain types of scribal copies have a strong claim to authenticity'. I have chosen examples that represent 'in-house memoranda' (e.g. October 1586, to William Cecil and Francis Walsingham, QEIC correspondence) and letters expressing more personal sentiments, such as the affectionate letter addressed to 'Rob' (e.g. 19th July 1586, to Robert Dudley, QEIC correspondence), or letters of condolence (e.g. 1590, to Lady Knyvett, QEIC correspondence).

May (2004a: xxvi) also suggests that official royal correspondence (letters with the opening and closing conventions 'trusty and well-beloved', 'given under our signet') may also be classified as those with a 'strong claim to authenticity'. However, I believe that Elizabeth's involvement in official letters is likely to be less direct than an autograph document; for example, she may have dictated the letter, or made brief notes from which a scribe independently composed the text. The corpus requires texts of the highest level of authenticity possible, and thus compositions of this type are excluded from QEIC (despite their undoubted historical value). Future work should certainly explore the linguistic evidence in relation to Elizabeth's participation, and enrich our appreciation of her secretariat.

The correspondence sub-section also includes transcriptions made from published editions, as access to the original manuscripts—such as those in private collections—was not always possible. Editions consulted include Bruce (1849), Harrison (1935), Perry (1990), Mueller & Marcus (2003), Pryor (2003) and May (2004a). In the best cases (Perry (1990) and Pryor (2003)), the editions included photographic images of the manuscript, and I could make my transcription from the reproduced original. Otherwise, I cross-checked the differences and similarities between the transcriptions of the same documents. Typically, the differences were negligible. For the occasional lexical discrepancy, I compared all available transcripts to establish and make a judgement on the most likely reading. Whilst this is not an ideal solution, it was a necessary compromise to ensure sufficient material for analysis. My careful assessments of the letters' provenance and the accuracy of the transcriptions mean that QEIC contains enough letters of satisfactory authenticity for an analysis of Elizabeth's idiolect.

19.2. *Speeches*

My decision to include Elizabeth's speeches as a sub-section in QEIC was influenced by the attention they have received in literary-historical analysis, often described as the most public or performative examples of Elizabeth's writing (see Heisch 1975; Reynolds 2010). They also contribute some of the more popular and enduring images and quotations associated with Elizabeth I. However, preliminary research indicated that many of the most famous speeches were not suitable for my corpus. The Tilbury speech, for instance, survives in several versions made after the event by third-party writers, but there is no extant autograph draft or copy (see Green 1997). The 1601 so-called Golden Speech, in which Elizabeth states her commitment to her subjects, survives as four non-autograph (and very different) versions. May (2004a: 89–92, 2004b) discusses the accuracy of each account, suggesting that elements of each version probably represent what Elizabeth actually said, with the scribes working in teams to document the oration. However, whilst historically significant, the third-party accounts are unsuited to a corpus representing Elizabeth's idiolect.

In total, QEIC contains six parliamentary speeches covering the earlier decades of her reign. These texts offer the most convincing evidence of Elizabeth's involvement in their composition; they are either full autographs (1563, 1566, 1567) or scribal documents that contain Elizabeth's corrections, amendments and material approval (the two speeches from 1586). I have included only one apograph in this sub-section, a speech dating from 1576, because the decade is poorly represented in the QEIC corpus. Elizabeth endorsed the copy of this speech, which was later published from the Harington collection (May 2004a: 52–60).

19.3. *Translations*

QEIC includes four autograph translations. I recognise that including translations in a corpus of authentic idiolectal material is a debatable decision, given that the goal of translation is to reproduce another individual's words. Translations have been described as posing 'special problems' for historical linguistic study (Raumolin-Brunberg 1991: 41). However, I consider the genre appropriate for QEIC for several reasons. Firstly, modern scholars have noted Elizabeth's translations are 'phrase for phrase' rather than 'word by word', suggesting that she drew on her own linguistic preferences in their composition rather than simply substituting English for French or Latin (see Archer 1995; Mueller & Scodel 2009a). The fact that Elizabeth translated these works into her native tongue also acts in favour of including them in QEIC. Secondly, the act of translation was a self-conscious act during the sixteenth century. Whilst some scholars have suggested that translation was a 'safe' literary venture for women, representing their subservience to the master (text) (Goldberg 1990: 76), the more popular line of thought regarding Elizabeth's own translations is that they are a demonstration of her learning, and allow her to engage with the scholarly ambitions of contemporary society; a framing that aligns the queen with accounts of male translation (Goldberg 1990: 82). During Elizabeth's lifetime, these works 'often attracted as much attention [...] as her own compositions' (Marcus, Mueller & Rose 2000: xv).

A strong argument for their inclusion in QEIC is the insight they provide into Elizabeth's more literary language. As another point, the translations allow me to fulfil my initial 'autograph only' ambition to some degree, as the texts provide some lengthy specimens of autograph writing.

The earliest translation in QEIC is Elizabeth's well-known translation (written in 1544) of Margaret d'Navarre's *The Mirror of the Sinful Soul*. I transcribed this text from a facsimile of the original autograph (Ames 1897), and checked it against the edition by Marc Shell (1993). This early work has received much attention in literary-historical circles, and scholars argue that it reveals Elizabeth's precocious 'brilliance and vulnerability' (Demers 2005: 74). As Elizabeth's earliest known English translation, it provides valuable insight into her childhood idiolect in a literary context. The second text in the pre-accession section was written a year later, the first chapter of John Calvin's *De Institution*. The QEIC transcription is based on Mueller & Scodel (2009a).

The first post-accession translation is Cicero's *Pro M. Marcello* (1592). My transcription is based on Mueller & Scodel (2009b) and May (2004a). QEIC also includes the c.1593 version of Boethius' *De Consolatione*, transcribed from Pemberton (1899) and compared with the recent edition edited by Mueller and Scodel (2009b). I did not transcribe the whole text of Boethius, as there are repeated points in the manuscript where Elizabeth's autograph cedes to a scribal hand. The scribal sections reportedly contain a number of mistranslations and errors that could be the result of transmission or scribal error, rather than Elizabeth's own mistakes (Mueller & Scodel 2009b: 50, 54). The QEIC transcript of Boethius therefore includes only the autograph sections, and is a mix of verse and prose.

19.4. *Queen Elizabeth I Corpus: Text Information*

A = autograph; B = contemporary copy of autograph; C = autograph, based on modern edition; D = copy of autograph, based on modern edition.

Table 76. Correspondence Texts in QEIC

Date	Addressee	Source(s)	Status
1544, 31st December	Catherine Parr	Bodleian Library MS Cherry 36, fols 2r–4v. Mueller & Marcus 2003.	A
1548, May	Edward Seymour	TNA SP 10/5, fol.8a. May 2004a: 100.	B
1548, June	Catherine Parr	TNA SP Domestic, Edward VI 10/2, fol.84c. Image in Perry 1990: 55.	A
1548, June	Thomas Seymour	Pierpont Morgan Library, MS Rulers of England, Box III, Part 1, art. 6. Image in Marcus 2008: 212–213.	A
1548, 31st July	Catherine Parr	BL Cotton Ortho C.X. fol.236v.	A
1549, January/ February	Edward Seymour	Burghley Papers, Vol. 1 pg. 102. Malone 1796.	C
1549, 28th January	Edward Seymour	Hatfield House, Cecil Papers, 133/4/2. Mueller & Marcus 2003.	A
1549, 6th February	Edward Seymour	BL MS Ashmole 1729, art. 6. Mueller & Marcus 2003; May 2004a: 106.	C
1549, 21st February	Edward Seymour	BL MS Lansdowne 1236, fol.33.	A
1549, 7th March	Edward Seymour	BL MS Lansdowne 1236 fol.35r.	A
1551, 15th May	Edward VI	BL MS Cotton Vespasian F.III, fol.48.	A
1552, 21st April	Edward VI	Department of Printing and Graphic Arts, Houghton Library, Harvard University, MS Typ 686. Mueller & Marcus 2003.	C
1552, 27th October	Mary I	BL MS Lansdowne 1236, fol.39	A
1553, c. May	Edward VI	BL MS Harley 6986, art. 16, fol.23r.	A
1553, January	Catherine Knollys	BL MS Lansdowne 94, fol.21. May 2004a: 124-125.	C

Table 76. (Continued)

Date	Addressee	Source(s)	Status
1554, 17th March	Mary I	TNA SP Domestic, Mary I 11/4/2, fol.3. Image in Pryor 2003.	A
1555, 29th October	William Paulet	BL Harley 39, fol.14v. Harrison 1935: 21; Perry 1990: 108.	B
1556, 2nd August	Mary I	BL MS Lansdowne 1236, fol.37.	A
1562, 4th July	Ambrose Dudley	Archaeologia XIII (1800) 201-203. Perry 1990: 174.	C
1563, July	William Throckmorton	Private collection. Image courtesy of Steven W. May.	A
1565, c.	Henry Sidney	Malone 1796: 69.	C
1566, November	William Cecil	BL MS Lansdowne 1236, fols 42–42v.	A
1570	Catherine Knyvett, Lady Paget	BL Add. 4160 fol.23. Malone 1796.	C
1570, 26th February	Henry Carey	TNA SP addenda 1566–1579, 15/17/113.	B
1572, 11th April	William Cecil	BL MS Ashmole 1729, art. 7 fol.13.	A
1572, 21st October	George Talbot	Lambeth Palace Library MS 1397, fol.41r. Mueller & Marcus 2003; May 2004a: 143.	C
1575, 6th March	Walter Devereux	Harrison 1935: 125.	C
1576, March	John Harington	Nugae Antiquae II, 149. Perry 1990: 223.	C
1580, August	Edward Stafford	Hatfield House, Cecil Papers pers 135/21. Perry 1990: 247.	D
1581, September	Francis Walsingham	Hatfield House, Cecil Papers 2, 430. Harrison 1935: 149–150.	C
1582, 24th February	Henry Wallop	Malone 1796: 110 (Plate 1).	A
1583, 15th May	William Cecil	BL MS Harley 787 fol.66A. Copy in BL MS Lansdowne 1236, fol.49.	A
1583, 7th August	James Stuart	TNA SP Foreign 1583, no. 217. Harrison 1935: 159.	C
1585, January	James Stuart	BL MS Add. 23240, fol.7.	A

Table 76. (Continued)

Date	Addressee	Source(s)	Status
1585, January/ February	James Stuart	BL MS Add. 23240, 11r–11v.	A
1585, June	James Stuart	BL MS Add. 23240 15r–15v.	A
1585, August	James Stuart	BL MS Add. 23240, fols 19r–19v.	A
1585, November	James Stuart	BL MS Add. 23240, fol.23.	A
1586, January	James Stuart	BL MS Add. 23240, art. 10, fols 30r–31v.	A
1586, February	James Stuart	BL MS Add. 23240, fol.34.	A
1586, 10th February	Robert Dudley	BL MS Cotton Galba C.8, fols 27 and 106.	B
1586, March	James Stuart	BL MS Add. 23240, fols 38r–39v.	A
1586, 14th April	John Perrot	TNA SP Ireland 123/34. Harrison 1935: 175.	C
1586, 27th April	Thomas Heneage	BL MS. Galba C. IX, fol.197b.	B
1586, May	James Stuart	BL MS Add. 23240 fol.45	A
1586, 19th July	Robert Dudley	TNA SP 84/9, ff.85–86. May 2004a: 169–170.	D
1586, 21st July	James Stuart	MS Thompson p.69 (location unknown). Bruce 1849: 157.	D
1586, August	Amias Paulet	BL MS Cotton Caligula C.9, fol.654. May 2004a: 172–173.	B
1586, October	William Cecil and Francis Walsingham	BL MS Lansdowne 10, fol.213. May 2004a: 179.	B
1586, 4th October	James Stuart	BL MS Add. 23240, fol.49.	A
1586, 14th October	James Stuart	BL MS Add.23240, fol.53.	A
1587, January	James Stuart	BL MS Add.23240, fols 57v–58r.	A
1587, February	James Stuart	BL MS Add. 23240 fol.61–62.	A
1588, 15th May	James Stuart	BL MS Add. 23240, fol.67.	A
1588, 1st July	James Stuart	BL MS Add.23240, fol.71.	A
1588, August	James Stuart	BL MS Add.23240, fol.77.	A

Table 76. (Continued)

Date	Addressee	Source(s)	Status
1588, 8th October	James Stuart	MS Thompson p.71 (location unknown). Bruce 1849: 158.	D
1588, December	James Stuart	MS Thompson p.73 (location unknown). Bruce 1849: 160.	D
1589, 16th March	James Stuart	MS Thompson, p.75 (location unknown). Bruce 1849: 161.	D
1589,15th April	Robert Devereux	Perry 1990: 293.	C
1589, 4th May	John Norris and Francis Drake	BL MS Cotton Galba D. I, fol.283. Perry 1990: 293.	C
1589, 19th May	James Stuart	MS Thompson MS p.80 (location unknown). Bruce 1849: 163.	D
1589, September	James Stuart	BL MS Add. 23240, fol.81.	A
1589, 1st December	Peregrine Bertie	Historical Manuscripts Commission Reports, MS Ancaster, p.297. Marcus, Mueller & Rose 2000: 360, fn.1.	D
1589, 6th December	Peregrine Bertie	TNA SP France, 70/20/119, fol.228. Marcus, Mueller & Rose 2000: 360.	D
1590	James Stuart	BL MS Add. 23240, fols 85–87.	A
1590, January	Elizabeth Drury	Malone 1796: 113–114.	C
1590, 16th April	James Stuart	MS Thompson, p.85 (location unknown). Bruce 1849: 165.	D
1590, May	James Stuart	BL MS Add. 23240, fol.90.	A
1590, 29th May	James Stuart	Boyd & Meikle 1936: 304.	C
1590, 6th July	James Stuart	BL MS Add.23240, fol.94.	A
1591, April	James Stuart	BL MS Add. 23240, fol.98.	A
1591, 12th August	James Stuart	Boyd & Meikle 1936: 561.	D
1591, 25th November	James Stuart	Boyd & Meikle 1936: 591–592.	D
1592, January	James Stuart	BL MS Add. 23240, fol.104.	A
1592, 11th September	James Stuart	MS Thompson, p.88 (location unknown). Bruce 1964: 75; Harrison 1935: 221–222.	D
1592, 26th November	James Stuart	MS Thompson, p.91 (location unknown). Bruce 1849: 77.	D
1593, January	James Stuart	BL MS Add.23240, fols 108r–109r.	A

Table 76. (Continued)

Date	Addressee	Source(s)	Status
1593, 16th March	James Stuart	Folger Shakespeare Library, MS X fol.1v. Image in May 2004a: 201-204.	C
1593, May	James Stuart	BL MS Add. 23240, fol.118.	A
1593, July	James Stuart	MS Thompson, p.93 (unknown location). Bruce 1849: 83.	D
1593, August	James Stuart	BL MS Add. 23240, fol.122.	A
1593, October	James Stuart	BL MS Add. 23240, fol.126.	A
1593, 29th October	James Stuart	BL MS Add. 23240, fol.131.	A
1593, October	Edward Norris	TNA SP 84/47, fol.128. May 2004a: 207.	D
1593, 22nd December	James Stuart	Cameron 1936: 248.	C
1594, May	James Stuart	BL MS Add. 23240, fol.132.	A
1594, May	James Stuart	Hatfield House, Cecil Papers, 133/80, fol.120. Mueller & Marcus 2003.	D
1594, October	James Stuart	BL MS Add. 23240 fols 136–137.	A
1596, January	James Stuart	BL MS Add. 23240, fol.140.	A
1596, 26th January	Anne of Denmark	Edinburgh University MS de 1.12/9. May 2004a: 221–222.	C
1596, 14th April	Robert Devereux	TNA SP 12/257, fol.46. May 2004a: 223.	D
1596, 29th June	James Stuart	MS Thompson, p.100 (location unknown). Bruce 1849: 114.	D
1596, July	James Stuart	MS Thompson, p.102 (location unknown). Bruce 1849: 116.	D
1596, 21st September	James Stuart	Giuseppi 1952: pp.319–320.	D
1597, 5th January	James Stuart	MS Thompson, p.104 (location unknown). Bruce 1849: 119.	D
1597, March	James Stuart	Giuseppi 1952: 497–8.	D
1597, 8th July	Robert Devereux	Harrison 1935: 248.	D

Table 76. (Continued)

Date	Addressee	Source(s)	Status
1597, 24th July	Robert Devereux	Hatfield House, Cecil Papers 56/46. Marcus, Mueller & Rose 2000: 388; Harrison 1935: 249–250.	D
1597, 22nd September	Margaret Norris	BL MS Add. 38137, fol.160. May 2004a: 225.	B
1598, 4th January	James Stuart	BL MS Cotton Caligula VIII, fol.210. Harrison 1935: 257–258.	B
1598, July	Robert Cecil	Hatfield House, Cecil Papers 133, fol.187. May 2004a: 228.	C
1598, 1st July	James Stuart	MS Thompson, p.128 (location unknown). Bruce 1849: 125.	D
1598, 26th December	James Stuart	MS Thompson, p.109 (location unknown). Bruce 1849: 127.	D
1600, 3rd December	Charles Blount	Lambeth Palace, Carew Papers 604, ff.242–242v. May 2004a: 235–236.	D
1601, April	James Stuart	MS Thompson, p.110 (location unknown). Bruce 1849: 134.	D
1601, December	James Stuart	MS Thompson, p.118 (location unknown). Bruce 1849: 141.	D
1601, 2nd December	James Stuart	MS Thompson, p.116 (location unknown). Bruce 1849: 140.	D
1602, 3rd February	James Stuart	MS Thompson, p.119. Bruce 1849: 142.	D
1602, 4th July	James Stuart	TNASP Scotland 52/68/75. Marcus, Mueller & Rose 2000: 402.	D
1602, 15th July	Charles Blount	Parry 1990: 316. Harrison 1935: 294.	C
1603, 6th January	James Stuart	MS Thompson, p.120 (location unknown). Bruce 1849: 154. Harrison 1935: 295–296.	D

Table 77. Speeches in QEIC

Date	Source	Status
1563, 10th April	BL MS Lansdowne 94, art. 15B, fol.30. Mueller & Marcus 2003: 34; May 2004a: 42–43.	A
1566, 5th November	TNA SP Domestic, Elizabeth 12/41/5. Mueller & Marcus 2003: 38; May 2004a: 45.	A
1567, 2nd January	BL MS Cotton Charter IV.38 (2), formerly Cotton Titus F.1, fol.92. Mueller & Marcus 2003: 40; May 2004a: 47–49.	A
1576, 15th March	May 2004a: 52–57.	D
1586, 12th November	BL MS Lansdowne 94, ff.84–85. May 2004a: 61–69; Heisch 1975.	B
1586, 24th November	BL MS Lansdowne 94, ff.86–88v. May 2004a: 70–75.	B

Table 78. Translations in QEIC

Date	Title	Source	Status
1544	The Mirror of the Sinful Soul	Ames 1897; Shell 1993; Mueller & Scodel 2009a.	A
1545	Calvin's Institutione, Chapter 1	National Archives of Scotland, MS RH 13/78, fols 1r–89v. Mueller & Scodel 2009a.	A
1592	Cicero's Pro M. Marcello	Bodleian MS 900, fols 2–8v. Mueller & Scodel 2009b; May 2004a: 268–280.	A
1593	Boethius' De Consolatione	Pemberton 1899; Mueller & Scodel 2009b.	A

20. Textual sources

MS Additional 23240; MS Additional 38137; MS Ashmole 1729; MS Cotton Caligula VIII; MS Cotton Caligula C. IX; Cotton Galba C.VIII; MS Cotton Galba C. IX; MS Cotton Galba D. I; MS Cotton Vespasian F.III; MS Lansdowne 8; MS Lansdowne 10; MS Lansdowne 94; MS Lansdowne 1236; MS Harley 39; MS Harley 787, British Library.

SP 10/2, SP 10/5, SP 12/41, SP 15/17, SP 84/47, MS Cotton Otho C. X, The National Archives of the UK, State Papers Online < http://gale.cengage.-co.uk/state-papers-online > .

Corpus of Early English Correspondence, 1998. Compiled by Terttu Nevalainen, Helena Raumolin-Brunberg, Jukka Keränen, Minna Nevala, Arja Nurmi and Minna Palander-Collin at the Department of English, University of Helsinki.

Parsed Corpus of Early English Correspondence, 2006. Compiled by Terttu Nevalainen, Helena Raumolin-Brunberg, Jukka Keränen, Minna Nevala, Arja Nurmi and Minna Palander-Collin, with additional annotation by Anne Taylor. Helsinki: University of Helsinki and York: University of York. Distributed through the Oxford Text Archive.

REFERENCES

ADAMSON, SYLVIA, 2007. 'Prescribed reading: pronouns and gender in the eighteenth century', *Historical Sociolinguistics and Sociohistorical Linguistics* 7.

ALLEN, WILL, BEAL, JOAN, CORRIGAN, KAREN, MAGUIRE, WARREN & MOISL, HERMANN, 2007. 'A linguistic "time capsule": the Newcastle electronic corpus of Tyneside English', in Joan Beal, Karen Corrigan and Hermann Moisl (eds.), *Creating and Digitizing Language Corpora: volume 2 diachronic databases*, Basingstoke: Palgrave Macmillan, 16–48.

ALLINSON, RAYNE, 2007. 'These latter days of the world: the correspondence of Elizabeth I and James VI, 1590-1603', *Early Modern Literary Studies Special Issue* 16, 2, 1–27.

AMES, P. A. (ed.), 1897. *The Mirror of the Sinful Soul: A prose translation from the French of a poem by Queen Margaret of Navarre, made in 1544 by Princess (afterwards Queen) Elizabeth, then eleven years of age. Reproduced in fac-simile, with portrait, for the Royal Society of Literature of the United Kingdom, and edited, with an introduction and notes, by Percy W. Ames, F.S.A., Librarian and Secretary, R.S.L.*, London: Asher and Co.

ANTHONY, LAURENCE, 2012, *AntConc* < http://www.antlab.sci.waseda.ac.jp/software.html >.

ARCHER, J., 1995. *The Translations of Queen Elizabeth I*. MA dissertation, University of Exeter.

ARIEL, MIRA, 2008. *Pragmatics and Grammar*. Cambridge Textbooks in Linguistics. Cambridge: Cambridge University Press.

BALL, CATHERINE, 1996. 'A diachronic study of relative markers in spoken and written English', *Language Variation and Change* 8, 227–258.

BARON, ALISTAIR, RAYSON, PAUL, & ARCHER, DAWN, 2012. 'Innovators of Early Modern English spelling change: Using DICER to investigate spelling variation trends', *Studies in Variation, Contacts and Change in English: Volume 10: Outposts of Historical Corpus Linguistics: From the Helsinki Corpus to a Proliferation of Resources* < www.helsinki.fi/varieng/journal/volumes/10/baron_rayson_archer >.

BAYLEY, ROBERT, 2002. 'The quantitative paradigm', in Jack. K. Chambers, Peter Trudgill and Natalie Schilling-Estes (eds.), *The Handbook of Language Variation and Change*. Blackwell Handbooks in Linguistics. Oxford: Blackwell Publishing, 117–141.

BAX, RANDY, 2002. 'Linguistic accommodation: the correspondence between Samuel Johnson and Hester Lynch Thrale', in Teresa Fanego, Belén Méndez-Naya & Elena Seoane (eds.), *Sounds, Words, Texts and Change:*

selected papers from 11 ICEHL. Amsterdam Studies in the Theory and History of Linguistic Science, Series IV Current Linguistic Theory. Amsterdam: John Benjamins, 9–24.

BEAL, JOAN, 2004. *English in Modern Times: 1700–1945*, London: Arnold.

BEAL, PETER, 2008. *A Dictionary of English Manuscript Terminology: 1450 to 2000*, Oxford: Oxford University Press.

BEESLY, E. S., 1892. *Queen Elizabeth*, London: Macmillan.

BENSKIN, MICHAEL, 2004. 'Chancery Standard', in Christian Kay, Carole Hough and Irené Wotherspoon (eds.), *New Perspectives on English Historical Linguistics: selected papers from 12 ICEHL Volume 2: Lexis and Transmission*. Amsterdam Studies in the Theory and History of Linguistic Science, Series IV Current issues in Linguistic Theory. Amsterdam; Philadelphia: John Benjamins, 1–40.

BLAKE, NORMAN. F., 2000. 'The English language of the Early Modern period', in Michael Hattaway (ed.), *A Companion to English Renaissance Literature and Culture*. Blackwell Companions to Literature and Culture 8. Oxford: Blackwell Publishing, 71–80.

BLAKE, NORMAN. F., 1965. 'English versions of "Reynard the Fox" in the fifteenth and sixteenth centuries', *Studies in Philology* 62, 63–77.

BLOCH, BERNARD, 1948. 'A set of postulates for phonemic analysis', *Language* 24, 1, 3–46.

BORMAN, TRACY, 2009. *Elizabeth's Women: The Hidden Story of the Virgin Queen*, London: Vintage Books.

BOYD, W. K. &. MEIKLE, H. W. (eds.), 1936. *Calendar of the state papers relating to Scotland and Mary, Queen of Scots, 1547–1603, preserved in the Public Record Office, The British Museum and elsewhere. Vol.10, A.D.1589–1593*, Edinburgh: H. M. General Register House.

BRUCE, J. (ed.), 1861. *Correspondence of James VI of Scotland with Sir Robert Cecil and others in England during the reign of Queen Elizabeth.* Camden Society Publications First Series 78. London: Camden Society.

BRUCE, J. (ed.), 1849. *Letters of Queen Elizabeth and King James VI of Scotland: some of them printed from originals in the possession of the Rev. Edward Ryder, and others from a ms. which formerly belonged to Sir Peter Thompson, kt.* Camden Society Publications First Series 46. London: Camden Society.

BUSSE, BEATRIX, 2010. 'Recent trends in new historical stylistics', in Daniel McIntyre and Beatrix Busse (eds.), *Language and Style*, New York: Palgrave Macmillan, 32–54.

CAON, LUISELLA. 2002. 'Final –E and spelling habits in the fifteenth-century versions of the Wife of Bath's Prologue', *English Studies* 83, 4, 296–310.

CAMERON, A. I. (ed.), 1936. *Calendar of the state papers relating to Scotland and Mary, Queen of Scots, 1547–1603, preserved in the Public Record Office, The British Museum and elsewhere. Vol.11, A.D.1593–1595*, Edinburgh: H. M. General Register House.

CASTIGLIONE, BALDASSARE, 1561. *The courtyer of Count Baldessar Castilio diuided into foure bookes. Very necessary and profitable for yonge gentilmen and gentilwomen abiding in court, palaice or place*, done into English by Thomas Hoby, London: Wyllyam Seres.

CAVANAGH, SHEILA, 1998. 'The bad seed: princess Elizabeth and the Seymour incident', in Julia Walker (ed.), *Dissing Elizabeth: Negative Representations of Gloriana*, Durham, NC: Duke University Press, 9–29.

CHAMBERS, JACK. K., 2003. *Sociolinguistic Theory: Linguistic Variation and its Social Significance*, 2nd ed., Language in Society 32, Oxford: Blackwell Publishing.

CHARLEBOIS, JUSTIN, 2009 'Language, Culture and Social Interaction', in Larry Samovar, Richard Porter and Edwin McDaniel (eds.), *Intercultural Communication: a Reader*, 12th ed., Boston: Wadsworth Cengage Learning, 237–243.

CHESHIRE, JENNY, 2002. 'Sex and gender in variationist research', in Jack. K. Chambers, Peter Trudgill and Natalie Schilling-Estes (eds.), *The Handbook of Language Variation and Change*. Blackwell Handbooks in Linguistics. Oxford: Blackwell Publishing,423–243.

CLEMENT, JENNIFER, 2008. 'The queen's voice: Elizabeth I's Christian prayers and meditations', *Early Modern Literary Studies* 13, 3, 1–26.

COULTHARD, MICHAEL & JOHNSON, ALISON, 2007. *An Introduction to Forensic Linguistics: Language in Evidence*, London: Routledge.

COUPLAND, NICHOLAS, 2007. *Style: Language Variation and Identity*. Key Topics in Sociolinguistics. Cambridge: Cambridge University Press.

CULPEPER, JONATHAN & KYTÖ, MERJA, 2010. *Early Modern English Dialogues: Spoken Interaction as writing*. Studies in English Language. Cambridge: Cambridge University Press.

CUSACK, B. (ed.), 1998. *Everyday English 1500–1700: A Reader*, Edinburgh: Edinburgh University Press.

D'ARCY, ALEXANDRA & TAGLIAMONTE, SALI, 2010. 'Prestige, accommodation, and the legacy of relative *who*', *Language in Society* 39, 383–410.

D'ARCY, ALEXANDRA & TAGLIAMONTE, SALI, 2009. 'Peaks beyond Phonology: Adolescence, Incrementation and Language Change', *Language* 85, 1: 58–198.

DAVIS, NORMAN, 1965. 'The litera troili and English letters', *R.E.S. New Series* 16, 63, 233–244.

DAYBELL, JAMES, 2009. 'Material meanings and the social signs of manuscript letters in Early Modern England', *Literature Compass* 6, 3, 647–667.

DAYBELL, JAMES, 2001. 'Female literacy and the social conventions of women's letter-writing in England, 1540–1603', in James Daybell (ed.), *Early Modern Women's Letter-writing: 1540–1700*. Early Modern Literature in History. Basingstoke: Palgrave, 59–76.

DAYBELL, JAMES, 1999. 'Women's Letters and Letter Writing in England 1540–1603: an introduction to the issues of authorship and construction', *Shakespeare Studies* 27, 161–186.

DEKEYSER, XAVIER, 1984. 'Relativizers in Early Modern English: a dynamic quantitative study', in Jacek Fisiak (ed.), *Historical Syntax*. Trends in Linguistics Studies and Monographs 23. Berlin: Mouton de Gruyter, 61–87.

DEMERS, PATRICIA, 2005. *Women's Writing in English: Early Modern England*, Toronto: University of Toronto Press.

DICKERMAN, EDMUND. H. & WALKER, ANITA, 1999. 'The language of blame: Henri III and the dismissal of his ministers', *French History* 13, 1, 77–98.

DORAN, SUSAN, 2005. 'Loving and affectionate cousins? The relationship between Elizabeth I and James VI of Scotland 1586–1603', in Susan Doran and Glenn Richardson (eds.), *Tudor England and its Neighbours*, London: Palgrave Macmillan, 203–234.

DORAN, SUSAN, 2000. 'Elizabeth I's religion: the evidence of her letters', *Journal of Ecclesiastical History* 51, 4, 699–720.

DORAN, SUSAN, 1998. 'Why did Elizabeth not marry?', in Julia Walker (ed.), *Dissing Elizabeth: Negative Representations of Gloriana*, Durham, NC: Duke University Press, 30–59.

DUNCAN-JONES, KATHERINE, 2007. 'Elizabeth I and her "good George": unpublished letters', in Peter Beal and Grace Ioppolo (eds.), *Elizabeth I and the culture of writing*, London: The British Library, 29–41.

ECKERT, PENELOPE, 2005. 'Stylistic practice and the adolescent social order', in Angie Williams and Crispin Thurlow (eds.), *Talking Adolescence: perspectives on communication in the teenage years*, New York: Peter Lang Publishing, 93–110.

ECKERT, PENELOPE, 2000. *Linguistic Variation as Social Practice: the Linguistic Construction of Identity at Belten High*, Oxford: Blackwell.

ECKERT, PENELOPE & RICKFORD, JOHN R., 2001. 'Introduction', in Penelope Eckert & John R. Rickford (eds.), *Style and Sociolinguistic Variation*, Cambridge: Cambridge University Press, 1–20.

ELLEGÅRD, ALVAR, 1953. *The Auxiliary 'do': The Establishment and Regulation of its Growth in English*. Gothenburg Studies in English 2. Stockholm: Almqvist and Wiksell.

ELZINGA, DIRK, 2006. 'English adjective comparison and analogy', *Lingua* 116, 757–770.

ETTENHUBER, KATRIN, 2007. 'Hyperbole: exceeding similitude', in Sylvia Adamson, Gavin Alexander & Katrin Ettenhuber (eds.), *Renaissance Figures of Speech*, Cambridge: Cambridge University Press, 196–214.

EVANS, MEL, 2012. 'Stories, style and identity: reconsidering the evidence from the Thomas Seymour affair'. Paper presented at the 25th Poetics and Linguistics Association annual conference, University of Malta.

FAGYAL, ZSUZSANNA, SWARUP, SAMARTH, ESCOBAR, ANNA MARÍA, GASSER, LES & LAKKARAJU, KIRAN, 2010. 'Centers and Peripheries: Network roles in language change', *Lingua* 120: 2061–2079.

FISHER, J. H., RICHARDSON, M. & FISHER, J. L. (eds.), 1984. *An Anthology of Chancery English*, Knoxville: University of Tennessee Press.

FRYE, SUSAN, 1993. *Elizabeth I: the Competition for Representation*, New York: Oxford University Press.

FURNIVALL, FREDERICK J., 1899. 'Note on queen Elizabeth's use of I for our long E', in Caroline Pemberton (ed.), *Queen Elizabeth's Englishings of Boethius, De consolatione philosophiae, A.D. 1593: Plutarch, de curiositate 1598; Horace, De arte poetica (part) A.D. 1598/edited from the unique ms., partly in the Queen's hand, in the Public Record Office, London by Caroline Pemberton*, EETS, London: K. Paul, Trench, Trübner and Co, xvi–xvii.

GADJA, ALEXANDRA, 2010. 'Political culture in the 1590s: the "second reign" of Elizabeth', *History Compass* 8, 1, 88–100.

GARRETT, PETER, 2010. *Attitudes to Language*. Key Topics in Sociolinguistics. Cambridge: Cambridge University Press.

GOLDBERG, JONATHAN, 1990. *Writing Matter: From the Hands of the English Renaissance*, Stanford: Stanford University Press.

GILES, J. A. (ed.), 1864. *The Whole Works of Roger Ascham, now first collected and revised, with a life of the author: volume II letters continued, and Toxophilus*, London: John Russell Smith.

GONZÁLEZ-DÍAZ, VICTORINA, 2008. *English Adjective Comparison: a historical perspective.* Amsterdam Studies in the Theory and History of Linguistic Science Series IV. Amsterdam; Philadelphia: John Benjamins.

GONZÁLEZ-DÍAZ, VICTORINA, 2007. 'On the nature and distribution of English double periphrastic comparison', *R.E.S. New Series* 57, 232, 623–664.

GONZÁLEZ-DÍAZ, VICTORINA, 2006. 'The origin of English periphrastic comparatives', *English Studies* 87, 6, 707–739.

GONZÁLEZ-DÍAZ, VICTORINA, 2003. 'Adjective comparison in renaissance English', *SEDERI* 13, 87–100.

GRANT, TIM, 2010. 'Text Messaging Forensics: Txt 4n6: Idiolect Free Authorship Analysis?', in Malcolm Coulthard and Alison Johnson (eds.), *The Routledge Handbook of Forensic Linguistics*. Routledge Handbooks in Applied Linguistics. Abingdon: Routledge, 508–522.

GREEN, JANET. M., 1997. 'I my self: Elizabeth I's oration at Tilbury camp', *The Sixteenth Century Journal* 28, 2, 421–445.

GIUSEPPI, M. S. (ed.), 1952. *Calendar of the state papers relating to Scotland and Mary, Queen of Scots, 1547–1603, preserved in the Public Record Office, The British Museum and elsewhere. Vol.12, A.D.1595–1597*, vol. 12., Edinburgh: H.M.S.O.

GUY, JOHN. A., 2004. *My Heart is My Own: the Life of Mary Queen of Scots*, London; New York: Fourth Estate.

GUY, JOHN. A., 1995. 'Introduction: the 1590s: the second reign of Elizabeth I?', in John A. Guy (ed.), *The Reign of Elizabeth I: Court and Culture in the Last Decade*, Cambridge: Cambridge University Press, 1–19.

HACKETT, HELEN, 2009. 'Shakespeare and Elizabeth I: icons and their afterlives', *Literature Compass* 6, 6, 1188–97.

HARRISON, G. B. (ed.), 1935. *The Letters of Queen Elizabeth I*, London: Cassell.

HAYNES, S. (ed.), 1740. *A collection of state papers, relating to affairs in the reigns of King Henry VIII. King Edward VI. Queen Mary, and Queen Elizabeth, from the year 1542 to 1570* [. . .] *Transcribed from original letters and other authentick memorials* [. . .], London: William Bowyer.

HEISCH, ALISON, 1980. 'Queen Elizabeth I and the persistence of patriarchy', *Feminist Review* 4, 45–56.

HEISCH, ALISON, 1975. 'Queen Elizabeth I: parliamentary rhetoric and the exercise of power', *Signs* 1,1, 31–55.

HEYWOOD, THOMAS, 1632. *Englands Elisabeth her life and troubles, during her minoritie, from the cradle to the crown. Historically laid open and interwoven with such eminent passages of state, as happened under the reigne of Henry the eight, Edward the sixt, Q. Mary; all of them aptly introducing to the present relation. By Thom. Heywood.* Cambridge: Philip Waterhouse.

HOOVER, DAVID, 2010. 'Authorial style', in Daniel McIntyre and Beatrix Busse (eds.), *Language and Style*, New York: Palgrave Macmillan, 250–271.

HOPE, JONATHAN, 1994. *The Authorship of Shakespeare's Plays: a Socio-Linguistic Study*, Cambridge: Cambridge University Press.

IHALAINEN, OSSI, 1983. 'On the notion of possible grammatical change: a look at a perfectly good change that did not quite make it', *Studia Anglia Posnaniensia* 15, 3–11.

INGHAM, RICHARD, 2008. 'Contact with Scandinavian and late Middle English negative concord', *Studia Anglia Posnaniensia* 44, 123–137.

IYEIRI, YOKO, 1998. 'Multiple negation in Middle English verse', in Ingrid Tieken Boon van Ostade, Gunnel Tottie, and Wim van der Wurff (eds.), *Negation in the History of English*. Topics in English Linguistics. Berlin: Walter de Gruyter, 121–146.

JOHNSTONE, BARBARA, 2000. 'The individual voice in language', *Annual Review of Anthropology* 29, 405–24.

KALLEL, AMEL, 2007. 'The loss of negative concord in Standard English: internal factors', *Language Variation and Change* 19, 27–49.

KALLEL, AMEL, 2002. 'The age variable in the rise of periphrastic "do" in English', *Reading Working Papers in Linguistics* 6, 161–185.

KANTOROWICZ, ERNST. H., 1957. *The King's Two Bodies: a Study in Mediaeval Political Theology*, Princeton: Princeton University Press.

KEENE, DEREK, 2000. 'Metropolitan norms: migration, mobility and cultural norms, London 1100–1700', in Laura Wright (ed.), *The Development of Standard English, 1300–1800: Theories, Descriptions, Conflicts*. Studies in English Language. Cambridge: Cambridge University Press, 93–116.

KYTÖ, MERJA, 1996. "'The best and most excellentest way'": The rivalling forms of adjective comparison in Late Middle and Early Modern English', in Jan Svartvik (ed.), *Words: Proceedings of an International Symposium Lund, 25–26 August 1995*. Konferenser 36. Stockholm: Almqvist and Wiksell International, 123–144.

KYTÖ, MERJA, 1993. 'Third-person present singular verb inflection in early British and American English', *Language Variation and Change* 5, 113–139.

KYTÖ, MERJA & RISSANEN, MATTI, 1993. 'General Introduction', in Matti Rissanen, Merja Kytö and Minna Palander-Collin (eds.), *Early English in the Computer Age: explorations through the Helsinki Corpus*. Topics in English Linguistics 11. Berlin: Mouton de Gruyter, 1–17.

KYTÖ, MERJA & ROMAINE, SUZANNE, 2000. 'Adjective comparison and standardization processes in American and British English from 1620 to the present', in Laura Wright (ed.), *The Development of Standard English, 1300-1800: Theories, Descriptions, Conflicts*. Studies in English Language. Cambridge: Cambridge University Press, 171–194.

KYTÖ, MERJA & ROMAINE, SUZANNE, 1997. 'Competing forms of adjective comparison in modern English: what could be more quicker and easier and more effective?', *The British National Corpus*, University of Oxford <www.natcorp.ox.ac.uk/archive/papers/kytorom.html>.

LABOV, WILLIAM, 2010. *Principles of Linguistic Change: Cognitive Factors*, vol. 3, Language in Society 39, Oxford: Blackwell Publishing.

LABOV, WILLIAM, 2006. *The Social Stratification of English in New York* City, 2nd ed., Cambridge: Cambridge University Press.

LABOV, WILLIAM, 2001. *Principles of Linguistic Change: Social Factors*, vol. 2, Language in Society 29, Oxford: Blackwell Publishing.

LABOV, WILLIAM, 1994. *Principles of Linguistic Change: Internal Factors*, vol. 1, Language in Society 20, Oxford: Blackwell Publishing.

LABOV, WILLIAM, 1972. *Sociolinguistic Patterns*, Philadelphia: University of Pennsylvania Press.

LASS, ROGER, 1999. 'Phonology and morphology', in Roger Lass (ed.), *The Cambridge History of the English Language 1476–1776*, vol. 3, Cambridge: Cambridge University Press, 56–186.

MAGNUSSON, LYNNE, 2011. 'Cicero Effects in sixteenth-century English letters', Paper presented at Culture of Correspondence in Early Modern Britain, 1550–1640, University of Plymouth, April 14th–16th 2011.

MALONE, EDMOND, 1796. *An Inquiry into the Authenticity of certain Miscellaneous Papers and Legal Instruments, published Dec. 24, MDCCXCV and attributed to Shakespeare, Queen Elizabeth and Henry, Earl of Southampton*, London: T. Cadell and W. Davies.

MARCUS, LEAH, 2008. 'Elizabeth on Elizabeth: underexamined episodes in an overexamined life', in Kevin Sharp and Steven. N. Swicker (eds.), *Writing Lives: Biography and Textuality: Identity and Representation in Early Modern England*, Oxford: Oxford University Press, 209–232.

MARCUS, L., MUELLER, J. & ROSE, M. B. (eds.), 2000. *Elizabeth I: Collected Works*, Chicago: University of Chicago Press.

MAY, STEVEN W., 2007. 'Queen Elizabeth prays for the living and the dead', in Peter Beal and Grace Ioppolo (eds.), *Elizabeth I and the culture of writing*, London: The British Library, 201–211.

MAY, S. W. (ed.), 2004a. *Elizabeth I: selected works*, New York: Washington Square Press.

MAY, STEVEN W., 2004b. 'Queen Elizabeth to her subjects: the Tilbury and Golden speeches', *EIRC* 30, 1, 23–39.

MAY, STEVEN W., 1991. *The Elizabethan Courtier Poets: their poems and their contexts*, London: University of Missouri Press.

MCINTOSH, ANGUS & OTHERS, 1986. *A Linguistic Atlas of Late Medieval English: General Introduction, Index of Sources, Dot Maps*, vol. 1, Oxford: Aberdeen University Press.

MCINTOSH, ANGUS & OTHERS, 1986. *A Linguistic Atlas of Late Medieval English: Item Maps*, vol. 2, Oxford: Aberdeen University Press.

MCINTOSH, ANGUS & WILLIAMSON, COLIN, 1963. 'King Lear act i, scene i: a stylistic note', *Review of English Studies: A Quarterly Journal of English Literature and the English Language* 14, 53, 54–58.

MCINTOSH, JERI L., 2008. *From Heads of Household to Heads of State: the preaccession households of Mary and Elizabeth Tudor, 1516-1558*, Gutenberg-e: Columbia University Press < www.gutenberg-e.org/mcintosh >.

MEYERHOFF, MIRIAM. 2002. 'Communities of Practice', in Jack. K. Chambers, Peter Trudgill and Natalie Schilling-Estes (eds.), *The Handbook of Language Variation and Change*. Blackwell Handbooks in Linguistics. Oxford: Blackwell Publishing, 526–528.

MILROY, JAMES, 2003. 'On the role of the speaker in language change', in Raymond Hickey (ed.), *Motives for Language Change*, Cambridge: Cambridge University Press, 143–157.

MILROY, JAMES, 1992. *Linguistic Variation and Change: on the Historical Sociolinguistics of English*, Oxford: Blackwell Publishing.

MILROY, JAMES & MILROY, LESLEY, 1985. 'Language Change, Social Network and Speaker Innovation', *Journal of Linguistics* 21, 2: 339–384.

MOORE, EMMA, 2012. 'The Social Life of Style', *Language and Literature* 21, 1: 66–83.

MONTROSE, LOUIS A., 2006. *The Subject of Elizabeth: Authority, Gender and Representation*, Chicago: University of Chicago Press.

MONTROSE, LOUIS A., 2002. 'Spenser and the Elizabethan Political Imaginary', *ELH* 69, 4, 907–946.

MUELLER, J. (ed.), 2011. *Katherine Parr: Complete Works and Correspondence*, Chicago: University of Chicago Press.

MUELLER, JANEL, 2001. 'Virtue and vitality: gender in the self-representations of Queen Elizabeth I', University of Chicago < fathom.lib.uchicago.edu/1/777777122145/ >.

MUELLER, JANEL, 2000. 'To my very good brother the King of Scots: Elizabeth I's correspondence with James VI and the question of succession', *PMLA*, 115, 5, 1063–1071.

MUELLER, J. & MARCUS, L. (eds.), 2003. *Elizabeth I: Autograph Compositions and Foreign Language Originals*, Chicago: Chicago University Press.

MUELLER, J. & SCODEL, J. (eds.), 2009a. *Elizabeth I: Translations 1544–1589*, Chicago: University of Chicago Press.

MUELLER, J. & SCODEL, J. (eds.), 2009b. *Elizabeth I: Translations 1592–1598*, Chicago: University of Chicago Press.

MURDIN, W. (ed.), 1759. *A Collection of State Papers relating to affairs in the reign of Queen Elizabeth, from 1571–1596. Transcribed from original papers and other authentic memorials never before published*, London: William Bowyer.

NAHKOLA, KARI & SAANILAHTI, MARJA, 2004. 'Mapping language changes in real time: a panel study on Finnish', *Language Variation and Change* 16, 2, 75–91.

NEALE, JOHN E., 1925. 'The sayings of queen Elizabeth', *History* 10, 212–233.

NEVALA, MINNA, 2004. *Address in Early English Correspondence: its forms and socio-pragmatic functions*. Mémoires de la Société Néophilologique de Helsinki 64. Helsinki: Société Néophilologique.

NEVALAINEN, TERTTU, 2012. 'Variable focusing in English spelling between 1400 and 1600', in Susan Baddeley and Anja Voeste (eds.), *Orthographies in Early Modern Europe: a Comparative View*, Berlin: Mouton De Gruyter, 127–165.

NEVALAINEN, TERTTU, 2006a. 'Mapping change in Tudor English', in Linda Mugglestone (ed.), *The Oxford History of English*, New York: Oxford University Press, 178–211.

NEVALAINEN, TERTTU, 2006b. *An Introduction to Early Modern English*. Edinburgh Textbooks on the English Language. Edinburgh: Edinburgh University Press.

NEVALAINEN, TERTTU, 2006c. 'Negative concord as an English "vernacular universal": social history and linguistic typology', *Journal of English Linguistics* 34, 257–278.

NEVALAINEN, TERTTU, 2002. 'What's in a royal letter? Linguistic variation in the correspondence of King Henry VIII', in Katja Lena and Ruth Möhlig (eds.), *Of Dyuersitie and Chaunge: essays presented to Manfred Görlach on the occasion of his 65th birthday*, Heidelberg: Carl Winter, 169–179.

NEVALAINEN, TERTTU, 2000. 'Gender differences in the evolution of Standard English: evidence from the corpus of early English correspondence', *Journal of English Linguistics* 28, 38–59.

NEVALAINEN, TERTTU, 1996a. 'Gender Difference', in Terttu Nevalainen and Helena Raumolin-Brunberg (eds.), *Sociolinguistics and Language History: studies based on the corpus of early English correspondence*, Amsterdam: Rodopi, 77–92.

NEVALAINEN, TERTTU, 1996b. 'Social Stratification', in Terttu Nevalainen and Helena Raumolin-Brunberg (eds.), *Sociolinguistics and Language History: studies based on the corpus of early English correspondence*, Amsterdam: Rodopi, 57–76.

NEVALAINEN, TERTTU, 1991. 'Motivated archaism: the use of affirmative periphrastic do in Early Modern English liturgical prose', in Dieter Kastovsky (ed.), *Historical English Syntax*. Topics in English Linguistics. Berlin: Mouton de Gruyter, 303–320.

NEVALAINEN, TERTTU & RAUMOLIN-BRUNBERG, HELENA, 2003. *Historical Sociolinguistics: language change in Tudor and Stuart England*. Longman Linguistics Library. London: Longman Pearson.

NEVALAINEN, TERTTU & RAUMOLIN-BRUNBERG, HELENA, 2002. 'The rise of relative *who* in Early Modern English', in Patricia Poussa (ed.), *Relativisation on the North Sea Littoral*. LINCOM Studies in Language Typology. Muenchen: Lincom Europa, 109–124.

NEVALAINEN, TERTTU, RAUMOLIN-BRUNBERG, HELENA & MANNILA, HEIKKI, 2011. 'The diffusion of language change in real time: Progressive and conservative individuals and the time depth of change', *Language Variation and Change* 23, 1–43.

NURMI, ARJA, 1999. *A Sociolinguistic History of Periphrastic Do*. Mémoires de la Société Néophilologique de Helsinki 56. Helsinki: Société Néophilologique.

OSSELTON, NOEL, 1984. 'Informal spelling systems in Early Modern English: 1500-1800', in Norman Blake and Charles Jones (eds.), *English Historical Linguistics: Studies in Development*. CECTAL conference papers series 3. Sheffield: Centre for English Cultural Tradition and Language for the Department of English Language, University of Sheffield, 123–137.

Oxford Dictionary of National Biography, < http://www.odnb.com >.

Oxford English Dictionary Online, < http://www.oed.com >.

PALANDER-COLLIN, MINNA, JUVONEN, TEO & HAKALA, MIKKA, 2010. 'Normalizing the spelling of early English correspondence: levelling social differences?' Paper given at The Language of Nobility and Early Modern Letters, a video conference between the School of English, University of Sheffield and VARIENG, University of Helsinki, 10th May 2010.

PALANDER-COLLIN, MINNA, NEVALA, MINNA & NURMI, ARJA, 2009. 'The language of daily life in the history of English: studying how macro meets micro', in Arja Nurmi, Minna Nevala and Minna Palander-Collin (eds.), *The Language of Daily Life in England (1400-1800)*. Pragmatics and Beyond New Series 183. Amsterdam: John Benjamins, 1–26.

PEACHAM, HENRY, 1593. *The Garden of Eloquence*, 2nd edn., STC 19498, London: H. Jackson.

PEMBERTON, C. (ed.), 1899. *Queen Elizabeth's Englishings of Boethius, De consolatione philosophiae, A.D. 1593: Plutarch, de curiositate 1598 ; Horace, De arte poetica (part) A.D. 1598 / edited from the unique ms., partly in the Queen's hand, in the Public Record Office, London by Caroline Pemberton*, EETS, London: K. Paul, Trench, Trübner and Co.

PERRY, MARIA, 1990. *Elizabeth I: the word of a prince: a life from contemporary documents*, London: Folio Society.

PLOWDEN, ALISON, 1971. *The Young Elizabeth*, London: Macmillan.

PODESVA, ROBERT J., 2007. 'Phonation type as a stylistic variable: the use of falsetto in constructing a persona', *Journal of Sociolinguistics* 11, 4, 478–504.

POLLEN, J.H. (ed.), 1904. *A letter from Mary Queen of Scots to the Duke of Guise, January 1562*. Scottish History Society, Edinburgh: Edinburgh University Press.

POUND, LOUISE, 1901. *The Comparison of Adjectives in English in the XV and the XVI Century*. Anglistische Forschungen. Heidelberg: Winter.

PRYOR, FELIX, 2003. *Elizabeth I: her life in letters*, Berkley, Los Angeles: University of California Press.

PUTTENHAM, GEORGE, 1589/2007. *The Art of English Poesie*, Middlesex: Echo Library.

RAUMOLIN-BRUNBERG, HELENA, 2006. 'Leaders of linguistic change in Early Modern England', in Roberta Facchinetti and Matti Rissanen (eds.), *Corpus-based studies of diachronic English*. Linguistic Insights 31. Bern: Peter Lang, 115–134.

RAUMOLIN-BRUNBERG, HELENA, 2005. 'Language change in adulthood', *European Journal of English Studies* 9, 1, 37–51.

RAUMOLIN-BRUNBERG, HELENA, 2000. 'which and the which in Late Middle English: free variants?', in Irma Taavitsainen and others (eds.), *Placing Middle English in Context*, Berlin and New York: Mouton de Gruyter, 209–226.

RAUMOLIN-BRUNBERG, HELENA, 1991. *The Noun Phrase in Sixteenth-Century English: a Study Based on Sir Thomas More's Writings*. Mémoires de la Société Néophilologique de Helsinki 50. Helsinki: Société Néophilologique.

RECORD COMMISSION, 1849. *State Papers Published under the authority of His Majesty's Commission: Henry the Eighth*, vol. 6, London: G. Eyre and A. Strahan.

REYNOLDS, PAIGE, MARTIN, 2010. 'George Peele and the judgement of Elizabeth I', *Studies in English Literature 1500–1900* 50, 2, 263–280.

RICHARDSON, MALCOLM, 2007. 'The ars dictaminis, the formulary and medieval epistolary practice', in Carol Poster and Linda. C. Mitchell (eds.), *Letter-writing Manuals and Instruction from Antiquity to the Present: Historical and Bibliographic Studies*. Studies in Rhetoric/ Communication. Colombia: University of South Carolina Press, 52–66.

RISSANEN, MATTI, 2000. 'Standardisation and the language of early statutes', in Laura Wright (ed.), *The Development of Standard English, 1300–1800: Theories, Descriptions, Conflicts*. Studies in English Language. Cambridge: Cambridge University Press, 117–130.

RISSANEN, MATTI, 1999. 'Syntax', in Roger Lass (ed.), *The Cambridge History of the English Language 1476–1776*, vol. 3, Cambridge: Cambridge University Press, 187–326

RISSANEN, MATTI, 1994. 'The Helsinki Corpus of English texts', in Merja Kytö, Matti Rissanen, and Susan Wright (eds.), *Corpora across the Centuries: Proceedings of the First International Colloquium on English Diachronic Corpora St Catherine's College, Cambridge, 25–27 March 1993*. Language and Computers, Studies in Practical Linguistics 11. Amsterdam: Rodopi, 73–80.

RISSANEN, MATTI, 1991. 'Spoken language and the history of *do*-periphrasis', in Dieter Kastovsky (ed.), *Historical English Syntax*, Berlin; New York: Mouton de Gruyter, 321–342.

RISSANEN, MATTI, 1987. 'Variation and the study of English historical syntax', in David Sankoff (ed.), *Diversity and Diachrony*. Current Issues in Linguistic Theory 53. Amsterdam: John Benjamins, 97–109.

ROMAINE, SUZANNE, 1982. *Socio-historical linguistics: its status and methodology*, Cambridge: Cambridge University Press.

ROMAINE, SUZANNE, 1980. 'The relative clause marker in Scots English: diffusion, complexity and style as dimensions of syntactic change', *Language in Society* 9, 221–47.

ROSE, MARY BETH, 2000. 'The gendering of authority in the public speeches of Elizabeth I', *PMLA* 115, 5, 1077–1082.

SAIRIO, ANNI, 2009. *Language and Letters of the Blue-stocking Network: Sociolinguistic Issues in Eighteenth-Century Epistolary English*. Mémoires de la Société Néophilologique de Helsinki 75. Helsinki: Société Néophilologique.

SALMON, VIVIAN, 1999. 'Orthography and punctuation', in Roger Lass (ed.), *The Cambridge History of the English Language 1476–1776*, vol. 3, Cambridge: Cambridge University Press, 13–55.

SAMUELS, MICHAEL, 1991. 'Scribes and manuscript traditions', in Felicity Riddy (ed.), *Regionalism in Late Medieval Manuscripts and Texts: Essays Celebrating the Publication of A Linguistic Atlas of Late Mediaeval English*. York Manuscripts Conferences Proceedings, Series 2. Cambridge: D.S. Brewer, 1–7.

SAMUELS, MICHAEL, 1972. *Linguistic Evolution: with Special Reference to English*. Cambridge Studies in Linguistics, 5. Cambridge: Cambridge University Press.

SANKOFF, GILLIAN & BLONDEAU, HÉLÈNE, 2007. 'Language change across the lifespan: /r/ in Montreal French', *Language* 83, 3, 560–588.

SCHENDL, HERBERT, 1997. 'Morphological variation and change in Early Modern English: *my/mine, thy/thine'*, in Raymond Hickey and S. Puppel (eds.), *Language History and Linguistic Modelling: A festschrift for Jacek Fisiak on his 60th Birthday: language history*, vol. 2, Berlin; New York: Mouton de Gruyter, 179–191.

SCHILLING-ESTES, NATALIE, 2002. 'Investigating Stylistic Variation', in Jack K. Chambers, Peter Trudgill and Natalie Schilling-Estes (eds.), *The Handbook of Language Variation and Change*. Blackwell Handbooks in Linguistics. Oxford: Blackwell Publishing, 375–401.

SCHNEIDER, EDGAR W., 2002. 'Investigating Variation and Change in Written Documents', in Jack K. Chambers, Peter Trudgill and Natalie Schilling-Estes (eds.), *The Handbook of Language Variation and Change*. Blackwell Handbooks in Linguistics. Oxford: Blackwell Publishing, 67–96.

SCHREIER, DAVID, 2006. 'The backyard as a dialect boundary: individuation, linguistic heterogeneity, and sociolinguistic eccentricity in a small speech community', *Journal of English Linguistics* 34, 26–57.

SCRAGG, DONALD G., 1974. *A History of English Spelling*. Mont Fellick Series 3. Manchester: Manchester University Press.

SEBBA, MARK, 2007. *Spelling and Society: the Culture and Politics of Orthography Around the World*, Cambridge: Cambridge University Press.

SHAKESPEARE, WILLIAM, 1994. *The Complete Works of William Shakespeare*. Project Gutenberg E-Text #100 < http://www.gutenberg.org/cache/epub/100/pg100.html > .

SHARMA, DEVYANI, 2011. 'Style Repertoire and social change in British Asian English', *Journal of Sociolinguistics* 15, 4: 464–492.

SHELL, M. (ed.), 1993. *Elizabeth's Glass: with 'The Glass of the Sinful Soul' (1544) by Elizabeth I, and 'Epistle Dedicatory' & 'Conclusion' (1548) by John Bale*, London: University of Nebraska Press.

SHENK, LINDA, 2007. '"To Love and Be Wise": the Earl of Essex, Humanist Court Culture, and England's Learned Queen', *Early Modern Literary Studies Special Issue* 16, 3, 1–27.

SHENK, LINDA, 2003. 'Turning learned authority into learned supremacy: Elizabeth I's learned persona and her University Orations', in Carole Levine, Jo Eldrige-Carney, and Debra Barrett-Graves (eds.), *Elizabeth I: Always Her Own Free Woman*, Aldershot: Ashgate Publishing, 78–96.

SHRANK, CATHY, 2010. 'This fatall Medea, this Clytemnestra: reading and the detection of Mary Queen of Scots', *Huntingdon Library Quarterly*, 73, 3, 523–541.

SHRANK, CATHY, 2000. 'Rhetorical constructions of a national community: the role of the King's English in mid-Tudor writing', in Alexandra Shepard and Phil Withington (eds.), *Communities in Early Modern England: Networks, Place, Rhetoric*, Manchester, New York: Manchester University Press, 180–198.

SMITH, JEREMY, 1996. *An Historical Study of English: Function, Form and Change*, London and New York: Routledge.

SOMERSET, ANNE, 1991. *Elizabeth I*, London: Phoenix Press.

SÖNMEZ, MARGARET, 2000. 'Perceived and real differences between men's and women's spellings of the early to mid-seventeenth century', in Dieter Kastovsky and Arthur Mettinger (eds.), *The History of English in a social context: a contribution to historical sociolinguistics*. Trends in Linguistics Studies and Monographs 129. Berlin: Mouton de Gruyter, 405–440.

STARKEY, DAVID, 2000. *Elizabeth: Apprenticeship*, Oxford: Chatto and Windus.

STEIN, DIETER, 1991. 'Semantic aspects of syntactic change', in Dieter Kastovsky (ed.), *Historical English Syntax*. Topics in English Linguistics. Berlin: Mouton de Gruyter, 355–366.

STRYPE, JOHN, 1821. *The Life of the Learned John Cheke, kt.: First Instructor, afterwards Secretary of State, to King Edward VI: One of the Great Restorers of Good Learning and True Religion in this Kingdom*, Oxford: Clarendon Press.

STRYPE, J. (ed.), 1738. *Annals of the Reformation and the Establishment of Religion, in the Church of England*, vol. 4, 2nd edn., London: Edward Symon.

SUMMIT, JENNIFER, 1996. '"The arte of a ladies penne": Elizabeth I and the poetics of queenship', *English Literary Renaissance* 26, 3, 395–422.

TAAVITSAINEN, IRMA, 2000. 'Scientific language and spelling standardisation 1375–1550', in Laura Wright (ed.), *The Development of Standard English, 1300–1800: Theories, Descriptions, Conflicts*. Studies in English Language. Cambridge: Cambridge University Press, 131–154.

TANG BOYLAND, JOYCE, 2001. 'Hypercorrect pronoun case in English? Cognitive processes that account for pronoun usage', in Joan Bybee and Paul Hopper (eds.), *Frequency and the Emergence of Linguistic Structure*. Typological Studies in Language. Amsterdam: John Benjamins, 383–404.

TAYLOR, ANN & SANTORINI, BARBARA, 2006. 'PCEEC annotation and manual' < http://www.users.york.ac.uk/~lang22/PCEEC-manual/ > .

TAYLOR-SMITHER, LARISSA J., 1984. 'Elizabeth I: a psychological profile', *The Sixteenth Century Journal* 15, 1, 47–72.

TEAGUE, FRANCIS, 2000. 'Elizabeth's Hand in The Glass of the Sinful Soul', in Peter Beal and Margaret. J. M. Ezell (eds.), *English Manuscript Studies, 1100–1700: Writings by Early Modern Women*. English manuscript Studies, 9. London: The British Library, 33–48.

TILLYARD, EUSTACE MANDEVILLE W., 1944. *Shakespeare's History Plays*, London: Chatto and Windus.

TRILL, SUZANNE, 1996. 'Sixteenth-century women's writing: Mary Sidney's Psalmes and the "femininity" of translation', in William Zunder and Suzanne Trill (eds.), *Writing and the English Renaissance*, Essex: Longman, 140–58.

THE LANGUAGE, OF QUEEN ELIZABETH I

TRUDGILL, PETER, 1974. *The Social Differentiation of English in Norwich.* London: Cambridge University Press.

VANHOUTTE, JACQUELINE, 2009. 'Elizabeth I as stepmother', *English Literary Renaissance* 39, 2, 315–335.

VUORINEN, ANNI, 2002. 'The gender role of Queen Elizabeth I as reflected by her language', *The Electronic Journal of the Department of English at the University of Helsinki: Corpora: Today's English Studies 2.*

WALES, KATIE, 1996. *Personal pronouns in Present-Day English.* Studies in English Language, Cambridge: Cambridge University Press.

WARDHAUGH, RONALD, 2010. *An Introduction to Sociolinguistics*, 6th edn., Chichester: Wiley Blackwell.

WARNER, ANTONY, 2005. 'Why DO dove: evidence for register variation in Early Modern English negatives', *Language Variation and Change* 17, 257–280.

WEINREICH, URIEL, LABOV, WILLIAM & HERZOG, MERVIN, 1968. 'Empirical Foundations for a Theory of Language Change', in W. P. Lehmann and, Y. Malkiel (eds.), *Directions for Historical Linguistics*, Austin: University of Texas Press, 95–195.

WIGGINS, ALISON, 2011. 'Bess of Hardwick's letter bearers and enclosures'. Paper presented at Culture of Correspondence in Early Modern Britain, 1550–1640, University of Plymouth, April 14th–16th 2011.

WILLIAMS, GRAHAM, 2010. '"Yr scribe can proove no nessecarye consiquence for you"?: the social and linguistic implications of Joan Thynne's using a scribe in letters to her son, 1607–11', in A. Lawrence-Mathers and P. Hardman (eds.), *Women and Writing, c.1340–1650: the Domestication of Print Culture,* York: York Medieval Press, 131–145.

WILSON, R. M., 1963. 'The orthography and provenance of Henry Machyn', in A. Brown and P. Foote (eds.), *Early English and Norse Studies: presented to Hugh Smith in honour of his sixtieth birthday*, London: Methuen, 203–216.

WISCHER, ILSE, 2008. 'What makes a syntactic change stop? On the decline of periphrastic do in Early Modern English affirmative declarative sentences', *Studies Anglia Posnaniensia* 44, 139–154.

WOUDHUYSEN, HENRY, 2007. 'The Queen's own hand: a preliminary account', in Peter Beal and Grace Ioppolo (eds.), *Elizabeth I and the culture of writing*, London: The British Library, 1–28.

INDEX